THE
EASTERN
FELLS

WALKERS EDITIONS

Published 2015		First published	First revision
Book One:	The Eastern Fells	1955	2005
Book Two:	The Far Eastern Fells	1957	2005
Published 2016		First published	First revision
Book Three:	The Central Fells	1958	2006
Published 2017		First published	First revision
Book Four:	The Southern Fells	1960	2007
Published 2018		First published	First revision
Book Five:	The Northern Fells	1962	2008
Published 2019		First published	First revision
Book Six:	The North-Western Fells	1964	2008
Published 2020		First published	First revision
Book Seven:	The Western Fells	1966	2009

PUBLISHER'S NOTE

Fellwalking can be dangerous, especially
in wet, windy, foggy or icy conditions.
Please be sure to take sensible precautions
when out on the fells. As A. Wainwright himself
frequently wrote : use your common sense
and watch where you are putting your feet.

A PICTORIAL GUIDE

TO THE

LAKELAND FELLS

WALKERS EDITION
REVISED BY CLIVE HUTCHBY

being an illustrated account
of a study and exploration
of the mountains in the
English Lake District
by

aWainwright

BOOK ONE
THE EASTERN FELLS

Originally published by Henry Marshall, Kentmere, 1955
First published by Frances Lincoln 2003
Second (revised) Edition published by Frances Lincoln, 2005
Reprinted with minor corrections 2007

Walkers Edition published in 2015 by Frances Lincoln,
an imprint of The Quarto Group
The Old Brewery, 6 Blundell Street
London N7 9BH, United Kingdom
T (0)20 7700 6700 F (0)20 7700 8066
www.QuartoKnows.com

Printed and bound in the United Kingdom.

A CIP catalogue for this book
is available from the British Library

ISBN 978 0 7112 3628 8

2 4 6 8 8 9 7 5 3 1

THIS REVISED EDITION FOR WALKERS PUBLISHED BY
FRANCES LINCOLN, LONDON

THE EASTERN FELLS

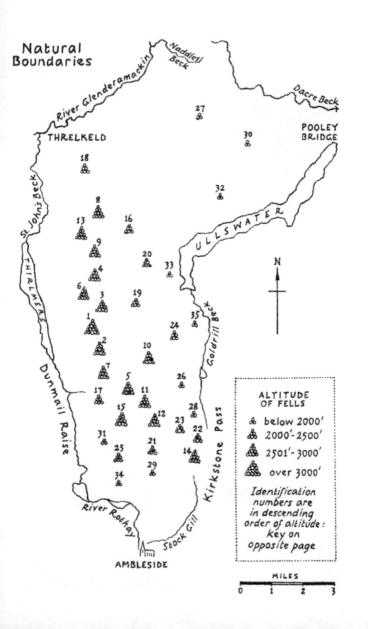

Natural Boundaries

River Glenderamackin

Naddlesl Beck

Dacre Beck

THRELKELD

POOLEY BRIDGE

St. John's Beck

ULLSWATER

N

THIRLMERE

Goldrill Beck

Dunmail Raise

Kirkstone Pass

River Rothay

Stock Gill

AMBLESIDE

ALTITUDE
OF FELLS

   below 2000'
   2000'- 2500'
   2501'- 3000'
   over 3000'

Identification
numbers are
in descending
order of altitude:
key on
opposite page

MILES
0   1   2   3

THE EASTERN FELLS

in the order of their appearance in this book

Reference to map opposite					Altitude in feet
over 3000'	2501'-3000'	2000'-2500'	below 2000'		
			35	ARNISON CRAG	1424
		19		BIRKHOUSE MOOR	2356
		24		BIRKS	2040
	3			CATSTYCAM	2917
		18		CLOUGH HEAD	2381
	7			DOLLYWAGGON PIKE	2815
	12			DOVE CRAG	2598
	5			FAIRFIELD	2863
			33	GLENRIDDING DODD	1450
			32	GOWBARROW FELL	1579
	8			GREAT DODD	2812
			27	GREAT MELL FELL	1760
	15			GREAT RIGG	2513
	11			HART CRAG	2698
		16		HART SIDE	2481
			26	HARTSOP ABOVE HOW	1903
1				HELVELLYN	3118
		25		HERON PIKE	2008
			28	HIGH HARTSOP DODD	1702
		21		HIGH PIKE	2155
		23		LITTLE HART CRAG	2091
			30	LITTLE MELL FELL	1657
			29	LOW PIKE	1667
		22		MIDDLE DODD	2146
			34	NAB SCAR	1450
	2			NETHERMOST PIKE	2920
	4			RAISE	2897
	14			RED SCREES	2546
	10			SAINT SUNDAY CRAG	2756
		17		SEAT SANDAL	2415
		20		SHEFFIELD PIKE	2215
			31	STONE ARTHUR	1652
	9			STYBARROW DODD	2770
	13			WATSON'S DODD	2589
	6			WHITE SIDE	2832
1	14	10	10		
		35			

Each fell is the subject of a separate chapter

INTRODUCTION
TO THE
WALKERS EDITION
BY CLIVE HUTCHBY

When I finished work on *The Wainwright Companion* in April 2012 I never expected that, less than two years later, I would be following literally in the footsteps of AW on his beloved Lakeland fells. And those of Chris Jesty, as well, whose Second Edition revisions of the guidebooks spurred me, at the end of 2010, to purchase the complete set for the umpteenth time — oh, how must the publishers have loved me down the years.

The full extent of Chris Jesty's updates might surprise many people, but to revise books that were half a century old really was a monumental task. A lot had happened in the previous fifty years, and almost as much has followed in the ten years since. Typical changes in that period have been stiles being replaced by gates, new footbridges, paths being repaired — and even re-aligned — by Fix the Fells, the construction of fences and planting of trees, as well as all the usual things that happen when thousands of people tramp the fells: some paths fall out of fashion and others spring up from nowhere.

I have largely succeeded in checking all the recommended routes without paths, despite some annoying footpath closures along the eastern side of Thirlmere because of tree felling. This has been a real eye-opener: some routes that I expected to now be popular are still without any trace of humans having been that way before, while other routes have now become so well used that new paths that have materialised have already had to be repaired. In the latter case, the path from the corner of the car park at the summit of Kirkstone Pass to the top of Red Screes is one of the most obvious examples. When you stand at the car park and look at the 1000' of crags and scree towering above you it seems inconceivable that there is a simple — and very clever, interesting and *safe* — route to the summit. Just changing the path on the ascent diagram from dots to a broken line didn't seem to me to be enough, which is why, on *Red Screes 6* you will find a new diagram showing the latter stages of the route. To create this space meant moving some elements of AW's original layouts, something I was unsure of doing but to which the publishers readily agreed. The brief was to make the Walkers Edition of Book One as up to date and informative as possible; among the changes, you will find a new two-page section about Striding Edge on *Helvellyn 18–19*, a detailed look at the wall from Low Pike to Dove Crag (familiar to anyone who has ever walked the Fairfield Horseshoe) on *High Pike 4*, and a feature about Castle Rock on *Watson's Dodd 5*.

AW said that he hoped people would use his guidebooks as a basis for their own notes; that is what I have tried to achieve with the changes made in this revision, plus, where space has allowed, I have added information that might be of interest. As in the Second Edition, paths remain in red, but this time a brighter tone and with bolder lines to make them stand out more. Also, I have used three criteria for the paths (formerly they were just *'clear'* and *'intermittent'*); now they are *'clear'*, *'intermittent or thin'* and *'sketchy'*. Of course, if you would like to use AW's original guidebooks as the basis for your own notes, you can still do so, as the original hardback editions remain in print. I'll always have a set in my bookcase.

The eastern fells are, of course, very popular among fellwalkers and not just because they are among the most easily accessible to visitors arriving via the M6/A591 or the A66. They include Helvellyn (Lakeland's most climbed mountain), the wonderful Catstycam, Fairfield, St Sunday Crag and Red Screes, and the lovely Great Mell Fell; this hill, with its unique summit landscape, is truly a special place to be on a sunny summer's day.

Some of the best walking anywhere in Lakeland can be found here, and invariably the most stunning walks start from the Patterdale side, where a profusion of lovely side valleys offer a wide variety of approaches. Everyone knows Striding Edge and Swirral Edge, but before you set out on any of these well trodden routes alongside hundreds of other walkers, consider the quieter delights of the east ridge of Nethermost Pike (awesome), the north-west ridge of Catstycam (spectacular) and my personal favourite, the east ridge of Dollywaggon Pike culminating in The Tongue, a place to which I could return again and again.

I would like to thank the following for their help and support in revising Book One: Margy Ogg, Chris Jesty, Sean McMahon, David Harrison, Chris Stanbury, Stan Hawrylak, Maggie Allan, Lesley Ritchie, Andy Beck, Derek Cockell, Jane King and Annie Sellar (from the Wainwright Estate), Richard Fox (from Fix the Fells) and (from publishers Frances Lincoln) John Nicoll, Andrew Dunn and Michael Brunström.

Clive Hutchby
Ambleside, January 2015

BOOK ONE

is dedicated to

THE MEN OF THE ORDNANCE SURVEY

whose maps of Lakeland
have given me much pleasure
both on the fells
and by my fireside

INTRODUCTION
BY
AWainwright

Surely there is no other place in this whole wonderful world quite like Lakeland ... no other so exquisitely lovely, no other so charming, no other that calls so insistently across a gulf of distance. All who truly love Lakeland are exiles when away from it.

Here, in small space, is the wonderland of childhood's dreams, lingering far beyond childhood through the span of a man's life: its enchantment grows with passing years and quiet eventide is enriched by the haunting sweetness of dear memories, memories that remain evergreen through the flight of time, that refresh and sustain in the darker days. How many, these memories .... *the moment of wakening, and the sudden joyful realisation that this is to be another day of freedom on the hills ...... the dawn chorus of bird song ...... the delicate lacework of birches against the sky .... morning sun drawing aside the veils of mist; black-stockinged lambs, in springtime, amongst the daffodils .... silver cascades dancing and leaping down bracken steeps ..... autumn colours .... a red fox running over snow .... the silence of lonely hills ...... storm and tempest in the high places, and the unexpected glimpses of valleys dappled in sunlight far beneath the swirling clouds .... rain, and the intimate shelter of lichened walls ....fierce winds on the heights and soft breezes that are no more than gentle caresses .... a sheepdog watching its master ...... the snow and ice and freezing stillnesses of*

tmidwinter: a white world, rosy-pink as the sun goes down ...... the supreme moment when the top cairn comes into sight at last, only minutes away, after the long climb .... the small ragged sheep that brave the blizzards ...... the symphonies of murmuring streams, unending, with never a discord .... curling smoke from the chimneys of the farm down below amongst the trees, where the day shall end ...... oil lamps in flagged kitchens, huge fires in huge fireplaces, huge suppers .... glittering moonlight on placid waters ...... stars above dark peaks ..... the tranquillity that comes before sleep, when thoughts are of the day that is gone and the day that is to come .... All these memories, and so many more, breathing anew the rare quality and magical atmosphere of Lakeland .... memories that belong to Lakeland, and could not belong in the same way to any other place .... memories that enslave the mind forever.

Many are they who have fallen under the spell of Lakeland, and many are they who have been moved to tell of their affection, in story and verse and picture and song.

This book is one man's way of expressing his devotion to Lakeland's friendly hills. It was conceived, and is born, after many years of inarticulate worshipping at their shrines.

It is, in very truth, a love letter.

Classification and Definition

Any division of the Lakeland fells into geographical districts must necessarily be arbitrary, just as the location of the outer boundaries of Lakeland must always be a matter of opinion. Any attempt to define internal or external boundaries is certain to invite criticism, and he who takes it upon himself to say where Lakeland starts and finishes, or, for example, where the Central Fells merge into the Southern Fells and *which* fells *are* the Central Fells and which the Southern and *why* they need be so classified, must not expect his pronouncements to be generally accepted.

Yet for present purposes some plan of classification and definition must be used. County and parochial boundaries are no help, nor is the recently defined area of the Lakeland National Park, for this book is concerned only with the high ground.

First, the external boundaries. Straight lines linking the extremities of the outlying lakes enclose all the higher fells very conveniently. There are a few fells of lesser height to the north and east, however, that are typically Lakeland in character and cannot properly be omitted: these are brought in, somewhat untidily, by extending the lines in those areas. Thus:

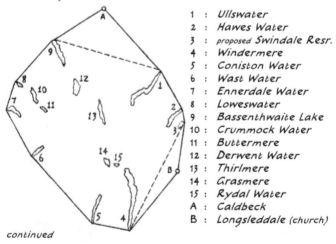

1	:	*Ullswater*
2	:	*Hawes Water*
3	:	proposed *Swindale Resr.*
4	:	*Windermere*
5	:	*Coniston Water*
6	:	*Wast Water*
7	:	*Ennerdale Water*
8	:	*Loweswater*
9	:	*Bassenthwaite Lake*
10	:	*Crummock Water*
11	:	*Buttermere*
12	:	*Derwent Water*
13	:	*Thirlmere*
14	:	*Grasmere*
15	:	*Rydal Water*
A	:	*Caldbeck*
B	:	*Longsleddale* (church)

continued

Classification and Definition

continued

The complete Guide includes all the fells in the area enclosed by the straight lines of the diagram. This is an undertaking quite beyond the compass of a single volume, and it is necessary, therefore, to divide the area into convenient sections, making the fullest use of natural boundaries (lakes, valleys and low passes) so that each district is, as far as possible, self-contained and independent of the rest.

This division gives seven areas, each with a well defined group of fells, and each area is the subject of a separate volume

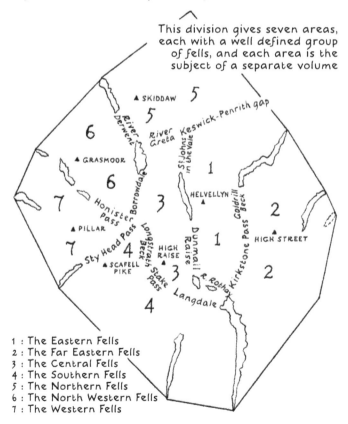

1 : The Eastern Fells
2 : The Far Eastern Fells
3 : The Central Fells
4 : The Southern Fells
5 : The Northern Fells
6 : The North Western Fells
7 : The Western Fells

INTRODUCTION

Notes on the Illustrations

THE MAPS .... Many excellent books have been written about
Lakeland, but the best literature of all for the walker is that
published by the Director General of Ordnance Survey, the 1" map
for companionship and guidance on expeditions, the 2½" map for
exploration both on the fells and by the fireside. These admirable
maps are remarkably accurate topographically but there is a
crying need for a revision of the paths on the hills: several
walkers' tracks that have come into use during the past few
decades, some of them now broad highways, are not shown at
all; other paths still shown on the maps have fallen into neglect
and can no longer be traced on the ground.

The popular Bartholomew 1" map is a
beautiful picture, fit for a frame, but this
too is unreliable for paths; indeed here
the defect is much more serious, for
routes are indicated where no paths
ever existed, nor ever could — the
cartographer has preferred to take
precipices in his stride rather than
deflect his graceful curves over easy
ground.

Hence the justification for the maps in this book: they have
the one merit (of importance to walkers) of being dependable as
regards delineation of *paths*. They are intended as supplements
to the Ordnance Survey maps, certainly not as substitutes.

THE VIEWS .... Various devices have
been used to illustrate the views from
the summits of the fells. The full
panorama in the form of an outline
drawing is most satisfactory generally,
and this method has been adopted for
the main viewpoints.

THE DIAGRAMS OF ASCENTS .... The routes of ascent of the
higher fells are depicted by diagrams that do not pretend to
strict accuracy: they are neither plans
nor elevations; in fact there is deliberate
distortion in order to show detail clearly:
usually they are represented as viewed
from imaginary 'space stations'. But it is
hoped they will be useful and interesting.

THE DRAWINGS .... The drawings at least are honest attempts
to reproduce what the eye sees: they illustrate features of
interest and also serve the dual purpose of breaking up the
text and balancing the layout of the pages, and of filling up
awkward blank spaces, like this:

THE
EASTERN
FELLS

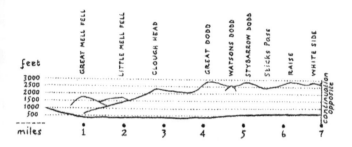

In the area of the Eastern Fells the greatest single mass of high ground in Lakeland is concentrated. It takes the form of a tremendous barrier running north and south, consistently high and steep throughout its length, mainly having an altitude between 2500'–3000', in two places only falling below 2000', and rising above 3000' on Helvellyn. In general the western slopes are steep, smooth and grassy and the eastern slopes are broken and craggy, but at the northern extremity the reverse obtains. The fells in this area may conveniently be classed in two groups divided by Grisedale Pass: in the south is the Fairfield group, pleasingly arrayed and with deep valleys cutting into the mass on both flanks; north is the bigger but less interesting Helvellyn range, with no valleys in the high western wall but several on the eastern side running down to Ullswater.

The geographical boundaries of the area are distinct. In shape it is a long inverted triangle, covering about fifty square miles of territory, based on Ambleside. The western boundary is formed by the deep trough of Dunmail Raise and Thirlmere, a great rift of which the principal road across the district takes advantage; the eastern boundary is the trench of Kirkstone Pass

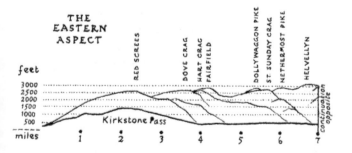

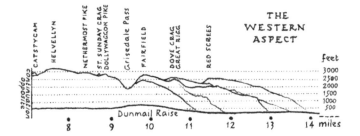

THE
WESTERN
ASPECT

and Ullswater, and the northern is the broad Keswick to Penrith gap. These boundaries are very satisfactory, enclosing all the dependencies of Helvellyn and Fairfield, and they are particularly convenient for the purposes of a separate guidebook because they are not crossed, normally, during the course of a day's fell-walk. Only at Kirkstone is there a link with fells outside the area but even here the breach is very pronounced.

This is an area easily accessible and (excepting the fells north of Sticks Pass) much frequented by walkers. It has in Helvellyn the most often climbed mountain in Lakeland and in Grisedale Pass one of the best known footpaths.

Ambleside and Grasmere are favourite resorts for those who frequent these fells, but, because the most dramatic features are invariably presented to the east, the quiet and beautiful Patterdale valley is far superior as a base for their exploration: the eastern approaches are more interesting, the surroundings more charming and the views more rewarding; furthermore, from Patterdale any part of the main ridge may be visited in a normal day's expedition.

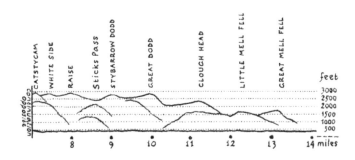

Arnison Crag 1424'

OS grid ref: NY394149

from Keldas

Glenridding •

Patterdale •

ARNISON CRAG ▲

BIRKS ▲

S.ᵗ SUNDAY CRAG
▲

MILES

0   1   2

The rough fellside curving out of Deepdale and bounding the highway to Patterdale village has an attractive rocky crown, often visited for the fine view it offers of the head of Ullswater. This is Arnison Crag, a low hill with a summit worthy of a mountain. It is a dependency of Sᵗ Sunday Crag, forming the lesser of the two prongs which constitute the north-east spur of that grand fell; Birks is the other. It starts as a grass shelf east of Cold Cove then takes the shape of a curving ridge of no particular interest except for the sudden upthrust of its craggy summit.

MAP

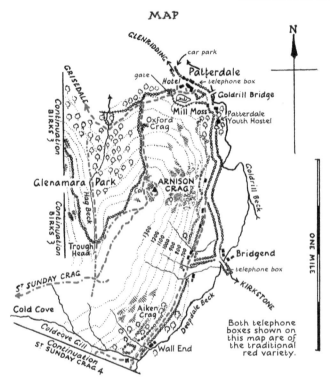

Both telephone boxes shown on this map are of the traditional red variety.

ASCENT FROM PATTERDALE
1000 feet of ascent : ¼ mile

Ascents from the south from Coldcove Gill or from the vicinity of Bridgend are not recommended. The best way up is from the village of Patterdale, starting from the lane opposite the telephone box, which heads uphill and bends right. After the bend, a path on the left skirts the attractive marshy area of Mill Moss. Go left at a T-junction and through a gate. Then follow the wall of Glenamara Park up the hill, past the rocky outcrop of Oxford Crag which is a lovely viewpoint. Stay on the path until you come to a col and then take a curving path to the left which swings round to the south of the western-facing summit rocks and approaches the summit from the south, with just an easy final scramble.

Alternatively, before the col is reached, a thin path leaves the main track to the left and reaches the summit area at the gap between the two main outcrops; a scramble up rocks to the right leads to the top.

Although a short and easy walk, the ascent may lead to difficulties in mist and should not be attempted.

THE SUMMIT

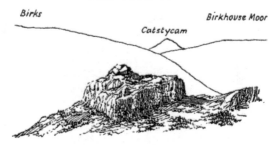

Birks   Catstycam   Birkhouse Moor

The summit is a rock platform, inaccessible to the walker on the west side and attained from other directions only by breaches in a low wall of crag defending it. A rock gateway (seen from the road near Hartsop as a clean-cut notch on the skyline) separates this platform from another of a slightly lower elevation, which has the principal cairn and overlooks the approach from Patterdale.

The summit is, in fact, not the highest point on the fell. Along the ridge from Arnison Crag to the depression at Trough Head are a series of knolls, one of which — about halfway along — is the true summit; it is clearly higher than the accepted top, but its grassy dome is a poor substitute for the rocky summit of Arnison Crag that walkers prefer.

The lower cairn (now collapsed)

The summit from the south

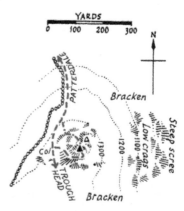

DESCENTS : The ridge should be followed down, for Patterdale. Short cuts are likely to encounter rougher ground. A longer alternative follows the wall to Trough Head, where a very awkward stile gives access to the wooded Glenamara Park and pleasant paths which lead back to Patterdale.

In mist, make a wide detour to the wall and follow it northwards.

THE VIEW

Arnison Crag is surrounded by higher fells, and the view is very restricted. A feature is the fine grouping of the hills above the pastures of Hartsop.

Ullswater is the only lake seen, its upper reach being well displayed. This is not, however, the best viewpoint for Ullswater by any means.

Principal Fells

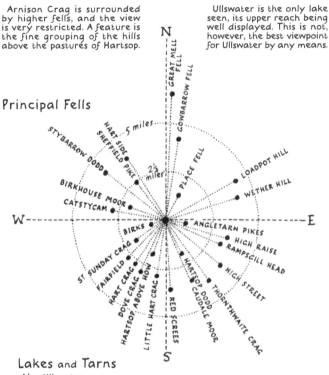

N

GREAT MELL FELL
GOWBARROW FELL
5 miles
HART SIDE
SHEFFIELD PIKE
STYBARROW DODD
2½ miles
PLACE FELL
LOADPOT HILL
WETHER HILL
BIRKHOUSE MOOR
CATSTYCAM
W
E
ANGLETARN PIKES
BIRKS
HIGH RAISE
RAMPSGILL HEAD
ST SUNDAY CRAG
HIGH STREET
FAIRFIELD
HART CRAG
DOVE CRAG
HARTSOP ABOVE HOW
HARTSOP DODD
CAUDALE MOOR
THORNTHWAITE CRAG
LITTLE HART CRAG
RED SCREES
S

Lakes and Tarns

N: *Ullswater*
SSE: *Brothers Water*

Ullswater

Birkhouse Moor 2356'

OS grid ref: NY363160

from Lanty's Tarn

RAISE
▲
Glenridding
●
BIRKHOUSE MOOR
●
Patterdale
●
▲
HELVELLYN

▲ FAIRFIELD
MILES
0   1   2   3   4

NATURAL FEATURES

The east ridge of Helvellyn starts as a narrow rock arête, known to all walkers as Striding Edge, and then gradually widens into the broad sprawling mass of Birkhouse Moor. A long grassy promenade is the main characteristic of the top, but the southern slopes soon steepen to form a natural wall for Grisedale for two miles; this flank is traversed by one of the most popular paths in the district. Northwards, Red Tarn Beck and Glenridding Beck form its boundaries; there are crags on this side, mainly concentrated around the only defined ridge descending from the summit, north-east. The name 'moor' is well suited to this fell, the top particularly being grassy and dull; below, eastwards, there are patches of heather, and in this direction the fell ends abruptly and craggily above Ullswater, the lower slopes being beautifully wooded.

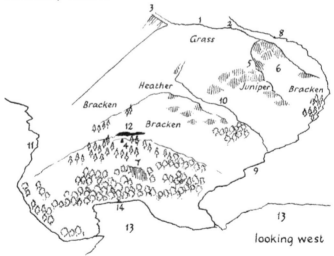

looking west

1 : The highest point
2 : The cairn at 2318'
3 : Ridge continuing to Helvellyn
4 : Keldas
5 : The north-east ridge
6 : Blea Cove
7 : Raven Crag
8 : Red Tarn Beck
9 : Glenridding Beck
10 : Mires Beck
11 : Grisedale Beck
12 : Lanty's Tarn
13 : Ullswater
14 : St Patrick's Well

The north-east ridge is sometimes referred to as The Nab. The depression from which Mires Beck flows, a small corrie separated by The Nab and Keldas, is known as Little Cove.

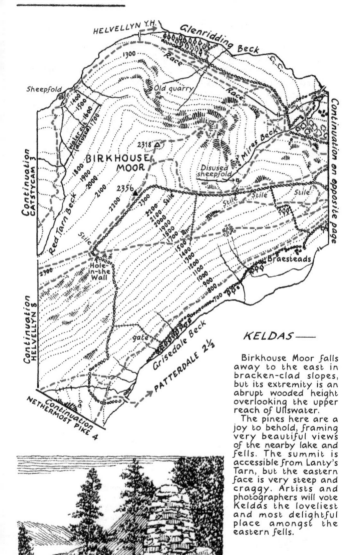

KELDAS——

Birkhouse Moor falls away to the east in bracken-clad slopes, but its extremity is an abrupt wooded height overlooking the upper reach of Ullswater.

The pines here are a joy to behold, framing very beautiful views of the nearby lake and fells. The summit is accessible from Lanty's Tarn, but the eastern face is very steep and craggy. Artists and photographers will vote Keldas the loveliest and most delightful place amongst the eastern fells.

The summit of Keldas as it appeared in 1954. The fine cairn has long since gone.

MAP

ONE MILE

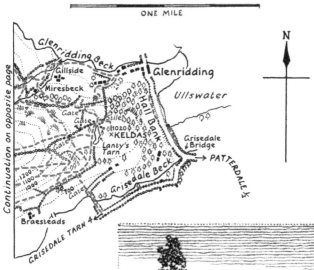

N

The most beautiful way up Keldas is from Glenridding, leaving via the lane on the south side of Glenridding Beck and turning left ahead of Gillside where the main path to Helvellyn goes straight on. A delightful climb through trees follows before reaching open fellside where an inviting path to the left should be ignored: this leads to private land. Continue on a simple climb to Lanty's Tarn; the summit is a short distance beyond a wall.

Ullswater from Keldas

ASCENT FROM GRISEDALE
1900 feet of ascent : 3½ miles from Patterdale village

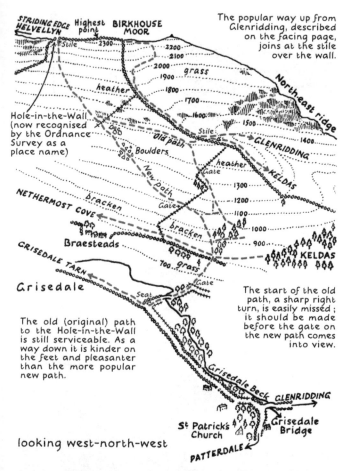

The popular way up from Glenridding, described on the facing page, joins at the stile over the wall.

STRIDING EDGE
HELVELLYN
Highest point
BIRKHOUSE MOOR

Stile
2300
2200
2100
2000
1900
1800
1700
1600
grass
heather

Northeast ridge

Hole-in-the-Wall
(now recognised by the Ordnance Survey as a place name)

Old path
Boulders
New path
Stile
1500
1400
GLENRIDDING
KELDAS
heather
Gate
1300
Gate
1200

NETHERMOST COVE
bracken
bracken
1100
1000
900

Braesteads
GRISEDALE TARN

Keldas

700 grass

Grisedale
Seat
Gate

The old (original) path to the Hole-in-the-Wall is still serviceable. As a way down it is kinder on the feet and pleasanter than the more popular new path.

The start of the old path, a sharp right turn, is easily missed ; it should be made before the gate on the new path comes into view.

Grisedale Beck
GLENRIDDING

St Patrick's Church
Grisedale Bridge

looking west-north-west

PATTERDALE

Birkhouse Moor may most easily be ascended by using the well-defined Patterdale-Striding Edge path climbing across its flank. The splendid views of Grisedale are the chief merits of the route via Hole-in-the-Wall; that via the stile and the wall is the shorter, and best in descent. Both routes are safe *in bad conditions*.

ASCENT FROM GLENRIDDING
1900 feet of ascent : 2 miles

The approach to the north-east ridge is hindered by tall bracken in summertime. This is a route for scramblers only. Pedestrians whose limbs are beginning to creak would be better advised to plod dully up by Mires Beck and follow the path to the top. This path has been paved for much of its length because of its popularity, primarily as a way to Striding Edge.

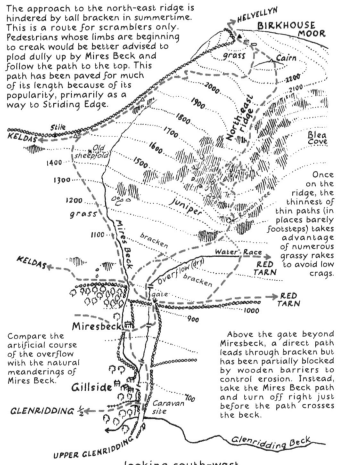

Once on the ridge, the thinnest of thin paths (in places barely footsteps) takes advantage of numerous grassy rakes to avoid low crags.

Compare the artificial course of the overflow with the natural meanderings of Mires Beck.

Above the gate beyond Miresbeck, a direct path leads through bracken but has been partially blocked by wooden barriers to control erosion. Instead, take the Mires Beck path and turn off right just before the path crosses the beck.

looking south-west

The north-east ridge, which is steep in places, offers a mild adventure and is a test in route-finding amongst low crags; as such, it most definitely needs clear weather. It is the best way up, with a beautiful view in retrospect, but *in bad weather* the Mires Beck route is preferable, and safer.

THE SUMMIT

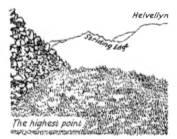

The highest point

Place Fell

The cairn at 2318'

The summit sits astride the path to Striding Edge and Helvellyn, marked by a small cairn ; the nearby wall, which follows the main ridge to Striding Edge, actually passes over slightly higher ground.

The north top (2318') lies 550 yards away at the meeting point of the well defined north-east ridge and the broader north ridge. A substantial cairn has been built here, somewhat larger than that illustrated above. The view from here of the High Spying How—Striding Edge—Helvellyn—Swirral Edge—Catstycam horseshoe is a much-photographed classic, and in the opposite direction the prospect of Ullswater is very pleasing.

A few small tarns relieve the monotony of the grassy expanse, but generally the summit area offers little of interest.

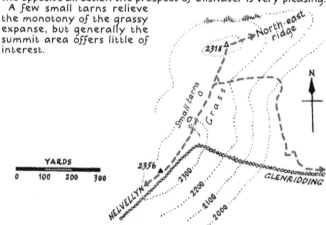

DESCENTS: The descent is best made by following the new path to the saddle above Mires Beck : here turn left for Glenridding, or (for Patterdale) cross the wall at the stile to join a path going down to the right. The rocky north-east ridge is not suitable for descent.

|||| *In bad weather conditions* follow the good path down to Glenridding. Avoid the east and north faces.

THE VIEW

The east face of Helvellyn, enclosed between the twin arms of Striding Edge and Swirral Edge, is the best feature of a rather dull panorama.

Lakes and Tarns

N: *Sticks Reservoir (dry)*
NE: *Ullswater*
  (better seen from the cairn at 2318')
ESE: *Angle Tarn*
 SE: *Hayeswater*
  S: *Grisedale Tarn*
WNW: *Keppelcove Tarn (dry)*

Principal Fells
(from the highest point)

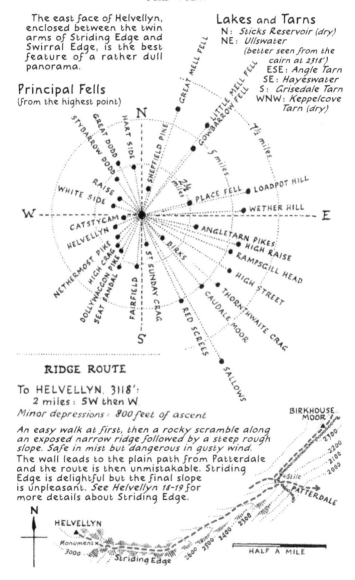

RIDGE ROUTE

To HELVELLYN, 3118':
2 miles: SW then W.

Minor depressions: 800 feet of ascent

An easy walk at first, then a rocky scramble along an exposed narrow ridge followed by a steep rough slope. Safe in mist but dangerous in gusty wind. The wall leads to the plain path from Patterdale and the route is then unmistakable. Striding Edge is delightful but the final slope is unpleasant. See Helvellyn 18-19 for more details about Striding Edge.

HALF A MILE

Birks

2040'

OS grid ref: NY382145

Glenridding

Patterdale

ARNISON CRAG ▲

BIRKS ▲

ST SUNDAY CRAG
▲

MILES
0   1   2

from Ullswater

The north-east shoulder of S.t Sunday Crag falls sharply to a depression beyond which a grassy undulating spur, featureless and wide, continues with little change in elevation towards Ullswater before finally plunging down to the valley through the enclosure of Glenamara Park. Although this spur lacks a distinctive summit it is sufficiently well defined to deserve a separate name; but, being an unromantic and uninteresting fell, it has earned for itself nothing better than the prosaic and unassuming title of Birks. It is rarely visited as the sole objective of an expedition, but walkers descending the ridge from S.t Sunday Crag often take it in their stride.

NATURAL FEATURES

Above the 1900' contour Birks is a half-mile's easy grass promenade and there is nothing here to suggest that there are formidable crags below on both sides. Yet the Grisedale flank has a continuous line of cliffs and round to the east are several tiers of rock above the lower wooded slopes of Glenamara Park. Beyond the hollow of Trough Head, where rises Birks' only stream of note, is a curving ridge which culminates in the rocky pyramid of Arnison Crag; both this lower ridge and Birks itself, together forming a high wedge of rough ground between Grisedale and Deepdale, are dependencies of St Sunday Crag, Birks especially being dominated by this fine mountain.

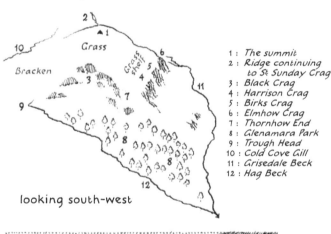

1 : *The summit*
2 : *Ridge continuing to St Sunday Crag*
3 : *Black Crag*
4 : *Harrison Crag*
5 : *Birks Crag*
6 : *Elmhow Crag*
7 : *Thornhow End*
8 : *Glenamara Park*
9 : *Trough Head*
10 : *Cold Cove Gill*
11 : *Grisedale Beck*
12 : *Hag Beck*

looking south-west

Ullswater from Thornhow End

MAP

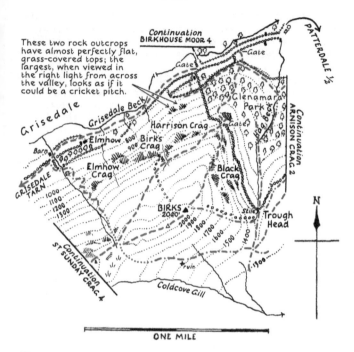

These two rock outcrops have almost perfectly flat, grass-covered tops; the largest, when viewed in the right light from across the valley, looks as if it could be a cricket pitch.

Continuation
BIRKHOUSE MOOR 4

PATTERDALE ½

Gate
Gate
Gate

Grisedale

Grisedale Beck

Glenamara
Park

Hog Beck

Harrison Crag

Continuation
ARNISON CRAG 2

Elmhow
Barn
1000
900

Birks
Crag

Gate

Elmhow
Crag

GRISEDALE
TARN

1000
1100
1200
1300

Black
Crag

BIRKS
2040
2000
1900
1800

Stile

Trough
Head

N

St Continuation
ST SUNDAY CRAG 4

ruin

1700
1600
1500
1400
1300

Coldcove Gill

ONE MILE

The path across the northern flank of Birks above Harrison Crag and Birks Crag is on a shelf sufficiently pronounced to be seen clearly from Lanty's Tarn, on the far side of Grisedale.

Place Fell from Glenamara Park

ASCENTS FROM PATTERDALE
1600 feet of ascent : 2½ miles (1¾ by short variations)

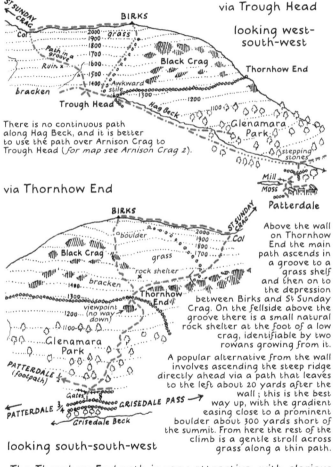

via Trough Head

looking west-south-west

ST SUNDAY CRAG

BIRKS

Col

2000 — grass
1900
1800
1700
Path in a groove
1600
Ruin x
1500
1400
Awkward stile
1300

Black Crag

Thornhow End

bracken

Trough Head

Hag Beck

1200

1100

Glenamara Park

stepping stones

There is no continuous path along Hag Beck, and it is better to use the path over Arnison Crag to Trough Head (*for map see Arnison Crag 2*).

Mill Moss

Patterdale

via Thornhow End

BIRKS

boulder

2000
1900
1800
1700

ST SUNDAY CRAG

Col

Black Crag

grass

rock shelter

bracken

Thornhow End

viewpoint (no way down)

1300

1200

1100

Glenamara Park

PATTERDALE ½ (footpath)

Gates

PATTERDALE ¾

GRISEDALE PASS

Grisedale Beck

looking south-south-west

Above the wall on Thornhow End the main path ascends in a groove to a grass shelf and then on to the depression between Birks and St Sunday Crag. On the fellside above the groove there is a small natural rock shelter at the foot of a low crag, identifiable by two rowans growing from it.

A popular alternative from the wall involves ascending the steep ridge directly ahead via a path that leaves to the left about 20 yards after the wall ; this is the best way up, with the gradient easing close to a prominent boulder about 300 yards short of the summit. From here the rest of the climb is a gentle stroll across grass along a thin path.

The Thornhow End path is very attractive, with glorious views, but it is steep, especially if the direct route is taken above the wall ; the easier approach via the col is very circuitous. The Trough Head route is without a path in places and, although very pleasant through Glenamara Park, is otherwise uninteresting. There is no pleasure, and some danger, in climbing Birks *in misty conditions*.

THE SUMMIT

Gavel Pike

St Sunday Crag

The summit has no interesting features. Do not believe out-of-date Ordnance Survey maps that promised a beacon here: all that can be found is a mound of stones. A more considerable heap of bigger stones further along the ridge appears to be a collapsed edifice of some kind. There is a narrow track along the crest to the west of the summit leading to the col between Birks and St Sunday Crag, and a clear but thin path to the north-east ridge and Thornhow End.

DESCENTS: The finest way down (because of the view of Ullswater) is by the ridge to the north, following a clear but steep path with zig-zags in places leading all the way down to the wall at Thornhow End.

‖ In bad weather conditions, search eastwards for the top of the broken wall and follow it down to Trough Head.

RIDGE ROUTE

To St SUNDAY CRAG
2756' : 1¼ miles : SW

*Minor depressions
800 feet of ascent*

An easy stroll on grass to the col is followed by steep climbing up the ridge to the sloping summit-plateau; the path that turns off left, to the depression to the west of Gavel Crag, is easier. *Not recommended in mist.*

ST SUNDAY CRAG

ONE MILE

THE VIEW

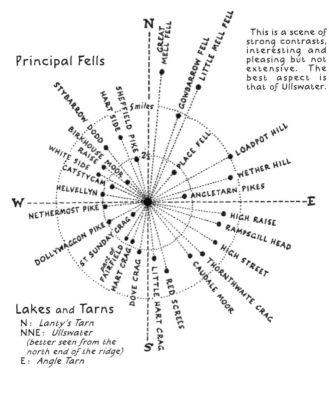

Principal Fells

This is a scene of strong contrasts, interesting and pleasing but not extensive. The best aspect is that of Ullswater.

N
GREAT MELL FELL
GOWBARROW FELL
LITTLE MELL FELL

STYBARROW DODD
HART SIDE
SHEFFIELD PIKE
BIRKHOUSE MOOR
RAISE
WHITE SIDE
CATSTYCAM
HELVELLYN
NETHERMOST PIKE
DOLLYWAGGON PIKE
ST SUNDAY CRAG
Part of FAIRFIELD
HART CRAG
DOVE CRAG
LITTLE HART CRAG
RED SCREES
CAUDALE MOOR
THORNTHWAITE CRAG
HIGH STREET
RAMPSGILL HEAD
HIGH RAISE
ANGLETARN PIKES
WETHER HILL
LOADPOT HILL
PLACE FELL

5 miles
2½

W
E
S

Lakes and Tarns
N: *Lanty's Tarn*
NNE: *Ullswater*
(better seen from the north end of the ridge)
E: *Angle Tarn*

Ullswater

Catstycam

2917'

sometimes called
Catchedicam or
Catstye Cam

OS grid ref: NY348158

from Glenridding Beck

RAISE ▲   ● Glenridding

CATSTYCAM ▲   ● Patterdale

HELVELLYN ▲

MILES
0   1   2   3   4

NATURAL FEATURES

If Catstycam stood alone, remote from its fellows, it would be one of the finest peaks in Lakeland. It has nearly, but not quite, the perfect mountain form, with true simplicity in its soaring lines, and a small pointed top, a real summit, that falls away sharply on all sides. From Birkhouse Moor especially it has the appearance of a symmetrical pyramid; and from the upper valley of Glenridding it towers into the sky most impressively. But when seen from other directions it is too obviously dominated by Helvellyn and although its sharp peak identifies it unmistakably in every view in which it appears, clearly it is no more than the abrupt terminus of a short spur of the higher mountain, to which it is connected by a fine rock ridge, Swirral Edge. Its best feature is the tremendous shattered face it presents to the valley to the north, riven by a great scree gully (one which attracts ice climbers in the winter months). The steep slopes are nearly dry, but there is marshy ground around its base; the waters from Catstycam drain into Red Tarn Beck and Glenridding Beck, which in turn meet just under one mile north-east of the summit.

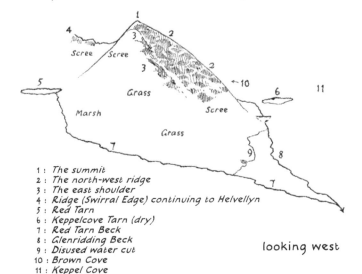

1 : *The summit*
2 : *The north-west ridge*
3 : *The east shoulder*
4 : *Ridge (Swirral Edge) continuing to Helvellyn*
5 : *Red Tarn*
6 : *Keppelcove Tarn (dry)*
7 : *Red Tarn Beck*
8 : *Glenridding Beck*
9 : *Disused water cut*
10 : *Brown Cove*
11 : *Keppel Cove*

looking west

MAP

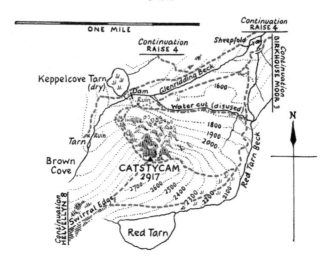

The paths to the summit via the north-west ridge and the east shoulder are well worn and simple to follow; navigating Catstycam in mist is far easier than in years gone by. However, for both paths the start (in ascent) is indistinct and both get very close to the precipitious north face. *In poor weather*, if in any doubt, go via Red Tarn/Swirral Edge.

Helvellyn and Swirral Edge

ASCENT FROM GLENRIDDING
2500 feet of ascent : 4 miles from Glenridding village

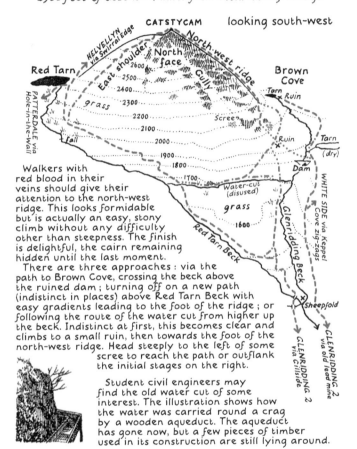

looking south-west

Walkers with red blood in their veins should give their attention to the north-west ridge. This looks formidable but is actually an easy, stony climb without any difficulty other than steepness. The finish is delightful, the cairn remaining hidden until the last moment.

There are three approaches : via the path to Brown Cove, crossing the beck above the ruined dam ; turning off on a new path (indistinct in places) above Red Tarn Beck with easy gradients leading to the foot of the ridge ; or following the route of the water cut from higher up the beck. Indistinct at first, this becomes clear and climbs to a small ruin, then towards the foot of the north-west ridge. Head steeply to the left of some scree to reach the path or outflank the initial stages on the right.

Student civil engineers may find the old water cut of some interest. The illustration shows how the water was carried round a crag by a wooden aqueduct. The aqueduct has gone now, but a few pieces of timber used in its construction are still lying around.

Of the two routes shown, that by Red Tarn Beck and the east shoulder is easy with a well worn path all the way to Red Tarn, in places repaired. The start of the climb of the east shoulder is not terribly distinct but a good path soon appears. The north-west ridge is steep and stony but a good airy climb in its later stages, giving a fine sense of achievement. This has become a popular alternative, as evidenced by the wear and tear on the path up the ridge. The easiest of all approaches is via Red Tarn, turning right at the depression between Swirral Edge and Catstycam.

THE SUMMIT

Catstycam is a true peak, and its small shapely summit is the finest in the eastern fells; if it were rock and not mainly grass it would be the finest in the district. Here the highest point is not in doubt!

DESCENTS: The north-west ridge is too steep for comfort. The quickest and easiest descent is by the east shoulder to Glenridding; for Patterdale, incline right from the east shoulder and cross Red Tarn Beck high up, to join the Striding Edge path.

In bad conditions use the east shoulder, keeping right rather than left in the mist, to Red Tarn Beck and so down to Glenridding. Or, for Patterdale, take the path to Helvellyn, turn left at the depression and follow the path below Red Tarn to Hole-in-the-Wall.

RIDGE ROUTE

To HELVELLYN, 3118' : 1 mile : SW

Depression at 2600' : 520 feet of ascent
A splendid walk with a fine rock scramble.
Safe in mist; dangerous in ice and snow.
Follow the grassy slope south-east from the summit. Soon after the depression there is a choice: the crest of Swirral Edge or a less exposed path to the left. The ridge narrows to an exciting but easy scramble, meeting the plateau at a cairn 200 yards north-west of Helvellyn's top.

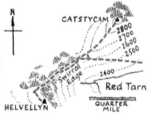

KEPPELCOVE TARN
AND ITS ENVIRONS
— a study in devastation

The burst banks

The breached dam

Keppelcove Tarn is now a marsh. Formerly it served as a reservoir for the Greenside lead mine. In October 1927, following a cloudburst, flooded waters burst the banks of the tarn, carved out a new ravine, and caused great damage. A replacement dam was breached later, in 1931, and has never been repaired.

The North-west Ridge, from White Side

THE VIEW

Catstycam, like all the satellites of Helvellyn, is robbed of a comprehensive view by Helvellyn itself, close at hand and higher. There is, however, an array of distant fells over the saddle between Helvellyn Lower Man and White Side. Eastwards the prospect is good.

Principal Fells

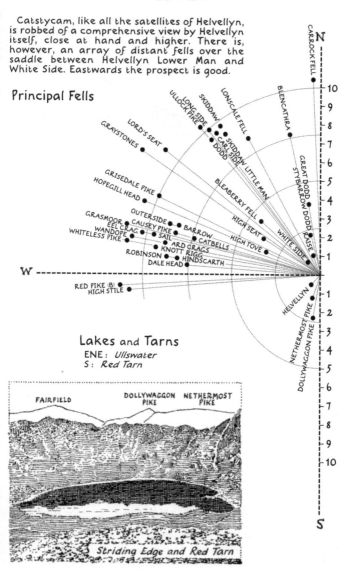

Lakes and Tarns

ENE: *Ullswater*
S: *Red Tarn*

Striding Edge and Red Tarn

THE VIEW

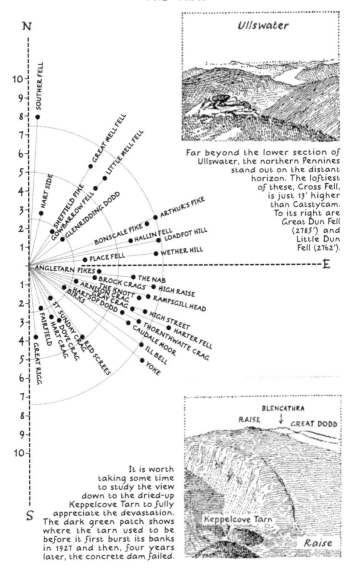

N

10
9
8 — SOUTHER FELL
7
6
5 — GREAT MELL FELL
4 — HART SIDE — LITTLE MELL FELL
3 — SHEFFIELD PIKE
2 — GOWBARROW FELL — GLENRIDDING DODD — ARTHUR'S PIKE
1 — BONSCALE PIKE — HALLIN FELL — LOADPOT HILL
— PLACE FELL — WETHER HILL
ANGLETARN PIKES - E
1 — BROCK CRAGS — THE NAB — HIGH RAISE
— ARNISON CRAG — THE KNOTT — RAMPSGILL HEAD
2 — GRAY CRAG — HARTSOP DODD
— BIRKS — HIGH STREET — HARTER FELL
3 — ST SUNDAY CRAG — THORNTHWAITE CRAG
— DOVE CRAG — CAUDALE MOOR
4 — FAIRFIELD — HART CRAG — RED SCREES — ILL BELL
5 — GREAT RIGG — YOKE
6
7
8
9
10

S

Ullswater

Far beyond the lower section of Ullswater, the northern Pennines stand out on the distant horizon. The loftiest of these, Cross Fell, is just 13' higher than Catstycam. To its right are Great Dun Fell (2785') and Little Dun Fell (2762').

RAISE   BLENCATHRA ↓   GREAT DODD

Keppelcove Tarn

Raise

It is worth taking some time to study the view down to the dried-up Keppelcove Tarn to fully appreciate the devastation. The dark green patch shows where the tarn used to be before it first burst its banks in 1927 and then, four years later, the concrete dam failed.

Clough Head 2381'

OS grid ref: NY334225

from High Rigg

• Threlkeld

Wanthwaite
•
▲ CLOUGH
HEAD

▲ GREAT
DODD

• Legburthwaite

MILES

0   1   2   3

From Kirkstone Pass the massive main ridge of the Fairfield and Helvellyn fells runs north, mile after mile, throughout maintaining a consistently high and a remarkably uniform altitude, and with a dozen distinct summits over 2500'. At its northern extremity the ground falls away swiftly to the deep valley of the Glenderamackin, and the last outpost of the ridge, although not so elevated as the summits to the south, occupies a commanding site: this is Clough Head.

NATURAL FEATURES

Contrary to the usual pattern of the Helvellyn fells, of which it is the most northerly member, Clough Head displays its crags to the west and grassy slopes to the east. These crags form a steep, continuous, mile-long wall above S! John's-in-the-Vale, with one breach only where a walker may safely venture; they are riven by deep gullies, one of which (Sandbed Gill) is the rockiest and roughest watercourse in the Helvellyn range. After initial steep scree, the northern slopes descend gently to the wide valley of the Glenderamackin at Threlkeld. Clough Head is an interesting fell, not only for walkers and explorers but for the ornithologist and botanist, the geologist and antiquarian also; while the merely curious traveller may content himself by puzzling out why and for what purpose Fisher's wife trod so persistently that remarkable path to Jim's Fold.

looking east

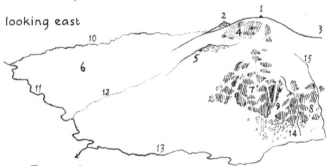

1 : *The summit*
2 : *White Pike*
3 : *Ridge continuing to Great Dodd*
4 : *Red Screes*
5 : *Threlkeld Knotts*
6 : *Threlkeld Common*
7 : *Wanthwaite Crags*
8 : *Bram Crag*
9 : *Fisher's Wife's Rake*
10 : *Mosedale Beck*
11 : *River Glenderamackin*
12 : *Birkett Beck*
13 : *S! John's Beck*
14 : *Sandbed Gill*
15 : *Beckthorns Gill*

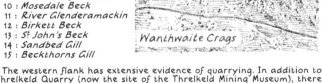

Wanthwaite Crags

The western flank has extensive evidence of quarrying. In addition to Threlkeld Quarry (now the site of the Threlkeld Mining Museum), there were granite quarries at Birkett Bank, Hill Top, Wanthwaite and Bram Crag. Behind Lowthwaite Farm lie the remains of Wanthwaite Crag Mine, mined for copper and lead up to the late 1800s.

MAP

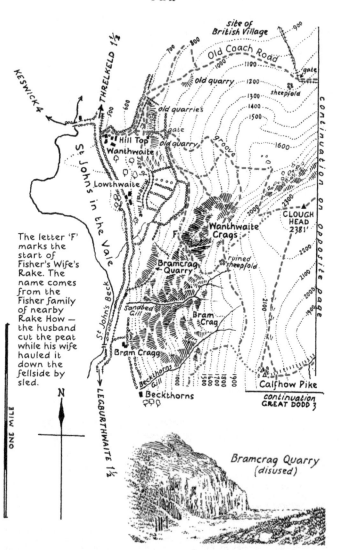

site of British Village

Old Coach Road

KESWICK 4

THRELKELD 1½

St Johns in the Vale

Hill Top
Wanthwaite
Lowthwaite

old quarry
old quarries
gate
old quarry
sheepfold

900
700
800
1000
1100
1200
1300
1400
1500
1600

groove

continuation on opposite page

2300
CLOUGH
HEAD
2381'

Wanthwaite
Crags

F

2000
2200
2100
2000
1900

Bramcrag
Quarry

ruined
sheepfold

The letter 'F'
marks the start
of Fisher's Wife's
Rake. The
name comes
from the
Fisher family
of nearby
Rake How —
the husband
cut the peat
while his wife
hauled it
down the
fellside by
sled.

St John's Beck

Sandbed
Gill

Bram
Crag

Bram Cragg

Beckthorns
Gill

1000
1100
1200
1300
1400
1500
900

Beckthorns

Calfhow Pike

continuation
GREAT DODD 3

ONE MILE

N

LEGBURTHWAITE 1½

Bramcrag Quarry
(disused)

'Wanthwaite' is pronounced 'Wanthet' and 'Lowthwaite' 'Lowthet'.

MAP

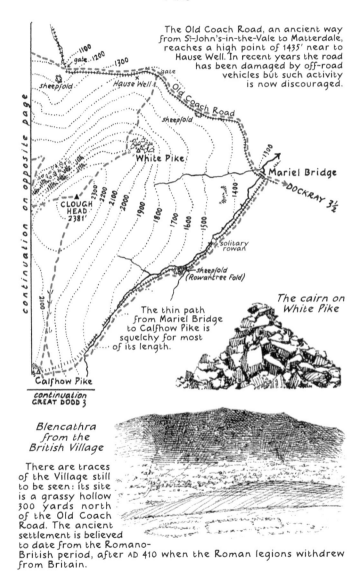

The Old Coach Road, an ancient way from St John's-in-the-Vale to Matterdale, reaches a high point of 1435' near to Hause Well. In recent years the road has been damaged by off-road vehicles but such activity is now discouraged.

1100
gate 1200
1300
gate
sheepfold
Hause Well
Old Coach Road
sheepfold
White Pike
1300
Mariel Bridge
DOCKRAY 3½
1400
CLOUGH HEAD 2381'
2300
2200
2100
2000
1900
1800
1700
1600
1500
solitary rowan
sheepfold (Rowantree Fold)
2100

continuation on opposite page

The thin path from Mariel Bridge to Calfhow Pike is squelchy for most of its length.

Calfhow Pike
continuation GREAT DODD 3

The cairn on White Pike

Blencathra from the British Village

There are traces of the Village still to be seen: its site is a grassy hollow 300 yards north of the Old Coach Road. The ancient settlement is believed to date from the Romano-British period, after AD 410 when the Roman legions withdrew from Britain.

ASCENT FROM WANTHWAITE
1900 feet of ascent : 2 miles ; 3 by way of White Pike

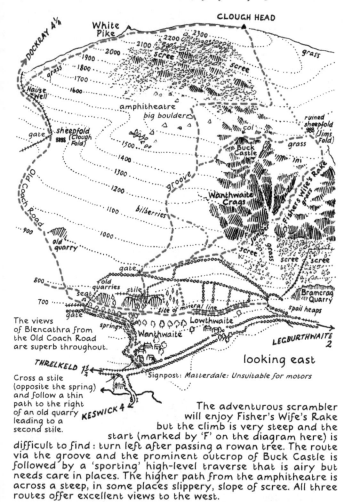

The views of Blencathra from the Old Coach Road are superb throughout.

Cross a stile (opposite the spring) and follow a thin path to the right of an old quarry leading to a second stile.

looking east

Signpost: Matterdale: Unsuitable for motors

The adventurous scrambler will enjoy Fisher's Wife's Rake but the climb is very steep and the start (marked by 'F' on the diagram here) is difficult to find : turn left after passing a rowan tree. The route via the groove and the prominent outcrop of Buck Castle is followed by a 'sporting' high-level traverse that is airy but needs care in places. The higher path from the amphitheatre is across a steep, in some places slippery, slope of scree. All three routes offer excellent views to the west.

The western aspect of Clough Head is dramatic, nowhere more so than from Fisher's Wife's Rake, but above the rough places it is all grass. The White Pike route is best used as a fast way down.

THE SUMMIT

The top of the fell is a pleasant grassy sward, adorned with a small wall shelter and an Ordnance Survey column.

Skiddaw

DESCENTS: Fisher's Wife's Rake is difficult to locate from above and in any case is too steep to provide a comfortable way down. The high-level path from Jim's Fold is an interesting route to the easier ground below the crags. Easiest of all is the grass slope to the Old Coach Road below Hause Well or the path to Hause Well from White Pike.

In bad weather conditions Clough Head is a dangerous place. All steep ground should be avoided and the descent made down the easy grass slope north-north-east to the Old Coach Road or the path below White Pike. A descent by Fisher's Wife's Rake should not be contemplated and the natural funnel of Sandbed Gill should be strictly left alone.

Two oddities on Clough Head

Unlike most Lakeland springs, which rise from grass, HAUSE WELL issues from a crevice in rocks. It is not easy to locate — its situation is near the fence bounding the Old Coach Road.

SANDBED GILL, a considerable stream in its rocky gorge, has an empty bed at valley level.

RIDGE ROUTE

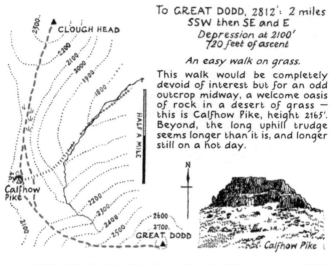

To GREAT DODD, 2812': 2 miles
SSW then SE and E
Depression at 2100'
720 feet of ascent

An easy walk on grass.

This walk would be completely devoid of interest but for an odd outcrop midway, a welcome oasis of rock in a desert of grass — this is Calfhow Pike, height 2165'. Beyond, the long uphill trudge seems longer than it is, and longer still on a hot day.

Calfhow Pike

Blencathra
from Clough Head

THE VIEW

Clough Head is sufficiently isolated from other fells to afford an uninterrupted prospect in every direction except south-east. A special feature, rare in views from the heights of the Helvellyn range, is the nice combination of valley and mountain scenery. This is an excellent viewpoint, the skyline between south and west being especially striking. To the north, the view of Blencathra's southern face is impressive.

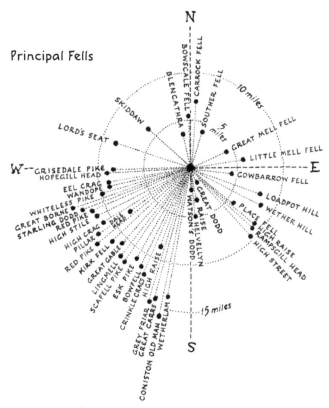

Principal Fells

Lakes and Tarns

SW: *Thirlmere*
W: *Derwent Water*
WNW: *Tewet Tarn*
WNW: *Bassenthwaite Lake*

Dollywaggon Pike   2815'

OS grid ref: NY346130

from Deepdale Hause

Patterdale

▲ HELVELLYN

Wythburn

DOLLYWAGGON PIKE

▲ FAIRFIELD

Grasmere

MILES

0   1   2   3   4   5

NATURAL FEATURES

Like most of the high fells south of the Sticks Pass, Dollywaggon Pike exhibits a marked contrast in its western and eastern aspects. To the west, uninteresting grass slopes descend to Dunmail Raise almost unrelieved by rock and scarred only by the wide stony track gouged across the breast of the fell by the boots of generations of pilgrims to Helvellyn. But the eastern side is a desolation of crag and boulder and scree : here are two silent recesses, Ruthwaite Cove and Cock Cove, which are rarely visited by walkers but well worth a detailed exploration, split by a narrow ridge (The Tongue), an ascent of the highest order. Rock climbers, too, are attracted by a pair of crags (Falcon Crag and Tarn Crag) that overlook the upper part of Grisedale.

looking north-west

1 : The summit of
    Dollywaggon Pike
2 : Ridge continuing to
    Nethermost Pike
3 : The Tongue
4 : Ruthwaite Cove
5 : Cock Cove
6 : Falcon Crag (or
    Dollywaggon Crag)
7 : The three gullies of
    Tarn Crag
8 : Tarn Crag
9 : Spout Crag
10 : Caves (artificial)
11 : Birkside Gill
12 : Raise Beck
13 : Ruthwaite Beck
14 : Grisedale Beck
15 : Grisedale Tarn

Falcon Crag

The figure 10 also indicates the position of Ruthwaite Lodge.

MAP

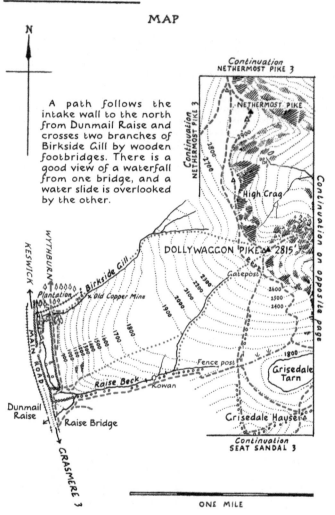

A path follows the intake wall to the north from Dunmail Raise and crosses two branches of Birkside Gill by wooden footbridges. There is a good view of a waterfall from one bridge, and a water slide is overlooked by the other.

ONE MILE

Grisedale Tarn, at an altitude of 1770' and a depth of 110', is thought to hold brown trout, perch and eels, together with something a lot more valuable: it is the supposed resting place of the crown of the kingdom of Cumberland, which was reputedly cast into the waters in 945 by soldiers of the last king, Dunmail, after he was killed in battle.

MAP

Ruthwaite Lodge has a long history. It was originally built in 1854 as a shooting lodge. For some years it was used by the Sheffield University Mountaineering Club, before again falling into disuse and disrepair. It was restored by the Ullswater Outward Bound School in 1993. The remains of several mine levels and some shallow open workings can still be traced near the lodge, close to the cascades of Ruthwaite Beck.

ONE MILE

Hard Tarn, which is more usually visited during an ascent or descent of Nethermost Pike's east ridge (see *Nethermost Pike 6*), can easily be visited from Ruthwaite Lodge, initially by taking the thin path to the right of the lodge into Ruthwaite Cove then following the beck on the right-hand side of the cove.

ASCENT FROM GRASMERE
2700 feet of ascent : 5 miles from Grasmere Church

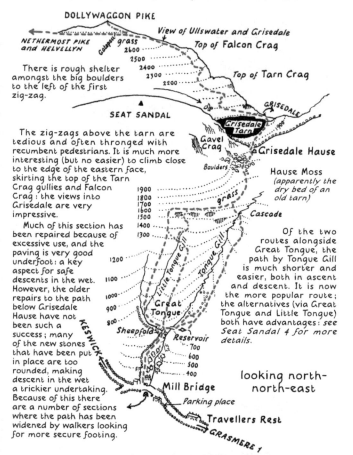

There is rough shelter amongst the big boulders to the left of the first zig-zag.

The zig-zags above the tarn are tedious and often thronged with recumbent pedestrians. It is much more interesting (but no easier) to climb close to the edge of the eastern face, skirting the top of the Tarn Crag gullies and Falcon Crag: the views into Grisedale are very impressive.

Much of this section has been repaired because of excessive use, and the paving is very good underfoot: a key aspect for safe descents in the wet. However, the older repairs to the path below Grisedale Hause have not been such a success; many of the new stones that have been put in place are too rounded, making descent in the wet a trickier undertaking. Because of this there are a number of sections where the path has been widened by walkers looking for more secure footing.

Of the two routes alongside Great Tongue, the path by Tongue Gill is much shorter and easier, both in ascent and descent. It is now the more popular route; the alternatives (via Great Tongue and Little Tongue) both have advantages: see Seat Sandal 4 for more details.

looking north-north-east

An alternative way up is to climb Seat Sandal first via its easy south Ridge. From the summit there are two options: a descent to Grisedale Hause, which joins the route illustrated, or a beeline for Dollywaggon Pike. (See Seat Sandal 4 and 8 for details.)

The route illustrated is the much-trodden path, almost a highway in places, from Grasmere to Helvellyn. It climbs the breast of Dollywaggon Pike and passes slightly below its summit, which is easily attained by a short detour.

ASCENT FROM DUNMAIL RAISE
2100 feet of ascent : 2 miles

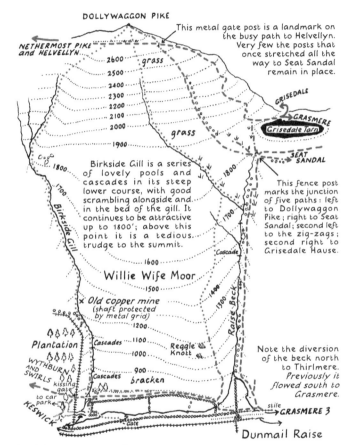

DOLLYWAGGON PIKE

NETHERMOST PIKE and HELVELLYN

This metal gate post is a landmark on the busy path to Helvellyn. Very few the posts that once stretched all the way to Seat Sandal remain in place.

2600
2500
2400
2300
2200
2100
2000
1900

grass

GRISEDALE

GRASMERE

Grisedale Tarn

grass

SEAT SANDAL

1800

Birkside Gill is a series of lovely pools and cascades in its steep lower course, with good scrambling alongside and in the bed of the gill. It continues to be attractive up to 1800'; above this point it is a tedious trudge to the summit.

This fence post marks the junction of five paths: left to Dollywaggon Pike; right to Seat Sandal; second left to the zig-zags; second right to Grisedale Hause.

1800

1700

Birkside Gill

Cascade

1700

Raise Beck

1600

Willie Wife Moor

1500

1400

× Old copper mine (shaft protected by metal grid)

1300

1200

Plantation

Cascades

1100

1000

Reggle Knott

1200

WYTHBURN AND SWIRLS

kissing gate

Cascades

900

bracken

Note the diversion of the beck north to Thirlmere. Previously it flowed south to Grasmere.

to car park

KESWICK

Gate

stile

GRASMERE 3

Dunmail Raise

looking east-north-east

The path beside Raise Beck is a delight up to the 1700' contour, the chief attraction being a pair of lovely cascades. A water slab crossing the path below the first cascade needs care when in spate.

The western slopes offer a short and direct route from the main road (the A591) but are monotonously grassy and of greater interest to sheep than walkers. Preferably one of the becks should be followed up, especially on a hot day.

ASCENT FROM GRISEDALE
2400 feet of ascent · 5 miles from Patterdale village

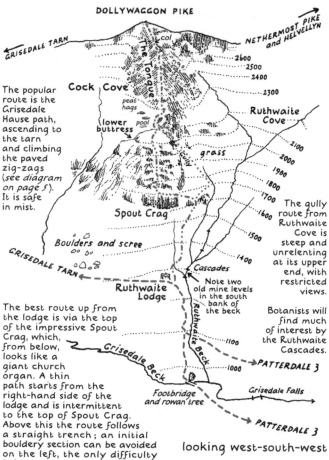

DOLLYWAGGON PIKE

GRISEDALE TARN

NETHERMOST PIKE and HELVELLYN

col

The Tongue

2600
2500
2400
2300

Cock Cove

peat hags

lower buttress

pool

Ruthwaite Cove

2100
2000
1900
1800
1700

gully

grass

1600
1500
1400

Spout Crag

Boulders and scree

GRISEDALE TARN

Cascades

Note two old mine levels in the south bank of the beck

Ruthwaite Lodge

Ruthwaite Beck

1100
1000

Grisedale Beck

Footbridge and rowan tree

PATTERDALE 3

Grisedale Falls

PATTERDALE 3

looking west-south-west

The popular route is the Grisedale Hause path, ascending to the tarn and climbing the paved zig-zags (*see diagram on page 5*). It is safe in mist.

The gully route from Ruthwaite Cove is steep and unrelenting at its upper end, with restricted views.

Botanists will find much of interest by the Ruthwaite Cascades.

The best route up from the lodge is via the top of the impressive Spout Crag, which, from below, looks like a giant church organ. A thin path starts from the right-hand side of the lodge and is intermittent to the top of Spout Crag. Above this the route follows a straight trench; an initial bouldery section can be avoided on the left, the only difficulty being a steep and damp grassy gully. Above the lower buttress, The Tongue looks daunting, but a thin path can soon be found to the left of the crest and the rest of the climb is a delight. A narrow grassy col near the summit is particularly pleasing.

This is much the most interesting and exhilarating way to the summit, but is relatively unknown and rarely used. The finish up the narrow Tongue is excellent. *This route should not be attempted in bad weather conditions.*

THE SUMMIT

The summit is a small grassy dome, narrowing to the east where the narrow ridge descending towards Grisedale (The Tongue) commences. The big cairn illustrated below is 30 yards west of the highest point. The fence post has gone.

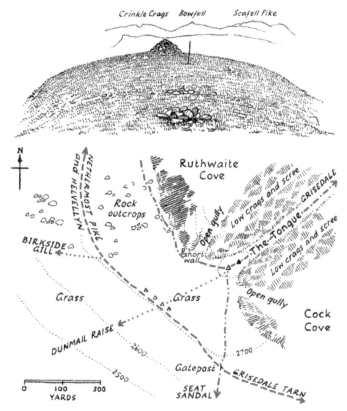

DESCENTS: The quickest and easiest way down is the direct descent to Dunmail Raise, but Birkside Gill should be avoided. The Tongue route should not be attempted unless it is already familiar, and even then is too steep in places to be comfortable, nor descents made into Cock Cove or Ruthwaite Cove, *in mist*: this side of the fell is extremely rough.

In bad weather conditions, the safest descent is the excellent zig-zag path to Grisedale Tarn, for either Grasmere or Patterdale.

THE VIEW

The view is extensive in most directions but restricted in the north and south-east by neighbouring fells of greater altitude. Westwards, the panorama is excellent.

Principal Fells

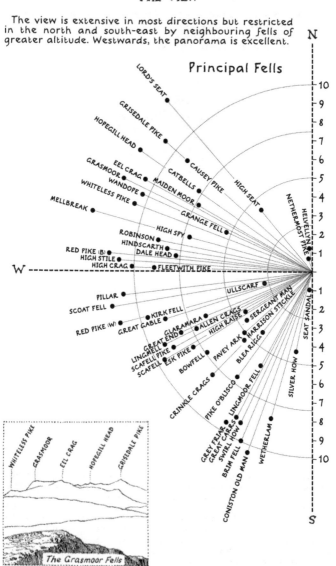

The Grasmoor Fells

THE VIEW

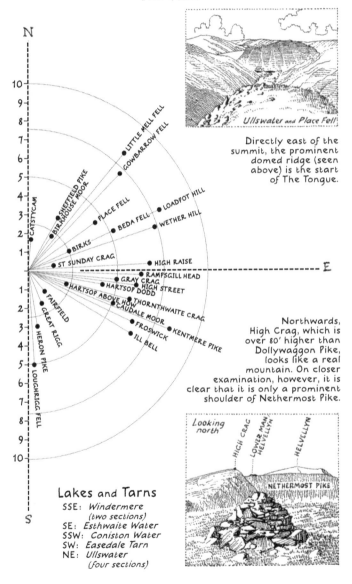

Ullswater and Place Fell

Directly east of the summit, the prominent domed ridge (seen above) is the start of The Tongue.

N

10
9
8
7
6
5
4
3
2
1

LITTLE MELL FELL
GOWBARROW FELL
SHEFFIELD PIKE
BIRKHOUSE MOOR
CATSTYCAM
PLACE FELL
BEDA FELL
LOADPOT HILL
WETHER HILL
BIRKS
ST SUNDAY CRAG
HIGH RAISE

E

RAMPSGILL HEAD
GRAY CRAG
HIGH STREET
HARTSOP DODD
HARTSOP ABOVE HOW
THORNTHWAITE CRAG
FAIRFIELD
CAUDALE MOOR
GREAT RIGG
FROSWICK
KENTMERE PIKE
HERON PIKE
ILL BELL

1
2
3
4
5
6
7
8
9
10

LOUGHRIGG FELL

S

Northwards, High Crag, which is over 80' higher than Dollywaggon Pike, looks like a real mountain. On closer examination, however, it is clear that it is only a prominent shoulder of Nethermost Pike.

Looking north

HIGH CRAG
LOWER MAN HELVELLYN
HELVELLYN
NETHERMOST PIKE

Lakes and Tarns

SSE: *Windermere* (two sections)
SE: *Esthwaite Water*
SSW: *Coniston Water*
SW: *Easedale Tarn*
NE: *Ullswater* (four sections)

Cave and Cascades, Ruthwaite

RIDGE ROUTES

To NETHERMOST PIKE, 2920' : 1 mile : NW then N.

Depression at 2700'
220 feet of ascent

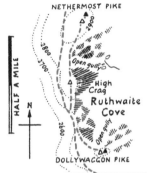

An easy walk with fine views. Safe in mist if the paths are followed closely.

An excellent path links Dollywaggon Pike and Nethermost Pike, skirting their actual summits to the west. A more interesting route, with a clear path for most of its length, lies along the edge of the crags overlooking Ruthwaite Cove.

To SEAT SANDAL, 2415'
1¼ miles : S

Depression at 1850'
600 feet of ascent

A steep but easy descent followed by a dull climb. The depression is marshy. Safe but unpleasant in mist.

Seat Sandal is the next fell to the south, but the direct route to it can hardly be called a ridge. From the gatepost a thin path becomes very distinct as the descent steepens alongside a broken wall which marks the former boundary of Cumberland and Westmorland. Of the row of fence posts down to the depression, only a few remain, one of which marks a crossroads of paths. A path heads up Seat Sandal's flank beside a broken wall.

The Tarn Crag gullies

Dove Crag

2598'

OS grid ref: NY375104

from Dovedale

Patterdale •

Hartsop •

▲ FAIRFIELD

DOVE ▲ CRAG

RED SCREES ▲

• Grasmere

Ambleside •

MILES

0   1   2   3   4

The lofty height that towers
so magnificently above Dovedale
is indebted for its name to a very
impressive vertical wall of rock
on the north-east flank: the crag
was named first and the summit
of the parent fell above, which
in the middle of the 20th century
was considered unworthy of
any official title, is now named
'Dove Crag' on the Ordnance
Survey maps.

NATURAL FEATURES

Dove Crag is a mountain of sharp contrasts. To the east, its finest aspect, it presents a scarred and rugged face, a face full of character and interest. Here, in small compass, is a tangle of rough country, a maze of steep cliffs, gloomy hollows and curious foothills gnarled like the knuckles of a clenched fist, with the charming valley of Dovedale below and the main crag of the fell frowning down over all. Very different is its appearance from other directions. A high ridge, part of the popular Fairfield Horseshoe, runs south, with featureless grass slopes flowing down from it to the valleys of Rydale and Scandale. The fell is a vertebra of the Fairfield spine and is connected to the next height in the system, Hart Crag, by a lofty depression.

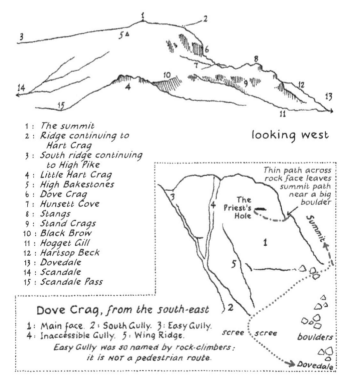

looking west

1 : The summit
2 : Ridge continuing to Hart Crag
3 : South ridge continuing to High Pike
4 : Little Hart Crag
5 : High Bakestones
6 : Dove Crag
7 : Hunsett Cove
8 : Stangs
9 : Stand Crags
10 : Black Brow
11 : Hogget Gill
12 : Hartsop Beck
13 : Dovedale
14 : Scandale
15 : Scandale Pass

The Priest's Hole

Thin path across rock face leaves summit path near a big boulder

Summit

scree   scree   boulders

Dovedale

Dove Crag, from the south-east

1 : Main face. 2 : South Gully. 3 : Easy Gully.
4 : Inaccessible Gully. 5 : Wing Ridge.
Easy Gully was so named by rock-climbers: it is NOT a pedestrian route.

MAP

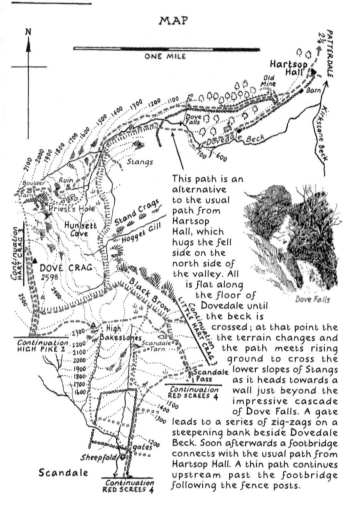

ONE MILE

N

PATTERDALE 2½

Hartsop Hall

Old Mine

Barn

Dove Falls

Dovedale Beck

Kirkstone Beck

Stangs

Boulder

Tarn

Ruin

Priest's Hole

Hunsett Cove

Stand Crags

Hogget Gill

Continuation HART CRAG

DOVE CRAG 2598

Black Brow

Continuation LITTLE HART CRAG 3

High Bakestones

Scandale Tarn

Scandale Pass

Continuation HIGH PIKE 2

Continuation RED SCREES 4

Sheepfold

gates

Scandale

Continuation RED SCREES 4

Dove Falls

This path is an alternative to the usual path from Hartsop Hall, which hugs the fell side on the north side of the valley. All is flat along the floor of Dovedale until the beck is crossed; at that point the the terrain changes and the path meets rising ground to cross the lower slopes of Stangs as it heads towards a wall just beyond the impressive cascade of Dove Falls. A gate leads to a series of zig-zags on a steepening bank beside Dovedale Beck. Soon afterwards a footbridge connects with the usual path from Hartsop Hall. A thin path continues upstream past the footbridge following the fence posts.

The Priest's Hole is a natural cave two thirds of the way up the sheer wall of Dove Crag's finest rock face, with a low wall across its entrance. It is hard to locate and requires strong nerves to reach; the ledge that indicates its position can be seen from the solitary boulder just below the tarn, and a thin path climbs from here across the rock face to the cave. It is safe if you take care, but one slip could be disastrous. Inside the cave there is a metal box containing messages from visitors.

ASCENT FROM PATTERDALE
2,200 feet of ascent: 5 miles from Patterdale village

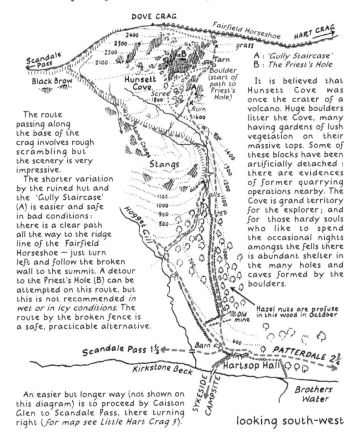

DOVE CRAG

Fairfield Horseshoe   HART CRAG

2400

2300

2200

2100

grass

Scandale Pass

Black Brow

Hunsett Cove

Scree 1800

Tarn

Boulder (start of path to Priest's Hole)

Ruin 1600

A: 'Gully Staircase'
B: The Priest's Hole

It is believed that Hunsett Cove was once the crater of a volcano. Huge boulders litter the Cove, many having gardens of lush vegetation on their massive tops. Some of these blocks have been artificially detached: there are evidences of former quarrying operations nearby. The Cove is grand territory for the explorer; and for those hardy souls who like to spend the occasional nights amongst the fells there is abundant shelter in the many holes and caves formed by the boulders.

The route passing along the base of the crag involves rough scrambling but the scenery is very impressive.

The shorter variation by the ruined hut and the 'Gully Staircase' (A) is easier and safe in bad conditions: there is a clear path all the way to the ridge line of the Fairfield Horseshoe — just turn left and follow the broken wall to the summit. A detour to the Priest's Hole (B) can be attempted on this route, but this is not recommended in *wet or in icy conditions*. The route by the broken fence is a safe, practicable alternative.

Stangs

1100
1000
900
800

Falls

Hogget Gill

Hazel nuts are profuse in this wood in October

Old mine

Barn   600   PATTERDALE 2¾

Scandale Pass 1½

Kirkstone Beck

Hartsop Hall

SYKESIDE CAMPSITE

Brothers Water

An easier but longer way (not shown on this diagram) is to proceed by Caiston Glen to Scandale Pass, there turning right (*for map see Little Hart Crag 3*).

looking south-west

The best way up is via the 'Gully Staircase'. This was once a slippery ascent on scree but a well constructed paved path now makes this steepest section of the ascent very easy.

Dove Crag is most often ascended from Ambleside on the popular tour of the 'Fairfield Horseshoe' — but the climb from Patterdale, by Dovedale, is far superior: it gives a much more interesting and intimate approach, the sharp transition from the soft loveliness of the valley to the desolation above being very impressive.

ASCENT FROM AMBLESIDE
2500 feet of ascent : 5 miles

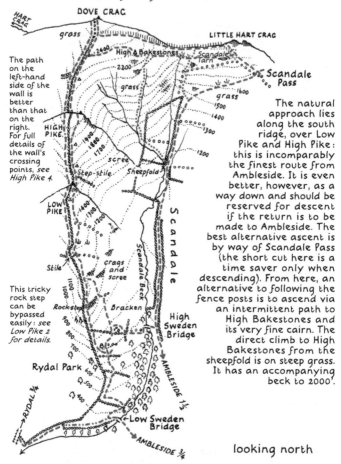

HART CRAG

DOVE CRAG

grass

LITTLE HART CRAG

2400

High Bakestones

Scandale Tarn

Scandale Pass

2200

grass

1600

1500

1400

1300

1200

The path on the left-hand side of the wall is better than that on the right. For full details of the wall's crossing points, *see High Pike 4.*

HIGH PIKE

1900

1800

1700

scree

Step-stile

Sheepfold

LOW PIKE

1600

1500

1400

1300

1200

Stile

crags and scree

Scandale Beck

Scandale

This tricky rock step can be bypassed easily: see Low Pike 2 for details.

1100

1000

Rockstep

Bracken

900

800

700

High Sweden Bridge

Rydal Park

600

500

500

AMBLESIDE 1½

RYDAL ¾

←Low Sweden Bridge

AMBLESIDE ¾

The natural approach lies along the south ridge, over Low Pike and High Pike: this is incomparably the finest route from Ambleside. It is even better, however, as a way down and should be reserved for descent if the return is to be made to Ambleside. The best alternative ascent is by way of Scandale Pass (the short cut here is a time saver only when descending). From here, an alternative to following the fence posts is to ascend via an intermittent path to High Bakestones and its very fine cairn. The direct climb to High Bakestones from the sheepfold is on steep grass. It has an accompanying beck to 2000'.

looking north

Leaving Ambleside by the Grasmere road, pass the Bridge House and turn right into Smithy Brow (the road leading to Kirkstone Pass). For Low Sweden Bridge, turn left into Nook Lane; for High Sweden Bridge, continue uphill and turn left into Sweden Bridge Lane.

Dove Crag cannot be seen from Ambleside, but rising from the fields north of the town is its clearly defined south ridge, offering an obvious staircase to the summit.

THE SUMMIT

The actual top of the fell is a small rock platform crowned by a cairn, twenty yards east of the crumbling wall crossing the broad summit plateau. It is of little distinction and there is nothing of interest in the immediate surroundings.

A visit to the top of the crag will repay walkers who have a liking for exploration. A quarter-mile north of the cairn, Easy Gully is reached by following down the natural slope of the fell: it can be identified by an overhang on the wall of the gully. A dividing buttress hides Inaccessible Gully, the upper exit of which will be found forty yards north. Just to the left of the top of Inaccessible Gully is a cross-wall which marks the limit of exploration, for beyond it is the precipitous main face of the crag.

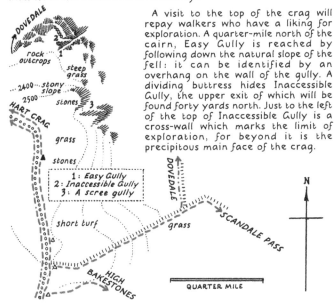

1: Easy Gully
2: Inaccessible Gully
3: A scree gully

QUARTER MILE

DESCENTS : All routes of ascent may be reversed for descent. The way down into Dovedale from the Dove Crag–Hart Crag depression used to be very rough but some fine paving through the worst section, the 'Gully Staircase', has made it good underfoot. The High Bakestones path to Scandale Pass is a little bumpy soon after the cairn, but easy enough, though not advised in bad weather.

In mist, whether bound for Ambleside or Patterdale, follow the broken wall south, soon turning left along the broken fence for Patterdale via Dovedale or continue to Scandale Pass. *Direct descents to Dovedale from the summit must not be attempted.*

THE VIEW
(with distances in miles)

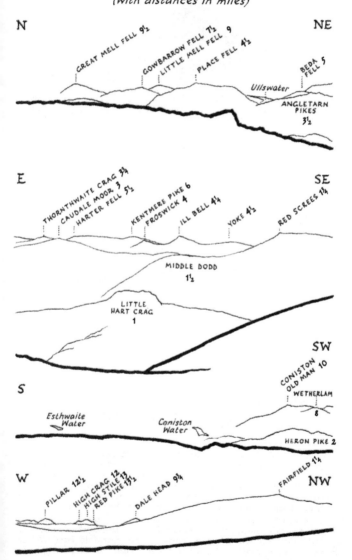

THE VIEW

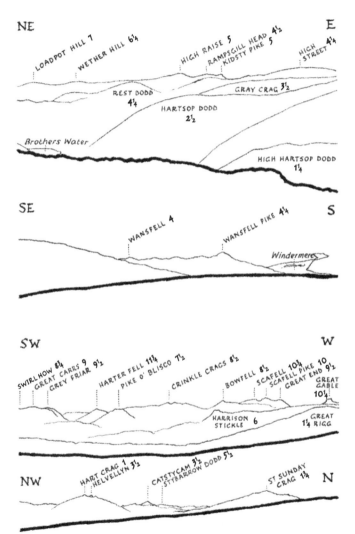

NE

LOADPOT HILL 7 WETHER HILL 6¼ HIGH RAISE 5 RAMPSGILL HEAD 5 KIDSTY PIKE 5 4½ HIGH STREET 4¼ E

REST DODD 4¼ GRAY CRAG 3½

HARTSOP DODD 2½

Brothers Water

HIGH HARTSOP DODD 1¼

SE

WANSFELL 4 WANSFELL PIKE 4¼ S

Windermere

SW

SWIRL HOW 8¾ GREAT CARRS 9 GREY FRIAR 9½ HARTER FELL 11¾ PIKE O' BLISCO 7½ CRINKLE CRAGS 8½ BOWFELL 8½ SCAFELL 10¾ SCAFELL PIKE 10 GREAT END 9½ GREAT GABLE 10¼ W

HARRISON STICKLE 6 GREAT RIGG 1¼

NW

HART CRAG 1 HELVELLYN 3½ CATSTYCAM 3½ STYBARROW DODD 5½ ST SUNDAY CRAG 1¾ N

Helvellyn comes more into view
by walking north from the cairn.

RIDGE ROUTES

To HART CRAG, 2698'; ¾ mile : NW
Depression at 2350'
350 feet of ascent

An easy walk, but Hart
Crag needs care in mist.

Follow the broken wall into the dip then up a rocky section until it comes to an end. Clamber up the rocks to the western (summit) cairn.

To HIGH PIKE, 2155'; 1 mile : S
Slight depression
Only a few feet of ascent

One of the easiest miles in Lakeland. Perfectly safe in mist.

Follow the wall south; a good path keeps a few yards to the left of it.

To LITTLE HART CRAG 2091'; 1¼ miles S then ENE and SE
Minor depressions
200 feet of ascent

Clear paths lead to the top of Little Hart Crag.

Head south beside the broken wall then follow the broken fence. A thin path turns off left while the main path makes a beeline to Scandale Pass.

The cairn on High Bakestones

This beautifully built 8' column, commanding a view of Scandale, is one of the finest specimens on these hills. It is more than a cairn. It is a work of art and a lasting memorial to its builder. The top has lost a few stones over the years, but the cairn has borne up well to the Lakeland elements.

Dovedale, from the top of Easy Gully

Fairfield

2863'

OS grid ref: NY 359117

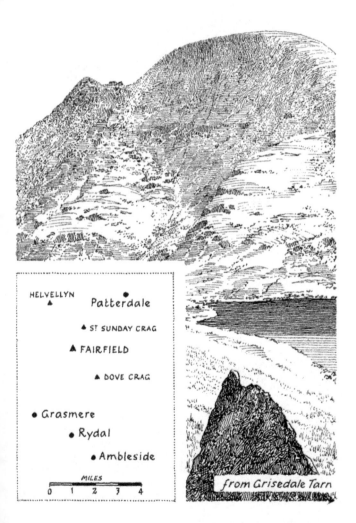

HELVELLYN
▲

Patterdale ●

▲ St SUNDAY CRAG

▲ FAIRFIELD

▲ DOVE CRAG

● Grasmere

● Rydal

● Ambleside

MILES
0   1   2   3   4

from Grisedale Tarn

NATURAL FEATURES

The rough triangle formed by Grisedale Pass, the Rothay valley and Scandale Pass, with the village of Patterdale as its apex, contains within its area a bulky mountain-system with five distinct summits over 2500'. High ridges link these summits; there are also subsidiary ridges and spurs of lesser altitude, massive rocky buttresses, gloomy coves and fine daleheads. The whole mass constitutes a single geographical unit and the main summit is Fairfield, a grand mountain with grand satellites in support. No group of fells in the district exhibits a more striking contrast in appearance when surveyed from opposite sides than this lofty Fairfield group. From the south it appears as a great horseshoe of grassy slopes below a consistently high skyline, simple in design and impressive in altitude, but lacking those dramatic qualities that appeal most to the lover of hills. But on the north side the Fairfield range is magnificent: here are dark precipices, long fans of scree, abrupt crags, desolate combes and deep valleys: a tangle of rough country, small in extent but full of interest, and well worth exploration. This grimmer side of the Fairfield group can only be visited conveniently from the Patterdale area. Fairfield turns its broad back to the south, to Rydal and Grasmere, and climbers from this direction get only the merest glimpse of its best features; many visitors to the summit, indeed, return unsuspecting, and remember Fairfield and its neighbours as mountains of grass. The few who know the head of Deepdale and the recesses of Dovedale, intimately, have a very different impression.

continued

looking south-east

1 : The summit
2 : Cofa Pike
3 : Deepdale Hause
4 : Ridge continuing to St Sunday Crag
5 : Greenhow End
6 : North face
7 : Ridge continuing to Great Rigg
8 : Grisedale Hause
9 : Grisedale Tarn
10 : Grisedale Beck
11 : Tongue Gill

NATURAL FEATURES

continued

Three ridges leave the top of Fairfield: one goes south over Great Rigg to end abruptly at Nab Scar above Rydal Water; another, the spine of the Fairfield system, keeps a high level to Dove Crag, traversing Hart Crag on the way, and the third, and best, runs north inclining east over the splintered crest of Cofa Pike and on to St Sunday Crag. On the west flank only is there no descending ridge: here an ill-defined gable-end falls steeply to Grisedale Hause.

The southern and western slopes are simple, the northern and eastern complicated and far more interesting. Here a mile-long face of alternating rock and scree towers high above the barren hollow of Deepdale. Crags abound: most impressive is the precipitous cliff of Greenhow End, scarped on three sides and thrusting far into the valley, and a wall of even steeper rock, with Scrubby Crag prominent, bounds Link Cove to the east.

Fairfield claims Deepdale Beck, Rydal Beck and the main branch of Tongue Gill as its streams, but is only one of many contributors to Grisedale Beck. It is without a tarn of its own, forming one side only of the green basin containing Grisedale Tarn.

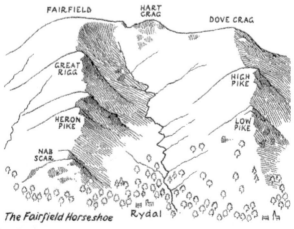

The Fairfield Horseshoe

The horseshoe is 11 miles in length between Rydal and Ambleside. Add another mile and a half for the return to the starting point. The total ascent is around 3500'.

Cofa Pike and the north-east ridge

Greenhow End

Scrubby Crag

The Crags of Fairfield

Black Crag, Rydal Head

Black Crag is renowned among rock climbers for its clean rock.
Its toughest route (very severe) is named Piglet's Wall.

Fairfield 5

MAP

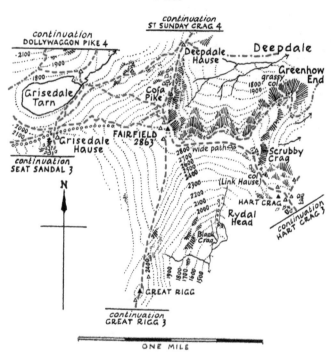

Cofa Pike

Of all the significant subsidiary summits in Lakeland, it is hard to think of one that is as distinctive as Cofa Pike. It is surely worth climbing if Fairfield is being ascended from Deepdale or Grisedale, and it stands in the way of the ridge walk from St Sunday Crag to Fairfield. Its bristly summit rocks can be bypassed, of course (but should not be), and it has a perched boulder on its western flank high above Grisedale Tarn.

Rocks on Cofa Pike

ASCENT FROM GRASMERE
2650 feet of ascent : 4¼ miles from Grasmere Church

Two longer variations are possible from Grisedale Hause: from the far end of Grisedale Tarn take the Deepdale Hause path and climb over stony Cofa Pike, or turn right off this path after 300 yards, where a steeper and more direct route bypasses the Pike.

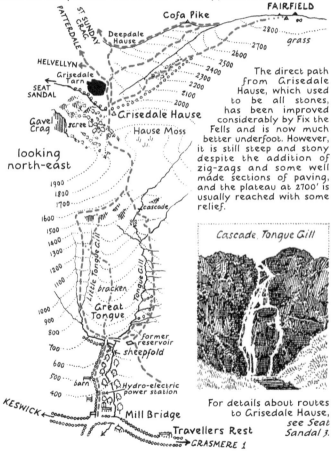

PATTERDALE

ST SUNDAY CRAG

Cofa Pike

FAIRFIELD

Deepdale Hause

2800

2700   grass

2600

2500

2400

2300

2200

2100

2000

HELVELLYN

Grisedale Tarn

SEAT SANDAL

Gavel Crag   scree

Grisedale Hause

Hause Moss

looking
north-east

The direct path from Grisedale Hause, which used to be all stones, has been improved considerably by Fix the Fells and is now much better underfoot. However, it is still steep and stony despite the addition of zig-zags and some well made sections of paving, and the plateau at 2700' is usually reached with some relief.

1900
1800
1700
1600
1500
1400
1300
1200
1100
1000
900
800
700
600
500
400

cascade

Little Tongue Gill

Tongue Gill

bracken

Great Tongue

former reservoir

sheepfold

barn

Hydro-electric power station

KESWICK ←

Mill Bridge

→ Travellers Rest

← GRASMERE 1

Cascade, Tongue Gill

For details about routes to Grisedale Hause, see Seat Sandal 3.

Tongue Gill is an interesting approach but the last 1000' of climbing is dull and, whichever route is taken from Grisedale Hause, arduous underfoot, with inescapable scree and stones. *The top of Fairfield is confusing in mist.*

ASCENT FROM PATTERDALE
2400 feet of ascent : 5¼ miles

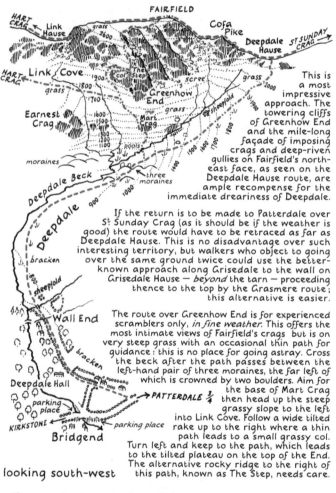

looking south-west

This is a most impressive approach. The towering cliffs of Greenhow End and the mile-long façade of imposing crags and deep-riven gullies on Fairfield's north-east face, as seen on the Deepdale Hause route, are ample recompense for the immediate dreariness of Deepdale.

If the return is to be made to Patterdale over St Sunday Crag (as it should be if the weather is good) the route would have to be retraced as far as Deepdale Hause. This is no disadvantage over such interesting territory, but walkers who object to going over the same ground twice could use the better-known approach along Grisedale to the wall on Grisedale Hause — *beyond* the tarn — proceeding thence to the top by the Grasmere route; this alternative is easier.

The route over Greenhow End is for experienced scramblers only, *in fine weather*. This offers the most intimate views of Fairfield's crags but is on very steep grass with an occasional thin path for guidance: this is no place for going astray. Cross the beck after the path passes between the left-hand pair of three moraines, the far left of which is crowned by two boulders. Aim for the base of Mart Crag then head up the steep grassy slope to the left into Link Cove. Follow a wide tilted rake up to the right where a thin path leads to a small grassy col. Turn left and keep to the path, which leads to the tilted plateau on the top of the End. The alternative rocky ridge to the right of this path, known as The Step, needs care.

The gradual revelation of the savage northern face of Fairfield as the view up Deepdale unfolds gives a high quality to this route. Deepdale itself is desolate, but has interesting evidences of glacial action; Link Cove is one of the finest examples of a hanging valley.

The head of Deepdale

The cliffs of Fairfield, from Greenhow End

The 'Deepdale Horseshoe' may not be as well known as the 'Fairfield Horseshoe', but is just as challenging and rewarding. The better way is clockwise: Hartsop above How, Hart Crag, Fairfield, Cofa Pike, St Sunday Crag, Birks and Arnison Crag. The purest route would omit the last two summits and include St Sunday Crag's east ridge.

THE SUMMIT

The summit of Fairfield is an extensive grassy plateau. The absence of distinguishing natural features makes it, in mist, particularly confusing, and the abundance of cairns is then a hindrance rather than a help. The actual top is flat and its surface is too rough to bear the imprint of paths, and the one definable point is a tumbledown windbreak of stones, built as a short wall and offering shelter only to persons of imagination. Thirty yards north of the shelter is the principal and largest cairn, which has five alcoves scooped out of it.

Mention should be made of the excellent turf on this wide top: weary feet will judge it delightful.

DESCENTS: Too many cairns are worse than too few, and it is fortunate that the piles of stones that once adorned the tops of the buttresses of the north face, snares in the mist to strangers to the fell, have now been removed. In clear weather there is no difficulty in identifying the various routes of descent, the best of which lies over Cofa Pike and St. Sunday Crag to Patterdale: an exhilarating and beautiful walk.

In mist, note that none of the usual routes descend over steep ground and that a cairn does not necessarily indicate a path. With care, all routes are quite practicable, but the safest way off, in bad weather and whatever the destination, is westwards to Grisedale Tarn, following a line of cairns until a path appears. (It doesn't matter much about finding a path if the walker is sure he is going either west or south, or between these points but he who wanders northward courts disaster.)

THE SUMMIT

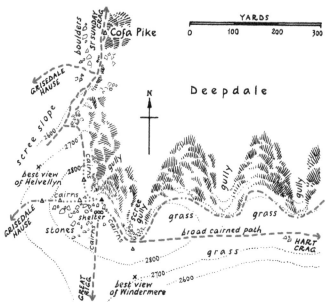

Travellers along the path to Hart Crag are urged to leave it *in clear weather* and skirt the edge of the cliffs just to the north, the glimpses of Deepdale down the gullies being very impressive. Over the years a thin but generally clear path has been formed by the feet of walkers who have decided to see Fairfield from this route. A detour to the top of Greenhow End, easily reached by a gradual descent over grass, is highly recommended, the rock scenery being especially good and the arête attractive. Most of the way there is a thin path, and a visit to the north face viewpoint is obligatory. *This place is dangerous in mist.*

THE VIEW

(with distances in miles)

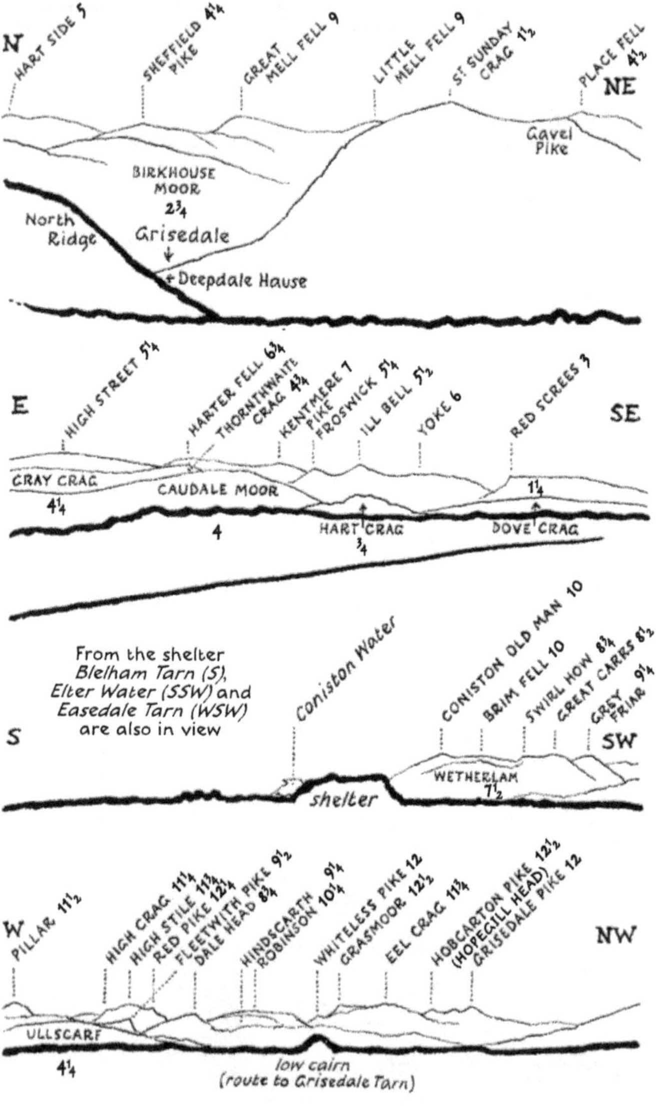
N
HART SIDE 5
SHEFFIELD PIKE 4¼
GREAT MELL FELL 9
LITTLE MELL FELL 9
St SUNDAY CRAG 1½
PLACE FELL 4½
NE
Gavel Pike
BIRKHOUSE MOOR 2¾
North Ridge
Grisedale
Deepdale Hause
E
HIGH STREET 5¼
HARTER FELL 6¾
THORNTHWAITE CRAG 4¾
KENTMERE PIKE 7
FROSWICK 5¼
ILL BELL 5½
YOKE 6
RED SCREES 3
SE
GRAY CRAG 4¼
CAUDALE MOOR 4
1¼
HART CRAG ¾
DOVE CRAG
From the shelter Blelham Tarn (S), Elter Water (SSW) and Easedale Tarn (WSW) are also in view
S
Coniston Water
CONISTON OLD MAN 10
BRIM FELL 10
SWIRL HOW 8¾
GREAT CARRS 8½
GREY FRIAR 9¼
SW
WETHERLAM 7½
shelter
W
PILLAR 11½
HIGH CRAG 11¼
HIGH STILE 11¾
RED PIKE 12¼
FLEETWITH PIKE 9½
DALE HEAD 8¾
HINDSCARTH 9¼
ROBINSON 10¼
WHITELESS PIKE 12
GRASMOOR 12½
EEL CRAG 11¾
HOBCARTON PIKE 12½ (HOPEGILL HEAD)
GRISEDALE PIKE 12
NW
ULLSCARF 4¼
low cairn (route to Grisedale Tarn)

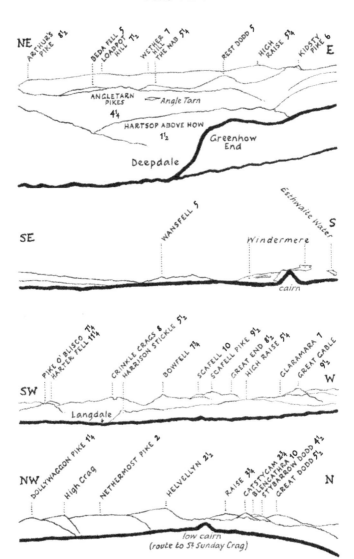

THE VIEW

RIDGE ROUTES

To St SUNDAY CRAG, 2756'
1½ miles : N then NE
Depression at 2150'
610 feet of ascent

*A rough stony descent followed
by an easy and pleasant climb.*

The grassy sward beyond the
north cairn is the start of an
excellent ridge walk. A steep
and rocky descent to the
depression ahead of Cofa
Pike can be avoided by
taking a zig-zag path
to the left, and the
top of the Pike can
similarly be bypassed
to its left (though the
direct route over its
rocky top is better).
The narrow ridge
descends steeply to Deepdale Hause;
a long gradual climb up a well defined
ridge then leads to the top of St Sunday
Crag. This is a fine walk, *but strangers
to Cofa Pike should not attempt it in mist.*

To GREAT RIGG, 2513'
1 mile : S
Depression at 2375'
140 feet of ascent

One of the easiest miles in Lakeland.

Leave the summit at the shelter and
proceed due south. There is no path at
first, but the objective is clear ahead.
The springy turf induces giant strides.
Safe in mist.

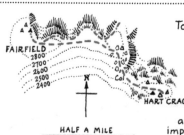

To HART CRAG, 2698'
1 mile : E then SE
Depression at 2550'
150 feet of ascent

An easy, interesting walk.

The path across the broad
top of Fairfield is as wide
as a road; it becomes steep
as the col is approached. It is
important, *in mist*, not to stray
from the path: danger lurks!

The north face of Fairfield

Glenridding Dodd

1450'

OS grid ref: NY380176

from Ullswater
(Sheffield Pike behind)

Glencoyne •

GLENRIDDING DODD ▲

Glenridding •

Patterdale •

MILES
0   1   2

Fashions change. When people climbed hills only for the sake of the views, the heathery summit of Glenridding Dodd must have been more frequented than it is today, though there are signs (clear paths to the summit) that it is regaining popularity. The fell occupies a grand position overlooking the upper reach of Ullswater. It is the end, topographically, of the eastern shoulder of Stybarrow Dodd.

MAP

This map is at a scale 20 per cent larger than that normally used throughout this book.

HALF A MILE

ASCENT FROM GLENRIDDING

via Greenside Road : 1000 feet of ascent : 1 mile

The Dodd is so conveniently situated and offers so delightful a view that it might be expected that walkers would have blazed a wide path to the top. Such is not the case, however, and it is not at all easy to find a way up. Starting from the crescent-shaped green in the centre of the village, the most straightforward route follows Greenside Road past the Travellers Rest pub, up a steep rise to a cattle grid and kissing gate just before a row of cottages. Bear right up a grassy slope that doubles back on itself. At a small signpost it is better to take the steep path to the right leading to the fine viewpoint of Blaes Crag, before continuing to the depression between Glenridding Dodd and Sheffield Pike. An easy path to the right leads to the summit.

via Stybarrow Crag and Mossdale Beck : 1100 feet of ascent : 1½ miles

An interesting and pretty alternative through delightful woodlands, but in descent the steep and mossy path can be very slippery. Take the lakeside route to Stybarrow Crag where a path from the back of the layby climbs to a rickety stile over a fence, then follows the beck on its south side. It joins the main path from Glenridding at the wall.

THE SUMMIT

On a sunny day in August the summit is a delectable place. Bilberries grow in profusion, and larches almost reach the top on the north side. Many cairns adorn this hummocky summit, the main one overlooking Glenridding village.

THE VIEW

Considering the low altitude of
the fell, the view is very pleasing:
it gains in charm and intimacy
what it lacks in extensiveness.
Ullswater takes pride of place.

Principal Fells

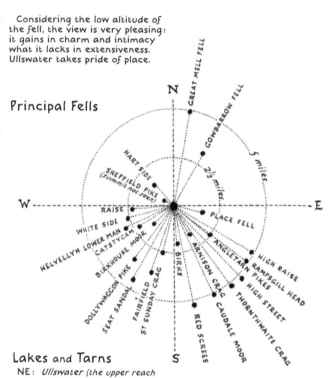

GREAT MELL FELL
GOWBARROW FELL
5 miles
2½ miles
HART SIDE
SHEFFIELD PIKE (summit not seen)
RAISE
PLACE FELL
WHITE SIDE
HELVELLYN LOWER MAN
CATSTYCAM
BIRKHOUSE MOOR
ANGLETARN PIKES
HIGH RAISE
RAMPSGILL HEAD
DOLLYWAGGON PIKE
SEAT SANDAL
ARNISON CRAG
HIGH STREET
FAIRFIELD
BIRKS
THORNTHWAITE CRAG
ST SUNDAY CRAG
CAUDALE MOOR
RED SCREES

N
W
E
S

Lakes and Tarns

NE: *Ullswater (the upper reach
can also be seen by walking east)*
S: *Lanty's Tarn*

*looking down
on Glenridding*

Stybarrow Crag

Ullswater and Birk Fell

Gowbarrow Fell

1579'

OS grid ref: NY408218

from Brown Hills

▲GREAT MELL FELL

LITTLE ▲
MELL
FELL

Pooley
Bridge ●

● Watermillock

● ▲GOWBARROW FELL

Dockray ●

● Glenridding

MILES

0   1   2   3   4

NATURAL FEATURES

Gowbarrow Fell is one of the best known of Lakeland's lesser heights, much of it being National Trust property and a favorite playground and picnic place. It is not the fell itself that brings the crowds, however, and its summit is lonely enough: the great attraction is Aira Force, on the beck forming its western boundary. The fell springs from a mass of high dreary ground in the north and takes the shape of a broad wedge, tapering as it falls to Ullswater, the middle reach of which is its south-eastern boundary throughout. The delightful lower slopes here are beautifully wooded, but low crags and bracken in abundance make them rather difficult of access except where they are traversed by the many pleasant green paths which add so much to Gowbarrow's charms.

The Head of Ullswater from Green Hill

In the 13th century, the fell was recorded as *Golbery* and *Golebergh*. The addition of 'fell' to the name is much more recent. The name probably derives from the Old Norse words *gol* ('windy hill') and *berg* ('rocky hill').

MAP

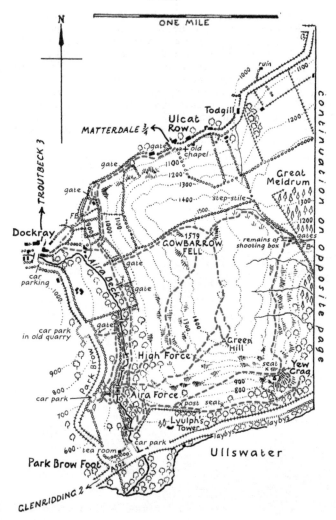

ONE MILE

N

TROUTBECK 3

MATTERDALE ¾

Dockray

car parking

car park in old quarry

car park

Park Brow Foot

GLENRIDDING 2

Ulcat Row

Todgill

old chapel

gate

gate

gate

FB

gate

gate

gate

Aira Beck

Park Brow

High Force

Aira Force

tea room

Lyulph's Tower

car park

post seat

laybys

laybys

1519

GOWBARROW FELL

ruin

Great Meldrum

step-stile

remains of shooting box

gates

FB

Green Hill

seat

Yew Crag

Ullswater

continuation on opposite page

The subsidiary summit of Green Hill and the rocky outcrop of Yew Crag are two of the best viewpoints for Ullswater, and are often the preferred destination of walkers rather than the actual summit of the fell.

MAP

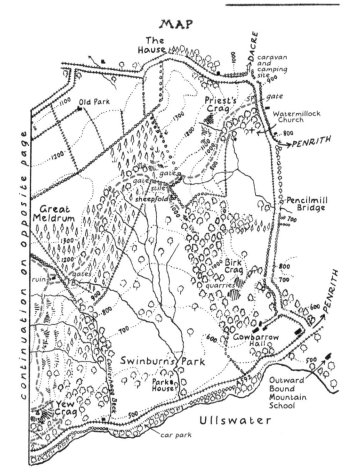

ASCENT FROM WATERMILLOCK CHURCH
850 feet of ascent : 2½ miles

There is very limited roadside parking near the start point, a signposted gate 300 yards north of the church. A clear path rises gently through bracken and gorse to the stile close to the sheepfold (turn left for a short stroll to a good viewpoint). Back on the main path, the route passes through the densely packed conifers of Swinburn's Park. An easy path on open ground leads from the shooting box ruins, approaching the summit from the north-east.

ASCENT FROM PARK BROW FOOT
via YEW CRAG and the SHOOTING BOX
1150 feet of ascent : 2½ miles
1½ miles (from the A592)

A path rises across the fellside behind Lyulph's Tower to the cairn above Yew Crag : this is the best way to the summit, and offers good views of Ullswater from the top of Yew Crag ; a gate gives access to this popular viewpoint. The path, always interesting, continues to what remains of the shooting box and can now be followed all the way to the summit.

Yew Crag can also be reached from the A592, but this shorter route is much steeper and offers no variation of return apart from the road.

via AIRA FORCE
1200 feet of ascent : 1½ miles

A visit to one of Lakeland's most spectacular waterfalls is the highlight of this ascent, with a short detour to High Force possible. The best way round is to ascend on a well worn path (repaired in places) to the summit direct, and return via the wonderful viewpoint of Green Hill, which has a substantial cairn on its summit. In their lower stages both paths may be obscured by bracken during the summer months.

ASCENT FROM DOCKRAY
650 feet of ascent : 1 mile

The ascent from Dockray direct (by following the wall up) is the quickest way to the summit and involves far less climbing, but is much less attractive than the routes described above. A better option is to walk south on the road to the car park in the old quarry. Then visit High Force and Aira Force on the way, joining the main path to the summit. Reserve the path by the wall for an easy descent.

Place Fell
and Ullswater
from Gowbarrow Park

Aira Force (above)

High Force (below)

AIRA FORCE

The most visited waterfall in Lakeland tumbles 66' as Aira Beck passes through a rocky gorge. The tiny arched bridge that spans the beck just as the stream goes over the edge offers a sense of scale for photographers at the foot of the falls (where there is another bridge).

Aira Force is situated in 750-acre Gowbarrow Park, which was purchased by the National Trust in 1908. There is parking for cars, a tea room and disabled access, with graded paths and viewing platforms that have been well integrated into the landscape.

Beside the path that passes up the wooded glen to the falls is a 'wish tree', a large fallen trunk. Over the years visitors have hammered so many coins into the bark that space is fast running out.

THE SUMMIT

Flowers, heather and bilberries bloom on the pleasant little ridge where the summit cairn depicted here once stood, but the neighbourhood is drab. This ridge is fringed on the side facing Ullswater by a wall of short broken crags and there are other outcrops nearby.

Great Mell Fell

NOTE: In the years since the illustrations on this page were prepared, Gowbarrow Fell has lost its summit cairn but gained an O.S. triangulation column (no. 10790).

DESCENTS: The best way off the fell is over the undulating top to Green Hill, descending from there to Aira Force. If the bracken is high, it is worth while to search for the path.

In mist, join the wall north of the summit, turning left for Dockray, right for the old shooting box (for Watermillock or Park Brow Foot via Yew Crag).

YARDS
0   100   200

The summit ridge

Cairn above Yew Crag

Yew Crag

The shooting box (now ruins)

THE VIEW

Gowbarrow Fell faces up Ullswater into the throat of the deep valley of Patterdale, and a feature of the view is the impressive grouping of the fells steeply enclosing it. Very little of the lake can be seen from the top of the fell because of the intervening high ground. Half a mile south from the summit is a far better viewpoint, Green Hill.

Principal Fells

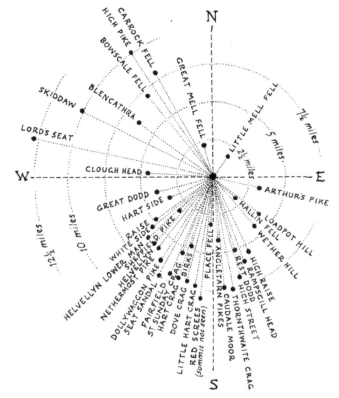

Lakes and Tarns

ENE: *Ullswater — the lower reach only. The more attractive middle and upper reaches come into view by walking across the top to Green Hill, where the lake is seen most impressively.*

Great Dodd

2812'

OS grid ref: NY342206

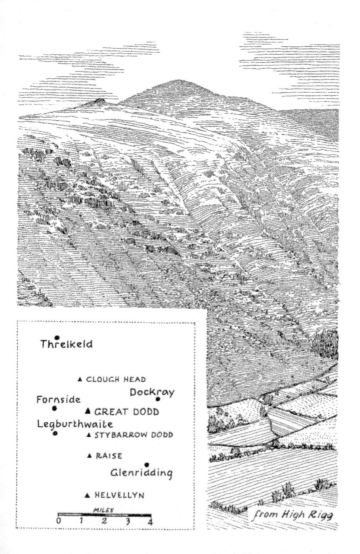

Threlkeld

▲ CLOUGH HEAD

Dockray

Fornside

▲ GREAT DODD

Legburthwaite

▲ STYBARROW DODD

▲ RAISE

Glenridding

▲ HELVELLYN

MILES

0   1   2   3   4

from High Rigg

NATURAL FEATURES

Great Dodd, well named, is the most extensive of the fells in the Helvellyn range. To the north-east, its long sprawling slopes fall away gradually in an undulating wilderness of grass to the old coach road; beyond is a wide expanse of uncultivated marshland, not at all characteristic of Lakeland and of no appeal to walkers. North and south, high ground continues the line of the main ridge, but steepening slopes reach valley level on both east and west flanks. Grass is everywhere: it offers easy and pleasant tramping but no excitements. Rocks are few and far between: there is a broken line of cliffs. Wolf Crags, overlooking the coach road, and the rough breast of High Brow above Dowthwaitehead breaks out in a series of steep crags (a favorite haunt of buzzards, and paragliders), while there are sundry small outcrops on both east and west flanks well below the summit.

Two of Great Dodd's streams are harnessed to provide water supplies: on the west side, Mill Gill, which has a fine ravine, is diverted to Manchester via Thirlmere; on the east, Aira Beck's famous waterfalls are robbed of their full glory to supply the rural districts of Cumbria. Mosedale Beck and Trout Beck drain the dreary wastes to the north.

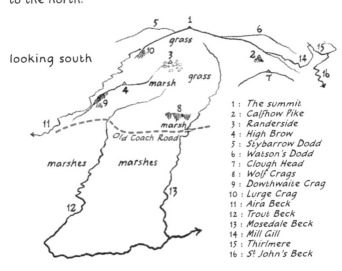

looking south

1 : The summit
2 : Calfhow Pike
3 : Randerside
4 : High Brow
5 : Stybarrow Dodd
6 : Watson's Dodd
7 : Clough Head
8 : Wolf Crags
9 : Dowthwaite Crag
10 : Lurge Crag
11 : Aira Beck
12 : Trout Beck
13 : Mosedale Beck
14 : Mill Gill
15 : Thirlmere
16 : St John's Beck

MAP

The subsidiary fell of Randerside (2392') is lower than Green Side (2608'), the equivalent subsidiary height on Stybarrow Dodd, but both have summit rocks that stand out on the largely grassy eastern slopes of their respective Dodds.

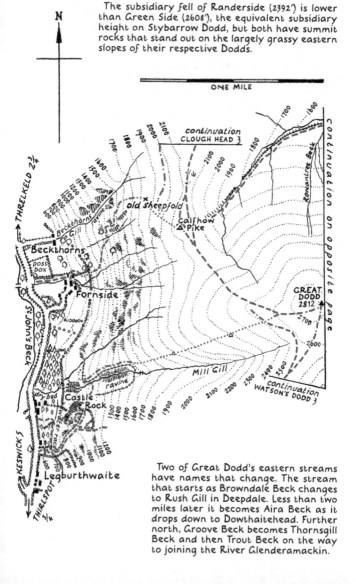

Two of Great Dodd's eastern streams have names that change. The stream that starts as Browndale Beck changes to Rush Gill in Deepdale. Less than two miles later it becomes Aira Beck as it drops down to Dowthaitehead. Further north, Groove Beck becomes Thornsgill Beck and then Trout Beck on the way to joining the River Glenderamackin.

MAP

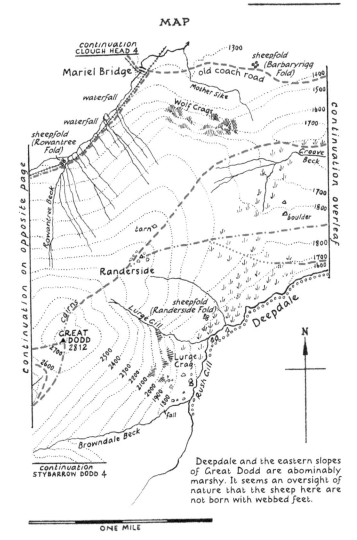

Deepdale and the eastern slopes of Great Dodd are abominably marshy. It seems an oversight of nature that the sheep here are not born with webbed feet.

ONE MILE

Most of the path from High Row direct to High Brow and then on to Randerside has either been created or enhanced by farmers' quad bikes. On the other side of Deepdale, the 'two-lane' path from Dockray over Common Fell and Watermillock Common, Common Fell and Brown Hills (*see Hart Side 5*) also shows evidence of them.

MAP

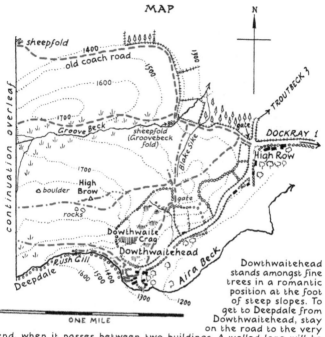

Dowthwaitehead stands amongst fine trees in a romantic position at the foot of steep slopes. To get to Deepdale from Dowthwaitehead, stay on the road to the very end, when it passes between two buildings. A walled lane will be found to the right of the right-hand building.

Wolf Crags

There is a good view of these crags from the Old Coach Road east of Mariel Bridge; they are a launching place for paragliders.

ASCENT FROM DOCKRAY
2000 feet of ascent : 4¾ miles

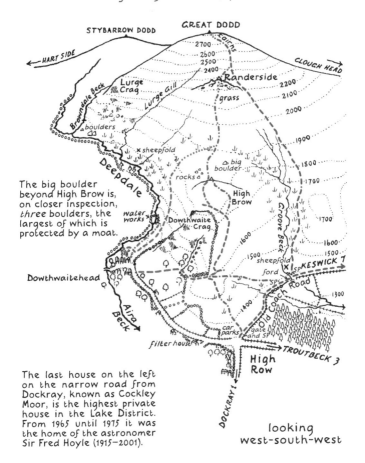

The big boulder beyond High Brow is, on closer inspection, *three* boulders, the largest of which is protected by a moat.

The last house on the left on the narrow road from Dockray, known as Cockley Moor, is the highest private house in the Lake District. From 1965 until 1975 it was the home of the astronomer Sir Fred Hoyle (1915–2001).

looking west-south-west

The ascent of Great Dodd via Groove Beck is one of the easiest climbs in Lakeland, the gradients being very gentle throughout, but otherwise it is without merit. The direct route, via a path turning off the old coach road 50 yards past the gate, has superior views. All routes from Dockray are most unpleasant *in wet weather*.

ASCENT FROM FORNSIDE
2300 feet of ascent : 2½ miles

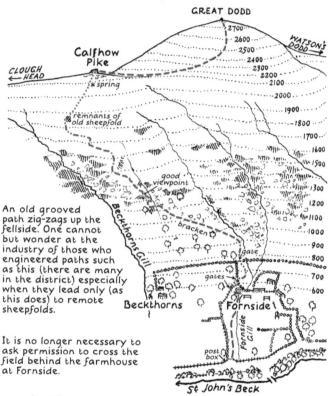

GREAT DODD

2700
2600
2500
2400
2300
2200
2100

WATSON'S DODD →

Calfhow Pike

CLOUGH HEAD ←

✱ spring

2000

1900

1800

1700

1600

1500

⊗ remnants of
old sheepfold

good
viewpoint

1300

1200

1100

1000

Beckthorns Gill

bracken

900

gate

800

gates

700

600

An old grooved
path zig-zags up the
fellside. One cannot
but wonder at the
industry of those who
engineered paths such
as this (there are many
in the district) especially
when they lead only (as
this does) to remote
sheepfolds.

Beckthorns

Fornside

Fornside Gill

It is no longer necessary to
ask permission to cross the
field behind the farmhouse
at Fornside.

post
box

St John's Beck

looking east

Use the northern entrance to Fornside Farm (near the post box)
and follow the signposts to the open fell: turn left at the
final barn and then right at the first gate. A map beside the
entrance gate at the road shows the route clearly.

This route is very rarely used. It is steep as far as
the ruined sheepfold, but there is recompense in the
lovely view of the valley above Fornside. Thereafter it is
monotonously grassy, with only the oddity of Calfhow
Pike to relieve the tedium of progress.

ASCENT FROM LEGBURTHWAITE
2300 feet of ascent : 2¼ miles

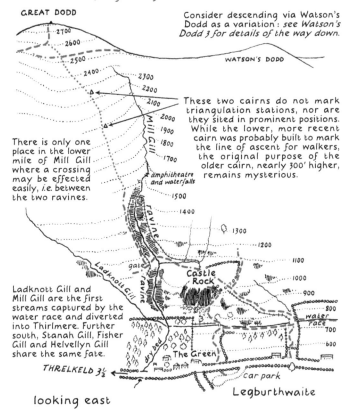

GREAT DODD

2700
2600
2500
2400
2300
2200
2100
2000
1900
1800
1700

WATSON'S DODD

Consider descending via Watson's Dodd as a variation : see *Watson's Dodd 3* for details of the way down.

Mill Gill

These two cairns do not mark triangulation stations, nor are they sited in prominent positions. While the lower, more recent cairn was probably built to mark the line of ascent for walkers, the original purpose of the older cairn, nearly 300' higher, remains mysterious.

amphitheatre and waterfalls

1500
1400
1300
1200
1100
1000
900
800
700
600

There is only one place in the lower mile of Mill Gill where a crossing may be effected easily, *i.e.* between the two ravines.

ravine

gate

ravine

Ladknott Gill

Castle Rock

water race

Ladknott Gill and Mill Gill are the first streams captured by the water race and diverted into Thirlmere. Further south, Stanah Gill, Fisher Gill and Helvellyn Gill share the same fate.

dry bed

The Green

THRELKELD 3½

car park

Legburthwaite

looking east

There are two ways to get onto Castle Rock : the direct route and that via the rear enclosure. *See Watson's Dodd 5 for details.* Castle Rock should not be climbed in mist.

If a visit to the water race is desired, start from the wooden steps opposite the United Utilities car park. A shorter variation begins from a solitary tree at an open patch of land where there is a seat.

The first part of this route is pleasant enough; it is interesting also if combined with an exploration of the environs of Castle Rock, but after crossing the attractive Mill Gill it develops into a trudge up a long grass slope: the gradient is easy.

THE SUMMIT

Catstycam Helvellyn Raise Stybarrow Dodd

On the north top is the main cairn, and on the south top is another cairn hollowed to provide shelter from the west wind. At one time this was the only cairn, and its builders must have felt twinges of conscience during their task: they selected as its site a most convenient rash of stones, ignoring the highest point a hundred yards distant, where all was grass. The summit is otherwise featureless.

DESCENTS: There are only very sketchy paths from the summit because of the hard-packed nature of the terrain underfoot, but the direction of the route to Dockray is marked by a small cairn, which appears on the skyline when viewed from the main cairn.

DOCKRAY

CLOUGH HEAD

▲ main cairn

△ shelter cairn

LEGBURTHWAITE

N

WATSON'S DODD and STICKS PASS

In mist, direction may be taken from the shelter in the cairn, which faces east.

There is no danger in leaving the top even in the thickest weather, but care must be taken to avoid descending into the inhospitable valley of Deepdale by mistake.

The cairn on Randerside

Clough Head

The cairn on High Brow

Hart Side Stybarrow Dodd Great Dodd

Deepdale

RIDGE ROUTES

To CLOUGH HEAD, 2381'
2 miles
W then NW and NNE
Depression at 2100'
300 feet of ascent

An easy walk on grass.

The curious tor of Calfhow Pike is the only interesting feature, but the excellent views are ample compensation for the dull trudge. *Clough Head should be avoided in bad weather conditions.*

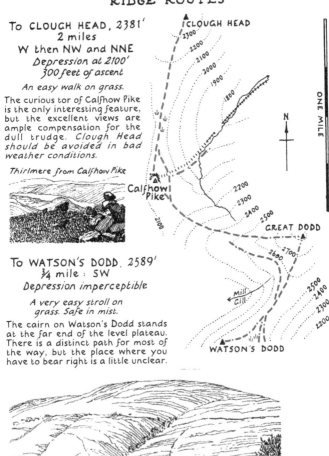

Thirlmere from Calfhow Pike

To WATSON'S DODD, 2589'
3/4 mile : SW
Depression imperceptible

A very easy stroll on grass. Safe in mist.

The cairn on Watson's Dodd stands at the far end of the level plateau. There is a distinct path for most of the way, but the place where you have to bear right is a little unclear.

Dowthwaitehead

THE VIEW
(with distances in miles)

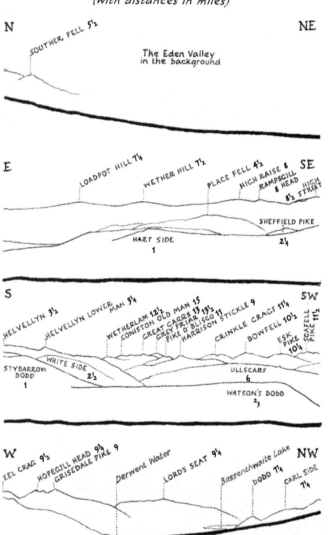

N   NE

SOUTHER FELL 5½

The Eden Valley
in the background

E   SE

LOADPOT HILL 7¼   WETHER HILL 7½   PLACE FELL 4½   HIGH RAISE 8   RAMPSGILL HEAD 8   HIGH STREET 8½

SHEFFIELD PIKE 2¼

HART SIDE 1

S   SW

HELVELLYN 3½   HELVELLYN LOWER MAN 3¼   WETHERLAM 12½   CONISTON OLD MAN 15   GREAT CARRS 13   GREY FRIAR 13½   PIKE O'BLISCO 11   HARRISON STICKLE 9   CRINKLE CRAGS 11¼   BOWFELL 10½   ESK PIKE 10¼   SCAFELL PIKE 11½

STYBARROW DODD 1

WHITE SIDE 2½

ULLSCARF 6

WATSON'S DODD 2¾

W   NW

EEL CRAG 9½   HOPEGILL HEAD 9½   GRISEDALE PIKE 9   Derwent Water   LORDS SEAT 9¼   Bassenthwaite Lake   DODD 7¼   CARL SIDE 7¼

THE VIEW

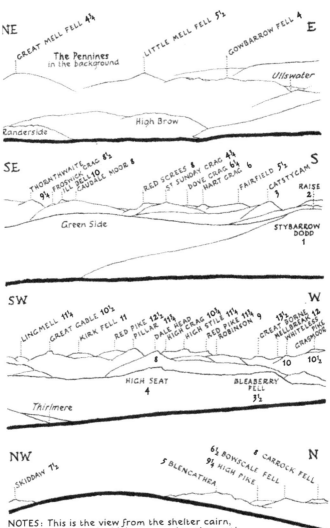

NE

GREAT MELL FELL 4¾

The Pennines
in the background

LITTLE MELL FELL 5½

GOWBARROW FELL 4

E

Ullswater

High Brow

Randerside

SE

THORNTHWAITE CRAG 8½
FROSWICK 9¼
ILL BELL 10
CAUDALE MOOR 8

RED SCREES 8
ST SUNDAY CRAG 4¾
DOVE CRAG 6¼
HART CRAG 6

FAIRFIELD 5½

CATSTYCAM 3

RAISE 2

S

Green Side

STYBARROW DODD 1

SW

LINGMELL 11¼
GREAT GABLE 10½
KIRK FELL 11
RED PIKE 12½
PILLAR 11½
DALE HEAD
HIGH CRAG 10¾
HIGH STILE 11¼
RED PIKE 11¾
ROBINSON 9

GREAT BORNE 13½
MELLBREAK 12
WHITELESS PIKE
GRASMOOR

W

8

10

10½

HIGH SEAT 4

BLEABERRY FELL 3½

Thirlmere

NW

SKIDDAW 7½

BLENCATHRA 5

HIGH PIKE 9¼

BOWSCALE FELL 6½

CARROCK FELL 8

N

NOTES: This is the view from the shelter cairn,
not from the higher ground to the north.
Thirlmere, Derwent Water and Bassenthwaite Lake
cannot actually be seen from this point, but come into view
a few yards to the west.

Great Mell Fell

1760'

OS grid ref: NY397254

from Great Meldrum

Troutbeck
Penruddock

GREAT ▲ MELL FELL

▲ LITTLE
MELL
FELL

Matterdale End

▲ GOWBARROW
FELL

Dockray

MILES
0 1 2 3 4

Great Mell Fell is a prominent object on the Penrith approach to Lakeland. With its lesser twin, Little Mell Fell, it forms the portals to the Helvellyn range on this side. Its round 'inverted pudding basin' shape does not promise much for the walker and it is rarely climbed. On closer acquaintance, however, it is rather more enjoyable than its appearance suggests, because of the presence of fine woodlands on the lower slopes; indeed, pines and larches persist almost to the summit. (Closer acquaintance was once frowned upon by the military authorities, but not any longer.)

NATURAL FEATURES

Great Mell Fell rises sharply from a wide expanse of desolate marshland to the north and west, territory not at all typical of Lakeland, the fell itself being much more fertile and colourful than its surroundings. Its rich red soil carries a wealth of timber, the eastern slopes especially being beautifully wooded. Bleached skeletons of trees near the top of the fell indicate that at one time it was more fully clothed; many of those that yet survive are battered by the prevailing wind into grotesque shapes.

MAP

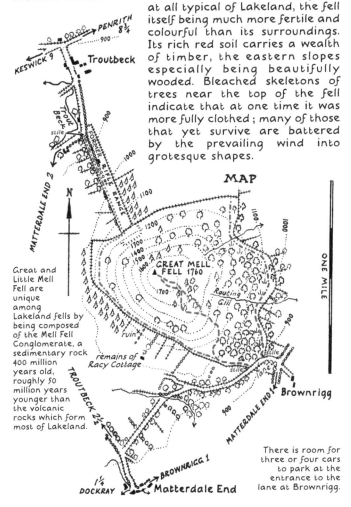

Great and Little Mell Fell are unique among Lakeland fells by being composed of the Mell Fell Conglomerate, a sedimentary rock 400 million years old, roughly 50 million years younger than the volcanic rocks which form most of Lakeland.

There is room for three or four cars to park at the entrance to the lane at Brownrigg.

The name Great Mell Fell probably derives from the Brittonic (Cumbic) word *mel* (Welsh *moel*), a bare hill, with Fell as a later addition.

ASCENTS

from BROWNRIGG : *900 feet of ascent : 1 mile*
from TROUTBECK : *900 feet of ascent : 1½ miles*

Above the 1100' contour, roughly, the fell is enclosed within a fence; everything above this is owned by the National Trust. Access may be gained at Troutbeck (along a muddy lane that follows the line of the former rifle range) and at two gates at the south-eastern corner. The danger signs (one such illustrated) that formerly guarded the entrances have been replaced by National Trust signs proclaiming this to be Mell Fell, without the 'Great'.

An intermittent path makes a circuit of the fell inside the fence, but is hard to follow in the bracken season. The path may be left anywhere for the climb to the top, but it is best by far to use the path that ascends from the south-east starting at Brownrigg. It is steep for just a short section before easing at a tilted grassy plateau. Ahead lies a wooded area through which there is a choice of paths, the most popular of which is that to the left. The summit is bare of foliage.

At one time the peripheral path gave a very pleasant walk, but now much of it has gone out of use and it is no longer recommended.

THE SUMMIT

Bilberries interspersed with cotton grass cover the level top. The decayed tree trunk in the illustration has gone, and the few stones on the summit have been made into a cairn. The highest tree is still recognisable, although it has twisted and grown a bit. The low mound on the summit is a tumulus.

DESCENTS : If Troutbeck is your destination, aim for the parallel fences of the former rifle range. Otherwise just follow the path.

the highest tree

THE VIEW

The highlight of the view is Blencathra undoubtedly, the noble proportions of this fine mountain being seen to great advantage. Otherwise the panorama is uneven, with a wide expanse of the Eden Valley, an impressive grouping of fells southwards, and a vista of the Grasmoor range in the west.

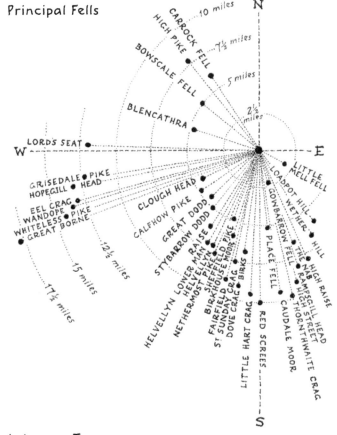

Principal Fells

Lakes and Tarns

S: *Ullswater*
   (a disappointing view, only a small section being visible)

Great Rigg

2513′

OS grid ref: NY356104

▲ FAIRFIELD

▲ GREAT
   RIGG

▲ STONE ARTHUR

▲ HERON PIKE

● Grasmere ▲ NAB SCAR

● Rydal

Ambleside ●

MILES

0 1 2 3 4

from Grasmere

NATURAL FEATURES

Great Rigg has no topographical secrets or surprises. It is a plain, straightforward, uninteresting fell on the southern spur of Fairfield, with gentle declivities linking the summit to the continuing ridge on either side (north to Fairfield, south to Heron Pike). East, stony slopes fall abruptly to Rydal Beck; ruined crags rise from wastes of scree. To the west the fellside is mainly grassy but there are occasional rocks low down on this flank, above Tongue Gill. From the ridge south of the summit a descending shoulder strikes off in the direction of Grasmere; this has a rocky terminus with the name of Stone Arthur. Between the shoulder and the ridge is a deep, narrow trough which carries Greenhead Gill, Great Rigg's only stream of note, down to the River Rothay.

The east face

Few people will climb Great Rigg without also ascending Fairfield, for the former is a stepping stone to its bigger neighbour when the Fairfield Horseshoe is being climbed clockwise. Whilst providing this humble service, however, the fell manages to retain a certain dignity, appreciated best from the west shore of Grasmere: seen from there, the dark dome of its summit appears to overtop all else.

looking north

1 : *The summit*
2 : *Ridge continuing to Fairfield*
3 : *Ridge continuing to Heron Pike*
4 : *Stone Arthur*
5 : *East face*
6 : *Greenhead Gill*
7 : *Tongue Gill*
8 : *River Rothay*

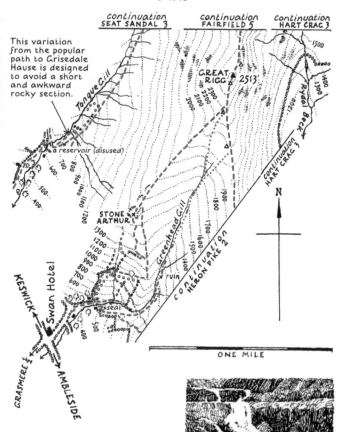

MAP

continuation
SEAT SANDAL 3

continuation
FAIRFIELD 5

continuation
HART CRAG 3

This variation from the popular path to Grisedale Hause is designed to avoid a short and awkward rocky section.

GREAT RIGG ▲ 2513

Tongue Gill

a reservoir (disused)

Rydal Beck

STONE ARTHUR ✕

continuation HART CRAG 3

Greenhead Gill

continuation HERON PIKE 2

KESWICK

Swan Hotel

ruin

seat

GRASMERE ½

AMBLESIDE

ONE MILE

N

As in many of the place names in Lakeland, Great Rigg's origins stem from Old English, the word *rigg* meaning a bumpy or knobbly ridge. The word is also a surname; Moses Rigg, the smuggler after whom Moses' Trod from Honister to Wasdale is named, is perhaps the most well known Lakeland character with this name.

Cascades, Greenhead Gill

ASCENT FROM GRASMERE
2300 feet of ascent : 3 miles

Greenhead Gill is deeply enclosed and uninteresting in its upper reaches; the slopes at its head are steep. It is better used for quick descent.

The route via Stone Arthur, although steep initially, is much better. By turning left at the gate, a path may be followed alongside a wall to the open fell. This slope is richly clothed with tall bracken.

At the final wall there is a choice: the original and direct path goes left. This ends with a rocky but simple scramble to the interesting summit of Stone Arthur. From there, an easy rising path leads to the ridge and the top of Great Rigg. The alternative path, to the right, bypasses the summit of Stone Arthur and is most often used by walkers in descent.

FAIRFIELD
GREAT RIGG
2400
2300
2200
2100
2000
HERON PIKE
1900
1800
1700
1600
1500
STONE ARTHUR
1400
1300
1200
1100
1000
900
800
700
600
500
400
x ruin
reservoir
ALCOCK TARN
1400
1300
1200
Greenhead Gill
gate
Swan Hotel
KESWICK
300
400
500
AMBLESIDE
GRASMERE 1/4

looking north-east

The Thirlmere aqueduct crosses Greenhead Gill just beyond the gate. A little further, around a bend in the stream, are pleasant cascades and an artificial pool of crystal-clear water.

If the Greenhead Gill route is chosen a decision needs to be made at the final confluence of streams (in a little amphitheatre): either go half right up a steep grass slope to reach the low point of the ridge or ascend via a green tongue (steeper but better underfoot) which leads more directly to the summit. A benefit of ascending via Greenhead Gill is a visit to the ruins of a former Elizabethan ore mine (see Stone Arthur 2 for details), passing some attractive cascades above the ruins.

Great Rigg is more often visited on the tour of the Fairfield Horseshoe, but it may be ascended directly from Grasmere by the routes illustrated, that by Stone Arthur being the more interesting.

THE SUMMIT

Helvellyn   Fairfield

The substantial cairn is sometimes given the name Greatrigg Man. It is now lower and wider than in this illustration.

The summit is comprehended at a glance. A well constructed cairn occupies the highest point and another is 60 yards south where the ridge steepens on its descent to Heron Pike. The top is a carpet of excellent turf which many a cricket ground would welcome.

RIDGE ROUTES

To FAIRFIELD, 2863': 1 mile : N
Depression at 2375' : 500 feet of ascent
An easy climb, needing care in mist.
A fair path, on grass, crosses the depression but peters out as the summit is approached. *Strangers to Fairfield should avoid it in mist.*

To HERON PIKE, 2008': 1½ miles SSW, then S
Minor depressions : 150 feet of ascent
A very easy high-level walk. Heron Pike is the *second* prominent rise on the ridge.

To STONE ARTHUR, 1652' 1¼ miles : SSW then SW
Downhill all the way.
Follow the wide grass shoulder branching from the main ridge. There is a path all the way.

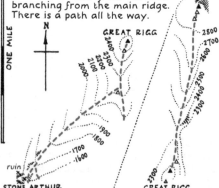

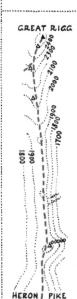

THE VIEW

The panorama is interesting and varied, a special feature being the large number of lakes and tarns in view. To the west the mountain skyline is very fine. There is an impressive vista of the Helvellyn group above the deep notch of Grisedale Hause, while closer to hand to the east, the far arm of the Fairfield Horseshoe (Hart Crag, Dove Crag, High Pike and Low Pike) encloses the deep recess of Rydale, far below.

Principal Fells

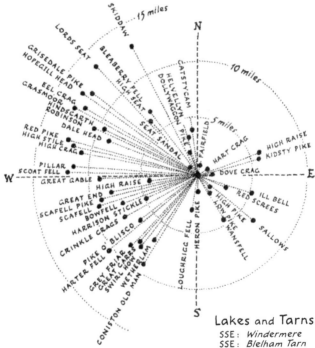

Lakes and Tarns

SSE: *Windermere*
SSE: *Blelham Tarn*
SSE: *Wise Een Tarn*
S: *Esthwaite Water*
SSW: *Alcock Tarn*
SSW: *Elterwater*
SSW: *Coniston Water*
SSW: *Grasmere*
WSW: *Easedale Tarn*
NNW: *Grisedale Tarn*

Visitors to the summit with a pair of binoculars can get a good view of the rock rib that has created the waterfall feature of Buckstones Jump (see *Low Pike 1 and 2*) by scanning the deep recesses of Ryedale.

Hart Crag

2698'

OS grid ref: NY369112

Patterdale ●

Hartsop ●

FAIRFIELD ▲
HART ▲ CRAG

DOVE CRAG▲

RED SCREES ▲

● Grasmere

● Rydal

Ambleside ●

MILES
0   1   2   3   4

from Dovedale

NATURAL FEATURES

Midway along the high-level traverse between Fairfield and Dove Crag is the rough top of Hart Crag, occupying a strategic position overlooking three valleys. To the north-east, Hart Crag follows usual mountain structure by sending out a long declining ridge, which forms a high barrier between desolate Deepdale and delectable Dovedale. North, a wall of crags defends the summit above the wild hollow of Link Cove, a hanging valley encompassed by cliffs: this is its finest aspect by far. South-west, after an initial fringe of broken crags, long stony slopes fall very steeply to Rydal Head. Although bounded by streams, Hart Crag itself is quite curiously deficient in watercourses.

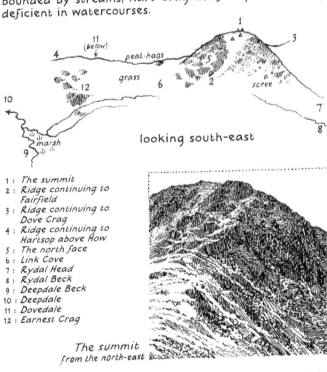

looking south-east

1 : The summit
2 : Ridge continuing to Fairfield
3 : Ridge continuing to Dove Crag
4 : Ridge continuing to Hartsop above How
5 : The north face
6 : Link Cove
7 : Rydal Head
8 : Rydal Beck
9 : Deepdale Beck
10 : Deepdale
11 : Dovedale
12 : Earnest Crag

The summit
from the north-east

The steep upper slopes of Hart Crag provide part of the headwalls to the three valleys of Deepdale, Dovedale and Rydale, but is not at the head of any of these.

MAP

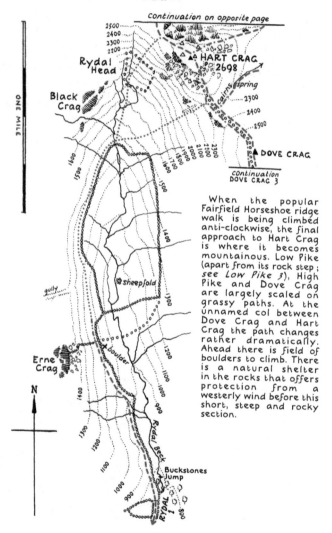

Continuation on opposite page

2500
2400
2300
2200

Rydal Head

Black Crag

△ HART CRAG 2698

spring

cairns

2300
2400
2500

● DOVE CRAG

continuation DOVE CRAG 3

ONE MILE

1600

1500

1500

1400

2300
2200
2100
2000
1900
1800
1700
1600
1500

gully

⊕ sheepfold

1300

Erne Crag

boulder

1200

N

1400

1100

1300

1200

1000

900

Rydal Beck

Buckstones Jump

1000

900

800

RYDAL

When the popular Fairfield Horseshoe ridge walk is being climbed anti-clockwise, the final approach to Hart Crag is where it becomes mountainous. Low Pike (apart from its rock step; see Low Pike 3), High Pike and Dove Crag are largely scaled on grassy paths. At the unnamed col between Dove Crag and Hart Crag the path changes rather dramatically. Ahead there is field of boulders to climb. There is a natural shelter in the rocks that offers protection from a westerly wind before this short, steep and rocky section.

Buckstones Jump is an attractive water feature that is well worth visiting. *For more details, see Low Pike 1 and 2.*

MAP

Greenhow End, while appearing
on the map to be part of
Hart Crag, belongs very
much to Fairfield, and,
indeed, offers
probably the best
way of climbing
the mountain.
*See Fairfield 7
for details.*

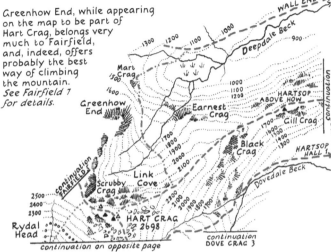

The sketchy and thin path from Mart Crag up to Link Cove and
then onto the Hart Crag–Hartsop above How ridge is *very* thin: it is
necessary to walk in single file for much of its length.

The north face

ASCENT FROM RYDAL
2,600 feet of ascent : 4½ miles

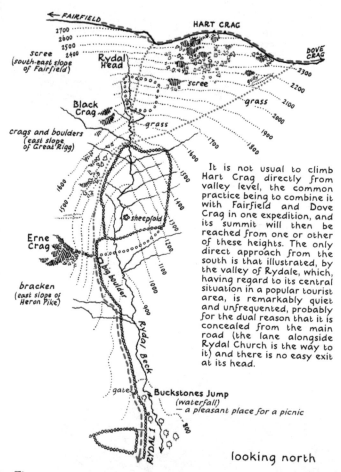

It is not usual to climb Hart Crag directly from valley level, the common practice being to combine it with Fairfield and Dove Crag in one expedition, and its summit will then be reached from one or other of these heights. The only direct approach from the south is that illustrated, by the valley of Rydale, which, having regard to its central situation in a popular tourist area, is remarkably quiet and unfrequented, probably for the dual reason that it is concealed from the main road (the lane alongside Rydal Church is the way to it) and there is no easy exit at its head.

Buckstones Jump (waterfall) — a pleasant place for a picnic

looking north

The approach by the Rydal Valley (Rydale) is attractive and interesting, but the climb out of it to the head of the valley between Fairfield and Hart Crag is steep; the alternative climb to the depression between Dove Crag and Hart Crag is not much easier. The valley lies entirely within the circuit of the Fairfield Horseshoe and is deeply enclosed.

ASCENT FROM PATTERDALE
2,300 feet of ascent : 4½ miles from Patterdale village

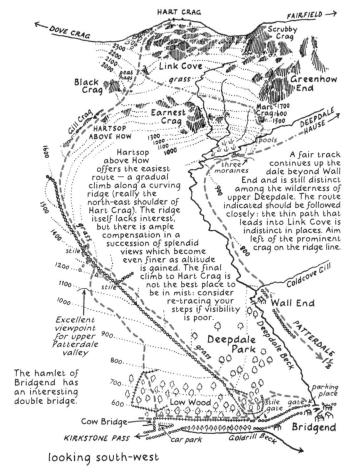

HART CRAG

FAIRFIELD

DOVE CRAG

Scrubby Crag

2300
2200
2100
2000
peat hags

Link Cove
grass

Black Crag

Greenhow End

Gill Crag

Earnest Crag

Hart 1700 Crag 1600 1500

HARTSOP ABOVE HOW

DEEPDALE HAUSE

1300
1200
1100
1000

pools

1600

Hartsop above How offers the easiest route — a gradual climb along a curving ridge (really the north-east shoulder of Hart Crag). The ridge itself lacks interest, but there is ample compensation in a succession of splendid views which become even finer as altitude is gained. The final climb to Hart Crag is not the best place to be in mist: consider re-tracing your steps if visibility is poor.

three moraines

A fair track continues up the dale beyond Wall End and is still distinct among the wilderness of upper Deepdale. The route indicated should be followed closely: the thin path that leads into Link Cove is indistinct in places. Aim left of the prominent crag on the ridge line.

1500

1400

stile

1200

1100

1000

stile

grass

900

grass

Coldcove Gill

900

Wall End

PATTERDALE

Excellent viewpoint for upper Patterdale valley

900

Deepdale Park

Deepdale Beck

PATTERDALE 1½

800

700

grass

600

The hamlet of Bridgend has an interesting double bridge.

Low Wood

parking place

stile   gate   gate

Cow Bridge

Bridgend

KIRKSTONE PASS

car park

Goldrill Beck

looking south-west

The ascent from Patterdale is far superior to that from the south. The Link Cove route especially is an interesting climb through the inner sanctuary of Hart Crag, the mountain scenery being impressive, but it is not recommended *in bad weather*: the thin path into the hanging valley is far too sketchy to be safely followed *in mist*.

THE SUMMIT

The summit area is relatively small, its level top being
about 120 yards long and having a cairn at each end.
Two other cairns indicate viewpoints. The top is stony
but a strip of grass running lengthwise across it to
the north of the main cairns offers an easy traverse.

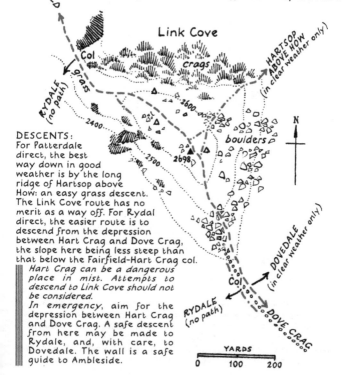

DESCENTS:
For Patterdale
direct, the best
way down in good
weather is by the long
ridge of Hartsop above
How: an easy grass descent.
The Link Cove route has no
merit as a way off. For Rydal
direct, the easier route is to
descend from the depression
between Hart Crag and Dove Crag,
the slope here being less steep than
that below the Fairfield-Hart Crag col.

*Hart Crag can be a dangerous
place in mist. Attempts to
descend to Link Cove should not
be considered.*

*In emergency, aim for the
depression between Hart Crag
and Dove Crag. A safe descent
from here may be made to
Rydale, and, with care, to
Dovedale. The wall is a safe
guide to Ambleside.*

THE VIEW

Hart Crag is a little too near to the great mass of Fairfield to provide a well balanced view. The panorama in other directions is extensive, but the picture as a whole is disappointing.

Principal Fells

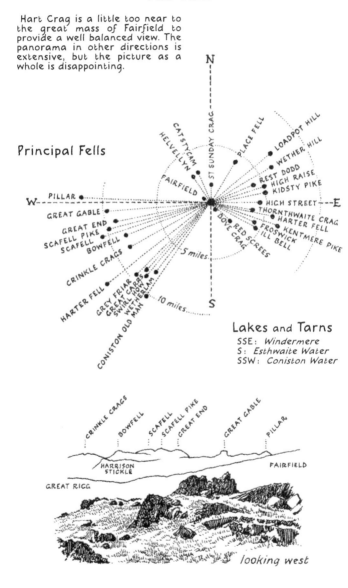

N

CATSTYCAM
HELVELLYN
ST SUNDAY CRAG
PLACE FELL
LOADPOT HILL
WETHER HILL
REST DODD
HIGH RAISE
KIDSTY PIKE
FAIRFIELD

W — PILLAR
GREAT GABLE
GREAT END
SCAFELL PIKE
SCAFELL
BOWFELL

HIGH STREET — E
THORNTHWAITE CRAG
HARTER FELL
FROSWICK
KENTMERE PIKE
ILL BELL
RED SCREES
DOVE CRAG

CRINKLE CRAGS

HARTER FELL
GREY FRIAR
GREAT CARRS
SWIRL HOW
WETHERLAM
CONISTON OLD MAN

5 miles
10 miles

S

Lakes and Tarns

SSE: *Windermere*
S: *Esthwaite Water*
SSW: *Coniston Water*

CRINKLE CRAGS
BOWFELL
SCAFELL
SCAFELL PIKE
GREAT END
GREAT GABLE
PILLAR

HARRISON STICKLE
FAIRFIELD
GREAT RIGG

looking west

RIDGE ROUTES

To FAIRFIELD, 2863' : 1 mile : NW, then W.
Depression at 2550' : 330 feet of ascent

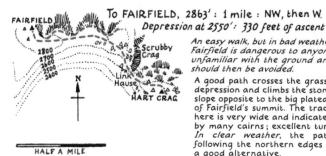

An easy walk, but in bad weather Fairfield is dangerous to anyone unfamiliar with the ground and should then be avoided.

A good path crosses the grassy depression and climbs the stony slope opposite to the big plateau of Fairfield's summit. The track here is very wide and indicated by many cairns; excellent turf. In clear weather, the path following the northern edges is a good alternative.

To DOVE CRAG, 2598' : ¾ mile : SE.
Depression at 2350' : 260 feet of ascent

An easy walk. Dove Crag is safe in mist, but care is then necessary in leaving Hart Crag.

A sketchy path, at first over grass and then, more clearly, among stones goes south from the eastern cairn to the wall at the depression. This wall continues over the summit plateau of Dove Crag: the summit cairn is a few yards to the east on a rock platform.

To HARTSOP ABOVE HOW, 1870' : 1½ miles : ENE
Depression at 1775' : 150 feet of ascent

An easy walk. In mist the natural way off Hart Crag is not easy to find (initially, what little path that exists is very sketchy) and this walk should not then be attempted.

Leave the summit near the main cairn, going down a patch of grass and crossing a band of scree before inclining slightly right down a shallow stony gully. Then work left to the ridge, which is broad and grassy, with many undulations and peat-hags. It narrows on the final rise, and the path bypasses the summit to the left. The top is beside the big cleft of Gill Crag.

Note that this ridge may be safely left *only* between Black Crag and Gill Crag (by descending *right*, to Dovedale)

ONE MILE

from the east ridge, St Sunday Crag

Hart Side

2481'

OS grid ref: NY359197

GREAT
DODD

Dockray

▲ HART SIDE

STYBARROW
DODD

Glencoyne

Glenridding

MILES

0   1   2   3

from Dockray

NATURAL FEATURES

The main watershed at Stybarrow Dodd sends out a long spur to the east which curves north from the subsidiary height of Green Side and continues at an elevated level until it is poised high above Ullswater before descending in wide slopes to the open country around Dockray. The principal height on this spur is Hart Side, which with its many satellites on the declining ridge forms the southern wall of the long valley of Deepdale throughout its sinuous course, its opposite boundary being the short deep trench of Glencoyne. The upper slopes of this bulky mass are unattractive in themselves, but, in strong contrast, the steep flank overlooking Ullswater is beautifully wooded, while the views of the lake from the Brown Hills, midway along the ridge, are of high quality.

Hart Side is rarely visited. Its smooth slopes, grass and marsh intermingling, seem very very remote from industry, but there is evidence that men laboured on these lonely heights a long time ago, and until 1962 the minerals far below its surface were being won by the enterprising miners of Glenridding.

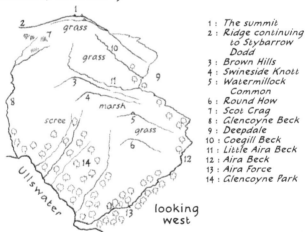

1 : The summit
2 : Ridge continuing to Stybarrow Dodd
3 : Brown Hills
4 : Swineside Knott
5 : Watermillock Common
6 : Round How
7 : Scot Crag
8 : Glencoyne Beck
9 : Deepdale
10 : Coegill Beck
11 : Little Aira Beck
12 : Aira Beck
13 : Aira Force
14 : Glencoyne Park

looking west

The fells of Watermillock Common

The ridge that extends east and north-east from Hart Side includes a number of fells known collectively as Watermillock Common. They are:

Swineside Knott (1814') — rounded, generally grassy but with some rocks on its steep eastern flank; known for its extensive view of Ullswater.

Common Fell (1811') — centrally placed on the ridge with a small cairn perched on the highest point, an attractive summit; nearby, a distinctive erratic boulder sits on a subsidiary mound.

Round How (1270') and Bracken How (1243') — a pair of grassy mounds, both with small cairns on their tops.

MAP

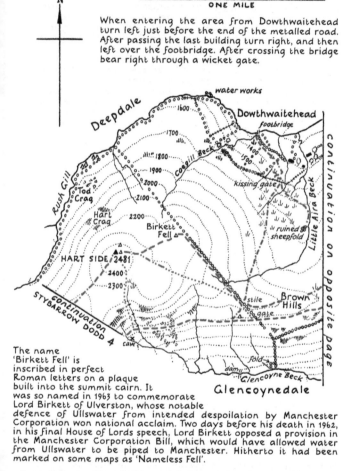

ONE MILE

When entering the area from Dowthwaitehead
turn left just before the end of the metalled road.
After passing the last building turn right, and then
left over the footbridge. After crossing the bridge
bear right through a wicket gate.

The name
'Birkett Fell' is
inscribed in perfect
Roman letters on a plaque
built into the summit cairn. It
was so named in 1963 to commemorate
Lord Birkett of Ulverston, whose notable
defence of Ullswater from intended despoilation by Manchester
Corporation won national acclaim. Two days before his death in 1962,
in his final House of Lords speech, Lord Birkett opposed a provision in
the Manchester Corporation Bill, which would have allowed water
from Ullswater to be piped to Manchester. Hitherto it had been
marked on some maps as 'Nameless Fell'.

According to the Ordnance Survey and Harvey maps, the
representation of a footpath thereon is no evidence of a right of way.
Nor, unfortunately, is it evidence that a footpath now exists at all!
Some of the paths marked on those maps in the district of Hart Side
were made originally by miners on their way to or from work at the
Glenridding lead mine, but the miners now use them no more : some
paths have become overgrown and cannot always be traced ; others
are starting to reappear.

MAP

TROUTBECK 3

Dockray

Pounder Sike

Bracken How

Round How

quarry

Park Brow

stile

Aira Beck

café

Common Fell

Watermillock Common

Glencoyne Park

continuation on opposite page

Little Aira Beck

fold

Swineside Knott

Brown Hills

fold

gate

gate

Glencoyne Beck   Glencoyne

GLENRIDDING 1

Ullswater

The 'cave' marked on the facing page (far left, near the continuation for *Stybarrow Dodd*) is, in fact, an emergency exit for the Greenside Lead Mine in Glenridding.

In 1953, following a serious fire at the mine the previous year, an emergency exit was constructed from the High Horse Level of the mine to the path around the top of Glencoyne, known as the Miners' Balcony Path.

The 'cave': the entrance is now smaller than illustrated here.

ASCENT FROM DOCKRAY
1600 feet of ascent : 4 miles

←STYBARROW DODD

HART SIDE

Green Side

2400

grass

dull, grassy trudges

2300

Birkett Fell

Deepdale

Glencoynedale Head

2200

2100

STICKS PASS

cave

1700

It is easy to go astray here: take the right-hand path.

1900

Dowthwaitehead

Coegill Beck

2000

1500
1400

stile

gate

Brown Hills

1800

Little Aira Beck

footbridge

DOCKRAY 2

Cameras out at this corner!

sheepfold

gate

Swineside Knott (best viewpoint for Ullswater)

Common Fell

1700

1600

Watermillock Common

1500

Aira Beck

Formerly the path through Glencoyne Park was both overgrown and neglected but now it is by far the best route of descent, with mature beechwoods and charming views that constantly change as you lose height.

gate

Glencoyne Park

bracken

1300

Round How

1200

1100

A path is picked up across the Common just before the stream and soon becomes much clearer.

DOWTHWAITEHEAD

stile

Park Brow

Parking

Dockray

TROUTBECK 3

car park

ULLSWATER ¼

AIRA FORCE

looking west-south-west

The joy of this walk is not to be found in the summit of Hart Side, which is dull, but in the splendid high-level route to it from Dockray, below Swineside Knott, which excels in views of Ullswater. An excellent alternative is via the summit of Common Fell and the historic cairn on Birkett Fell. The Dowthwaitehead route deserves no consideration.

THE SUMMIT

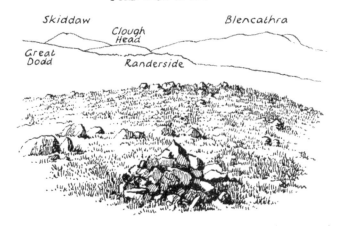

Skiddaw
Clough Head
Blencathra
Great Dodd
Randerside

The summit has nothing extraordinary to show in natural forms, being grassy with a few outcropping boulders. Yet this is a top that cannot be confused with any other, for here man has not contented himself merely with building a few cairns but has really got to work with pick and spade, and excavated a most remarkable ditch, rather like the Vallum of the Roman Wall. As the project was abandoned, the reason for the prodigious effort is not clear. An excavation below the summit, intended as the site of a building, has now been smoothed out. It is believed these were workings in connection with the Greenside lead mine in Glenridding.

The ditch on the summit as it appeared in 1954.

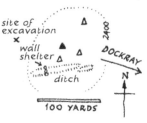

DESCENTS : Descents will usually be either to Dockray or Glencoyne. Walk ESE, over a minor rise, to the wall running across the fell, or avoid this shortcut and take the path to Birkett Fell on the way to the wall. Follow the wall down, joining the miners' path (at a gap) for Dockray. For Glencoyne, continue by the wall down into the valley. These are the best routes *in mist*.

RIDGE ROUTE

To STYBARROW DODD, 2770'
1½ miles : SW then W
Depressions at 2250' and 2525'
550 feet of ascent

*An easy walk on grass. Safe in mist.
Follow round the head of Deepdale,
skirting the intermediate summit of
Green Side. In mist, take care to keep
the rising slope on the left. It is also
possible to make a detour to White
Stones, Green Side's summit rocks.*

Ullswater, from the Brown Hills

THE VIEW

Principal Fells

The view is generally disappointing. Although Hart Side has a considerable altitude, it does not overtop the main ridge to the west, which hides all the high fells beyond. Intervening ground to the east conceals most of Ullswater.

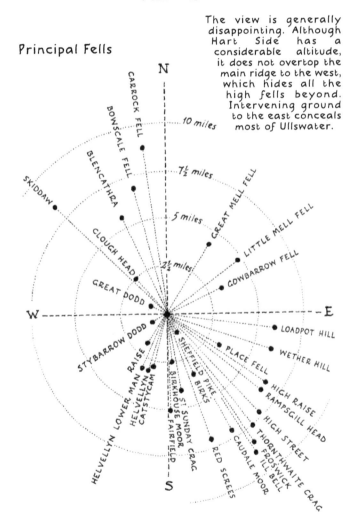

Lakes and Tarns
ENE: *Ullswater*

Hartsop above How

OS grid ref: NY383120

from Hunsett Cove

Patterdale ●

St SUNDAY CRAG ▲   Hartsop ●

FAIRFIELD ▲   ▲ HARTSOP ABOVE HOW

HART CRAG ▲

▲ DOVE CRAG

MILES
0   1   2   3

The long curving north-east ridge of Hart Crag rises to a separate summit midway, and this summit is generally referred to as Hartsop above How by guidebook writers and mapmakers. Sometimes the three words in the name are hyphenated, sometimes not. Probably the first two should be, but not the last two : the word 'How' is common, meaning low hill, and the distinctive title of this particular How is 'Hartsop-above', indicating its geographical relationship to the hamlet in the valley below. Most natives of Deepdale, however, know it not by this name, with or without hyphens, but they all know Gill Crag, which fringes the summit, and this would seem to be a more satisfactory name for the fell. But one cannot so wantonly ignore the authority of the guidebooks and maps : and the name Hartsop above How, without hyphens (in the belief that an error of omission is less a sin than an error of commission) will be used here in support of the Director General of Ordnance Survey.

NATURAL FEATURES

Hartsop above How is a simple ridge (really a part of Hart Crag) curving like a sickle to enclose the valley of Deepdale on the south and east. Only in the vicinity of the summit is it at all narrow, but both flanks are steep throughout most of its three-mile length, the slopes above Dovedale being especially rough. There are several crags on the fell, the most imposing being Black Crag above the rough hollow of Hunsett Cove; also prominent are the distinctive Gill Crag, immediately below the highest point, the grey rocks of Dovedale Slabs (looking as pleasant and attractive as steep rocks can look) below the eastern end of the summit, and, on the Deepdale side, the gloomy cliff of Earnest Crag (looking as unpleasant and unattractive as steep rocks can look). The slopes above Brothers Water are well wooded over an extensive area, and Deepdale Park also has some fine trees.

MAP

Hartsop Hall, now a farmhouse, dates from the 16th century. Local history records that when the hall was extended two centuries later it was built across an ancient right of way, a right which at least one local resident insisted on exercising, by walking through the hall.

ASCENT FROM PATTERDALE
1400 feet of ascent : 3 miles from Patterdale village

looking south-west

The path through Low Wood from Cow Bridge is steep, but it provides the opportunity to visit a grassy platform that offers superb views over Brothers Water.

If taking the track from the parking place at Bridgend, turn left at the sign: slight bumps in the ground in this area mark the boundary of an ancient settlement. Then follow the arrows and cairns up through the wood.

An easy, gradual climb, not attractive in itself but with views increasing in quality as altitude is gained. A detour to visit Dovedale Slabs and The Perch (a striking viewpoint) is recommended in clear weather.

Dovedale Slabs

THE SUMMIT

The highest point is a grassy knoll adjoining the top of the cleft splitting Gill Crag, a dramatic situation; it is without a cairn and is bypassed by the ridge path. Another knoll 200 yards north-east was once considered the summit, but this is clearly lower and much less exciting.

DESCENTS: The easiest way down *in any conditions* is by the ridge to the road. Direct descents, either to Deepdale or Dovedale, are too rough.

THE VIEW

There is no better place for appraising the ruggedness of the eastern crags and caves of the Fairfield group of fells.

Principal Fells

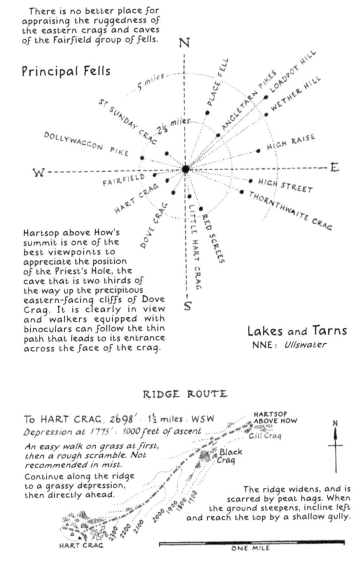

Hartsop above How's summit is one of the best viewpoints to appreciate the position of the Priest's Hole, the cave that is two thirds of the way up the precipitous eastern-facing cliffs of Dove Crag. It is clearly in view and walkers equipped with binoculars can follow the thin path that leads to its entrance across the face of the crag.

Lakes and Tarns
NNE: *Ullswater*

RIDGE ROUTE

To HART CRAG, 2698': 1½ miles: WSW
Depression at 1775': 1000 feet of ascent

An easy walk on grass at first, then a rough scramble. Not recommended in mist.
Continue along the ridge to a grassy depression, then directly ahead.

HARTSOP ABOVE HOW
Gill Crag
Black Crag

The ridge widens, and is scarred by peat hags. When the ground steepens, incline left and reach the top by a shallow gully.

HART CRAG

2300 2200 2100 2000 1900 1800 1700

ONE MILE

Helvellyn

3118'

OS grid ref: NY341152

from the south-west ridge of St Sunday Crag

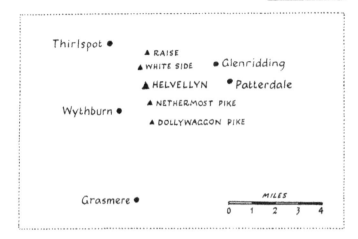

Thirlspot ●

▲ RAISE
▲ WHITE SIDE   ● Glenridding
▲ HELVELLYN   ● Patterdale
▲ NETHERMOST PIKE
▲ DOLLYWAGGON PIKE

Wythburn ●

Grasmere ●

MILES
0   1   2   3   4

Legend and poetry, a lovely name and a lofty altitude combine to encompass Helvellyn in an aura of romance; and thousands of pilgrims, aided by its easy accessibility, are attracted to its summit every year. There is no doubt that Helvellyn is climbed more often than any other mountain in Lakeland, and, more than any other, it is the objective and ambition of the tourist who does not normally climb; moreover, the easy paths leading up the western flanks make it particularly suitable for sunrise expeditions, and, in a snowy winter, its sweeping slopes afford great sport to the ski parties who congregate on these white expanses. There are few days in any year when no visitors call at the wall shelter on the summit to eat their sandwiches. It is a great pity that Helvellyn is usually ascended by its western routes, for this side is unattractive and lacking in interest. From the east, however, the approach is quite exciting, with the reward of an extensive panorama as a sudden and dramatic climax when the top is gained; only to the traveller from this direction does Helvellyn display its true character and reveal its secrets. There is some quality about Helvellyn which endears it in the memory of most people who have stood on its breezy top; although it can be a grim place indeed on a wild night, it is, as a rule, a very friendly giant. If it did not inspire affection would its devotees return to it so often?

NATURAL FEATURES

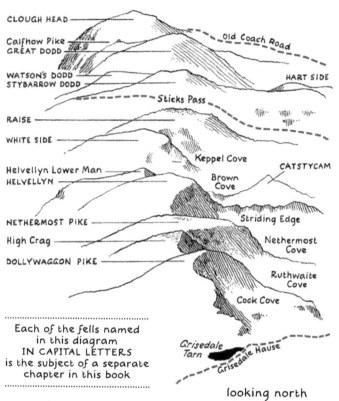

CLOUGH HEAD

Calfhow Pike
GREAT DODD

Old Coach Road

WATSON'S DODD
STYBARROW DODD

HART SIDE

Sticks Pass

RAISE

WHITE SIDE

Keppel Cove

CATSTYCAM

Helvellyn Lower Man
HELVELLYN

Brown
Cove

NETHERMOST PIKE

Striding Edge

High Crag

Nethermost
Cove

DOLLYWAGGON PIKE

Ruthwaite
Cove

Cock Cove

Each of the fells named
in this diagram
IN CAPITAL LETTERS
is the subject of a separate
chapter in this book

*Grisedale
Tarn*

Grisedale Hause

looking north

The Helvellyn Range

The altitude of these fells and the main connecting ridges is consistently above 2500 feet from Dollywaggon Pike (2815') to Great Dodd (2812') except for the depression of Sticks Pass, which is slightly below at 2420'. This is the greatest area of high fells in Lakeland, and the traverse of the complete range from south to north (the better way) is a challenge to all active walkers. (As a preliminary canter, strong walkers will include the Fairfield group, starting at Kirkstone Pass and reaching Grisedale Tarn over the tops of Red Screes, Little Hart Crag, Dove Crag, Hart Crag and Fairfield.)

NATURAL FEATURES

The Helvellyn range is extremely massive, forming a tremendous natural barrier from north to south between the deep troughs of the Thirlmere and Ullswater valleys. The many fells in this vast upland area are each given a separate chapter in this book, and the following notes relate only to Helvellyn itself, with its main summit at 3118' (the third highest in Lakeland) and a subsidiary at 3033'.

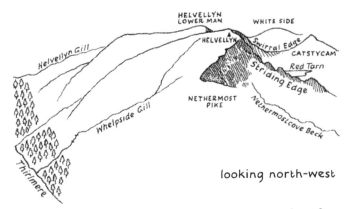

HELVELLYN LOWER MAN

WHITE SIDE

HELVELLYN

Swirral Edge

CATSTYCAM

Red Tarn

Striding Edge

Helvellyn Gill

NETHERMOST PIKE

Nethermostcove Beck

Whelpside Gill

Thirlmere

looking north-west

Helvellyn is a high point on a high ridge and therefore is substantially buttressed by neighbouring heights, the connecting depressions, north and south, being relatively slight. Westwards, however, after a gentle incline from the summit the slope quickens and finally plunges steeply down to Thirlmere, the total fall in height being nearly half a mile in a lateral distance of little more than one mile. This great mountain wall below the upper slopes is of simple design, consisting of two broad buttresses each bounded by swift-flowing streams and scarred by broken crags and occasional scree gullies. The base of the slope is densely planted with conifers.

continued

Two 'fell top assessors' employed by the Lake District National Park take it in turn to climb Helvellyn every day during the winter months of December to March to check the conditions at the summit. They prepare a report with information such as temperature, windchill, windspeed, snow depth, and dangers such as unstable snow, avalanche risks and icy footpaths. This report is published on Weatherline, which is a Met Office mountain weather forecast.

NATURAL FEATURES

continued

The smooth slopes curving up from the west break abruptly along the ridge, where, in complete contrast, a shattered cliff of crag and scree falls away precipitously eastwards : here are the most dramatic scenes Helvellyn has to offer. From the edge of the declivity on the summit Red Tarn is seen directly below, enclosed between the bony arms of Swirral Edge on the left and Striding Edge on the right. Swirral Edge terminates in the grassy cone of Catstycam, a graceful peak, but Striding Edge is all bare rock, a succession of jagged fangs ending in a black tower. The Edges are bounded by deep rough hollows, silent and very lonely.

Beyond the Edges is the bulky mass of Birkhouse Moor, Helvellyn's long east shoulder, a high wedge separating Grisedale and Glenridding and descending to the lovely shores of Ullswater.

Striding Edge

Early writers regarded Striding Edge as a place of terror; contemporary writers, following a modern fashion, are more inclined to dismiss it as of little account. In fact, Striding Edge is the finest ridge there is in Lakeland for walkers — its traverse is always an exhilarating adventure in fair weather or foul, and it can be made easy or difficult according to choice. The danger of accident is present only when a high wind is blowing or when the rocks are iced: in a mist on a calm day, the Edge is a really fascinating place.

Swirral Edge

Helvellyn from Red Tarn

MAP

continuation on next page

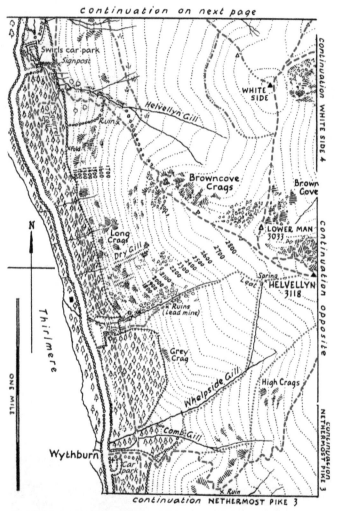

Wythburn car park is large and from the north end there is access to the fell path. The Swirls car park and Station Coppice car park, across the A591, are smaller; all are fee-paying. Free parking may be available at the layby midway between the King's Head and Swirls car park; it gets busy, so arrive early.

MAP

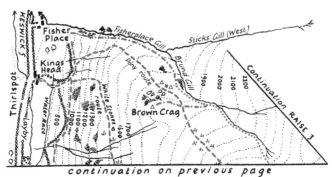

continuation on previous page

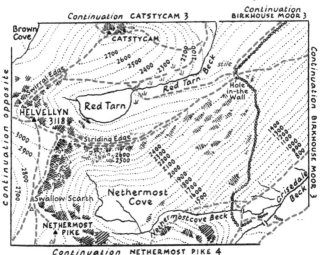

The path climbing from Grisedale beside Nethermostcove Beck into the hanging valley of Nethermost Cove is of no use when ascending Helvellyn. This is a way up Nethermost Pike via its east ridge (*see Nethermost Pike 6*); for ordinary walkers there is no way up from the cove onto the Striding Edge ridge; it is far too steep and stony.

Similarly, Brown Cove as a way of ascent onto the Swirral Edge ridge is not recommended, and as a possible way down from the depression to the south-east of Helvellyn Lower Man it is desperately steep and slippery.

THE WESTERN APPROACHES

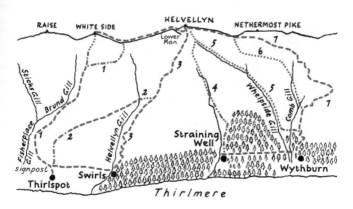

1 : The old pony route — 2700' of ascent : 4 miles

The original, longest and easiest route. The path has become intermittent owing to disuse and, in the upper stages towards the depression between White Side and Helvellyn Lower Man, disappears on an awkward grassy slope; it is hard to imagine ponies coming this way now.

2 : The 'White Stones' route — 2700' of ascent : 3½ miles

Once the usual and popular way up from Thirlspot, this route still has enough fellwalking devotees and useful cairns to make it clear once the start has been found. Turn right at the signpost for fifty paces and then head up the hill ; a path soon appears. In its latter stages this route follows the Browncove Crags route.

3 : via Browncove Crags — 2600' of ascent : 3 miles

With Route 7, one of the two most popular ways up Helvellyn from the west, as shown by the pitched path for much of its length. The original way was from Thirlspot above the wall, but now nearly everyone starts from the Swirls car park. The scenery in the vicinity of Browncove Crags is excellent.

4 : via the old lead mine — 2600' of ascent : 1½ miles

The shortest way to the top from the road, taking advantage of a breach in the plantation. Very steep and rough for 2200' and overgrown with brambles at the start. Solitary walkers with weak ankles should avoid this route: it is *not* recognised and is not attractive. It is linked to the car park at Wythburn by a forest road, which adds three quarters of a mile to the ascent.

5 : via Whelpside Gill — 2800' of ascent : 2⅓ miles

A good route on a hot day, with water close almost to the summit. The route initially follows the Birk Side path, turning off at the top of a short section of zig-zags where the plantation ends, then making a descent to the gill. The ascent follows the gill all the way to Whelpside Gill Spring. Mostly pathless, with a few sections where feet have worn out a sketchy track.

THE WESTERN APPROACHES

6 : via Comb Gill — 2600' of ascent : 2¼ miles
> A route of escape from the crowds on the Birk Side path. Steep up by the gill, but generally easy walking most of the way, on grass.

7 : 'Wythburn' route, via Birk Side — 2550' of ascent : 2¼ miles
> One of the most popular ways up Helvellyn, and the usual route from Wythburn. Good path throughout with some interesting twists and turns. Steep for the first mile, then much easier.

These routes are illustrated on pages 11 and 12 following.

Helvellyn Gill

In mist:

Route 1 is very difficult to find in descent.

Route 2 is difficult to find in ascent and not easy to locate in descent.

Route 3 is easy to find and easy to follow.

Route 4 is safe but seems even rougher in mist.

Route 5 is safe if the gill is kept alongside.

Route 6 is better avoided.

Route 7 is best of all, the path being distinct throughout its length.

Whelpside Gill

Browncove Crags

The most impressive crags on Helvellyn's western flank are oddly named, as Brown Cove is on the eastern side of the fell. This is the view from the old pony route near the White Side-Helvellyn ridge.

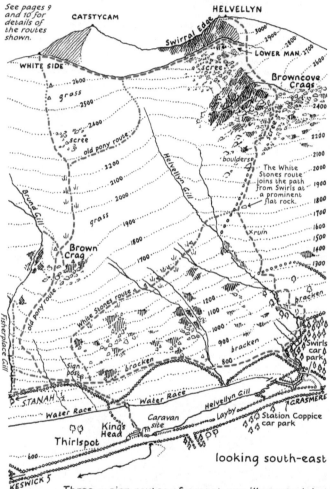

ASCENT FROM THIRLSPOT
2600 feet of ascent: 3½ - 4 miles

See pages 9 and 10 for details of the routes shown.

CATSTYCAM

HELVELLYN

Swirral Edge

LOWER MAN

WHITE SIDE

2600

2900
2800
2700
2600

grass

2500

scree

Browncove Crags

2400

scree

old pony route

2300

2200

2100

2000

boulders

The White Stones route joins the path from Swirls at a prominent flat rock.

1900
1800
1700
1600

Helvellyn Gill

Brund Gill

grass

2100

2000

1900

× ruin

1500
1400
1300

Brown Crag

1800

1700

White Stones route

1200

bracken

old pony route

1100

1000

900

bracken

800

Swirls car park

Fisherplace Gill

Sign post

bracken

Water Race

STANAH

Water Race

King's Head

Caravan site

Helvellyn Gill

Layby

GRASMERE

Station Coppice car park

Thirlspot

600

looking south-east

KESWICK 5

Three major routes of ascent are illustrated, but only one way up now attracts the crowds. The pony route and the 'White Stones' route were favourites of the Victorians but are now out of fashion. In contrast, the route from Swirls car park via Browncove Crags is probably the most popular way of ascending Helvellyn from the west.

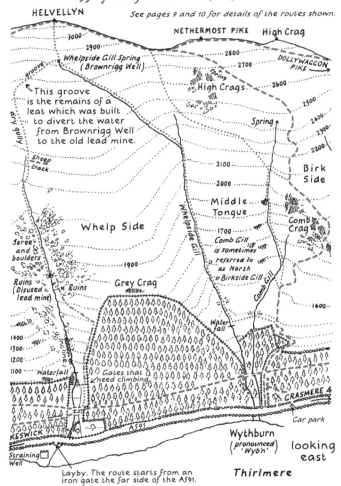

ASCENT FROM WYTHBURN
2550 feet of ascent : 2¼ - 2¾ miles

See pages 9 and 10 for details of the routes shown.

HELVELLYN
NETHERMOST PIKE High Crag
3000
2900
DOLLYWAGGON PIKE
Whelpside Gill Spring
(Brownrigg Well)
2800
2700
← This groove
is the remains of a
leat which was built
to divert the water
from Brownrigg Well
to the old lead mine.
High Crags.
Spring
2600
2500
2400
2300
2200
Spring
Sheep
track
Birk
Side
2100
2000
Whelpside Gill
Middle
Tongue
Comb
Crag
Whelp Side
1700
Comb Gill
is sometimes
referred to
as North
Birkside Gill
Comb Gill
1900
Scree
and
boulders
Grey Crag
Ruins
(Disused
lead mine)
Ruins
1400
Water
fall
Incline
1400
1300
1200
1100
Waterfall
Gates that
need climbing.
GRASMERE 4
Car park
KESWICK
Straining
Well
A591
Wythburn
(pronounced
'Wyb'n')
looking
east
Thirlmere
Layby. The route starts from an
iron gate the far side of the A591.

The Wythburn route via Birk Side is still one of the most
popular ways up Helvellyn. Steeper alternatives via the gills
offer solitude but at the expense of views and a decent path
underfoot; in this respect, the start of the old lead mine route
from an iron gate on the A591 offers no pleasure whatsoever
— an unpleasant climb through bracken and brambles.

THE EASTERN APPROACHES

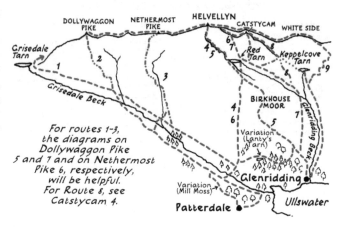

For routes 1-3,
the diagrams on
Dollywaggon Pike
5 and 1 and on Nethermost
Pike 6, respectively,
will be helpful.
For Route 8, see
Catstycam 4.

1 : via Grisedale Tarn — 3000' of ascent : 7⅓ miles

A long easy walk on a good path with variations initially, and only one steep section : the zig-zags from the tarn to the summit area of Dollywaggon Pike. An interesting and pleasant route.

2 : via Dollywaggon Pike direct — 3000' of ascent : 6¼ miles

A very fine route for the more adventurous walker, cutting off a big corner of Route 1 — but the variation is steep and pathless in places once the main Grisedale path is left behind.

3 : via Nethermost Pike direct — 2800' of ascent : 5 miles

Twin to Route 2, with a steep enjoyable scramble. Not for novices.

4 : via Striding Edge — 2700' of ascent : 5¼ miles

The best way of all (Route 5 is as good) ; well known, popular, and often densely populated in summer. The big attraction is an airy rock ridge, very fine indeed. Good paths throughout.

5 : via Striding Edge — 2800' of ascent : 4 miles

A shorter way to Striding Edge, starting from Glenridding and crossing Birkhouse Moor.

**6 : via Red Tarn and Swirral Edge,
from Patterdale — 2600' of ascent : 5½ miles**

An enjoyable walk with magnificent scenery in the vicinity of Red Tarn and a good scramble up the rock staircase of Swirral Edge.

**7 : via Red Tarn and Swirral Edge,
from Glenridding — 2600' of ascent : 4½ miles**

A shorter way to Swirral Edge starting at Glenridding. An easy walk as far as Red Tarn before the climb up to Swirral Edge and the final scramble to the summit plateau.

8 : via Catstycam direct — 3200' of ascent : 4½ miles

Just as Dollywaggon Pike, Nethermost Pike and White Side can be climbed first, so can the shapely Catstycam. There is a choice : the east shoulder or the adventurous north-west ridge.

THE EASTERN APPROACHES

9 : Old Pony Route via Keppel Cove — 3000' of ascent : 5½ miles
   The original route from Glenridding. Long, easy and interesting.

In mist:

Route 1 is easy to follow every inch of the way.
Routes 2 and 3 should be avoided.
Routes 4 and 5 are safe for anyone familiar with them.

Route 6 is safe, though there could be some uncertainty near Red Tarn.
Routes 7 and 9 are distinct all the way.
Route 8 should be avoided.

Routes 4-9 are illustrated on pages 16 and 17 following.
The ascent from Grasmere is described on page 15.

The summit, from Striding Edge

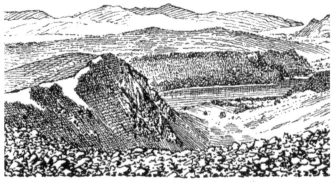

Looking north-west to Thirlmere, from Lower Man

ASCENT FROM GRASMERE
3050 feet of ascent : 6½ miles from Grasmere Church

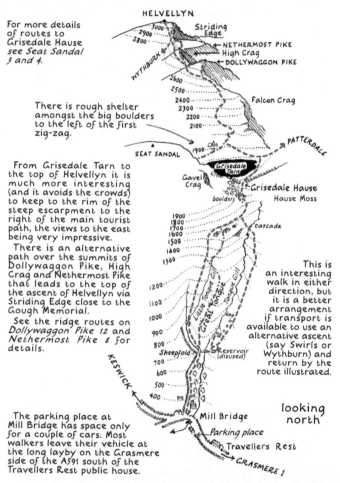

HELVELLYN

For more details
of routes to
Grisedale Hause
see *Seat Sandal
3 and 4.*

Striding
Edge

3000
2900
2800

NETHERMOST PIKE
High Crag
DOLLYWAGGON PIKE

WYTHBURN

2600
2500

Falcon Crag

2400
2300
2200
2100

PATTERDALE

There is rough shelter
amongst the big boulders
to the left of the first
zig-zag.

SEAT SANDAL

1900

Grisedale
Tarn

From Grisedale Tarn to
the top of Helvellyn it is
much more interesting
(and it avoids the crowds)
to keep to the rim of the
steep escarpment to the
right of the main tourist
path, the views to the east
being very impressive.

Gavel
Crag

boulders

Grisedale Hause

Hause Moss

1900
1800
1700
1600
1500
1400
1300

cascade

There is an alternative
path over the summits of
Dollywaggon Pike, High
Crag and Nethermost Pike
that leads to the top of
the ascent of Helvellyn via
Striding Edge close to the
Gough Memorial.

1200

1100

1000

This is
an interesting
walk in either
direction, but
it is a better
arrangement
if transport is
available to use an
alternative ascent
(say Swirls or
Wythburn) and
return by the
route illustrated.

See the ridge routes on
Dollywaggon Pike 12 and
Nethermost Pike 8 for
details.

KESWICK

Little Tongue Gill

Great Tongue

Tongue Gill

900

800

700

Sheepfold

Reservoir
(disused)

600

500

400

**looking
north**

The parking place at
Mill Bridge has space only
for a couple of cars. Most
walkers leave their vehicle at
the long layby on the Grasmere
side of the A591 south of the
Travellers Rest public house.

Mill Bridge

Parking place

Travellers Rest

GRASMERE 1

Most sojourners at Grasmere make this familiar pilgrimage
to Helvellyn: it is fast becoming a traditional custom for those
who stay there. For many it serves as a pleasant introduction
to the fells. If transport is available to Dunmail Raise, there is
a saving in time and distance by climbing to Grisedale Tarn
via Raise Beck. For details, see *Dollywaggon Pike 6.*

ASCENT FROM GLENRIDDING
2750 feet of ascent : 4½ or 5½ miles

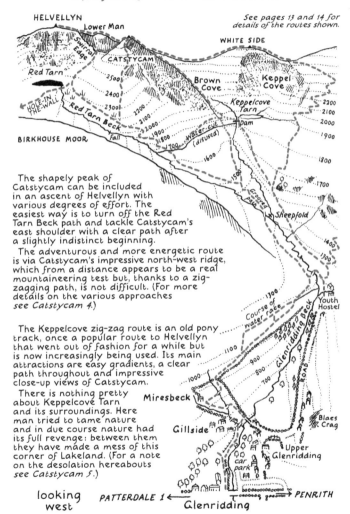

See pages 13 and 14 for details of the routes shown.

The shapely peak of Catstycam can be included in an ascent of Helvellyn with various degrees of effort. The easiest way is to turn off the Red Tarn Beck path and tackle Catstycam's east shoulder with a clear path after a slightly indistinct beginning.

The adventurous and more energetic route is via Catstycam's impressive north-west ridge, which from a distance appears to be a real mountaineering test but, thanks to a zig-zagging path, is not difficult. (For more details on the various approaches see *Catstycam 4*.)

The Keppelcove zig-zag route is an old pony track, once a popular route to Helvellyn that went out of fashion for a while but is now increasingly being used. Its main attractions are easy gradients, a clear path throughout and impressive close-up views of Catstycam.

There is nothing pretty about Keppelcove Tarn and its surroundings. Here man tried to tame nature and in due course nature had its full revenge: between them they have made a mess of this corner of Lakeland. (For a note on the desolation hereabouts see *Catstycam 5*.)

looking west

An excellent alternative to Striding Edge from Glenridding (usually via Birkhouse Moor, *see Birkhouse Moor 6*), the highlight being the rocky scramble up Swirral Edge.

ASCENT FROM PATTERDALE
2700 feet of ascent : 5 miles

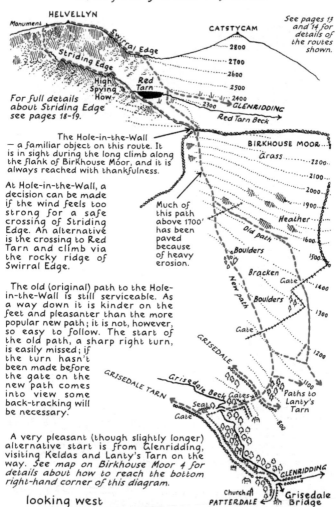

HELVELLYN

Monument

Swirral Edge

Striding Edge

CATSTYCAM

2800
2700
2600
2500
2400 GLENRIDDING
2300
Red Tarn Beck

High Spying How

Red Tarn

See pages 13 and 14 for details of the routes shown.

For full details about Striding Edge see pages 18-19.

The Hole-in-the-Wall
— a familiar object on this route. It is in sight during the long climb along the flank of Birkhouse Moor, and it is always reached with thankfulness.

At Hole-in-the-Wall, a decision can be made if the wind feels too strong for a safe crossing of Striding Edge. An alternative is the crossing to Red Tarn and climb via the rocky ridge of Swirral Edge.

The old (original) path to the Hole-in-the-Wall is still serviceable. As a way down it is kinder on the feet and pleasanter than the more popular new path; it is not, however, so easy to follow. The start of the old path, a sharp right turn, is easily missed; if the turn hasn't been made before the gate on the new path comes into view some back-tracking will be necessary.

A very pleasant (though slightly longer) alternative start is from Glenridding, visiting Keldas and Lanty's Tarn on the way. See map on Birkhouse Moor 4 for details about how to reach the bottom right-hand corner of this diagram.

BIRKHOUSE MOOR
Grass
2200
2100
2000
1900
Heather
1600
1500
Boulders
Bracken
Gate 1400
Boulders 1300
Gate 1200

Much of this path above 1700' has been paved because of heavy erosion.

Old path
New path

GRISEDALE
Grisedale Beck Gates
GRISEDALE TARN
Seat
Gate
1100
Paths to Lanty's Tarn
800

GLENRIDDING
Church
PATTERDALE
Grisedale Bridge

looking west

One of the definitive Lakeland routes of ascent; the spectacular Striding Edge is an iconic ridge and inevitably attracts hordes of walkers most days of the year.

Striding Edge

Whatever the conditions on the ridge and however many prior visits you have made, this is a route that always demands total respect.

The section from the Hole-in-the-Wall to point A (*see map, right*) is about 500 yards on an easy rising path; from here, you can go left on a sketchy path over Low Spying How to High Spying How, or continue on the main path. Most walkers choose the latter.

At point B comes the *big* decision: the path splits. You can go left, to High Spying How, or right, below the crest. The two paths meet again at crossover point C.

Striding Edge begins at the moment the top rocks of High Spying How are reached, and immediately there is a taste of things to come: the descent is rocky and sharply defined, and some boulder hopping is necessary. Progress is slow down to point C, with care required all the way. (Looking back, you may be able to spot the Dixon Memorial on a small platform of rock above Nethermost Cove.)

After the crossover comes the most exhilarating and photogenic stretch of Striding Edge (points C–D), as the ridge narrows and the path on the crest rises up and down four

For detailed map of the whole Helvellyn area, see pages 7 and 8.

towers, the second of which is particularly impressive. In a number of places there is a thin path to the left (just off the crest).

After the towers there are several less significant ups and downs, with the ridge mainly in a shallow decline to the final dip (point D). The path below the crest on the right is occasionally just a few feet away

Point D is the final big depression before the end of Striding Edge, and it used to be a second crossing point, with the lower path switching sides and offering the opportunity for walkers on the crest to avoid the Rock Chimney that marks the end of Striding Edge. However, in the summer of 2014 Fix the Fells undertook work to discourage walkers from this route because of the dangers of erosion — so *don't go left* at this point.

continued

The final challenge, and the toughest, is the Rock Chimney. This 25' descent requires a far greater degree of agility than earlier sections, but is not as difficult as it looks. From point D a path rises over the final tower and splits early on, but the routes reunite at the top of the chimney, where the generally light-coloured rock across the crest assumes a pinkish hue as rock walls close in on either side. As usual with steep rocky descents that are close to vertical in places, it is best to go down backwards; footholds and handholds have been worn smooth over the years, but still remain firm and easy to find.

All that now remains is to climb the steep slope to the summit plateau. It is best over the lightish rocks directly ahead, which form a distinctive outcrop known as The Castle. Resist the temptation to bypass it either side: over the years, this has caused serious erosion that has had to be repaired by helicopters lifting in tons of rock. Above The Castle there is a clear path that splits higher up with a choice of two routes that lead to the Gough Memorial.

The path below the crest

There is an alternative to walking along the narrow crest of Striding Edge, the well blazed path on the northern slope, and this has been in use for as long as anyone can remember, certainly since Victorian times, and is surprisingly interesting, with more ups and downs and little scrambles than might be expected.

This path ends at the final dip (*point D on the map on the previous page*) where it used to cross to the steep southern flank of

Striding Edge, as seen from south of the Gough Memorial.

Low Spying How

HIGH SPYING HOW

to Hole-in-the-Wall

Dixon Memorial

Crossover

Four towers

Path below crest

Path on crest

Final dip

Main path

Lower path

Rock Chimney

The Castle

to HELVELLYN

the Edge overlooking Nethermost Cove. That was a relatively new route, however, largely made by walkers in the early years of this century, but it was never going to be sustainable on such a slope and, inevitably, erosion set it, resulting in major repair work. Avoid the temptation to go this way — the fellside needs to be left alone.

Swirral Edge

If Swirral Edge were the only sharp ridge on Helvellyn's eastern flank it would rank among one of the great ascents in Lakeland. It has everything: a narrow, exciting ridge with some easy scrambling, an easy-to-follow route and superlative views. However, its position just across Red Tarn from Striding Edge means it will be forever in the shadow of its 'big brother'. Plenty of walkers do climb Helvellyn this way, but it is probably *descended* more often than it is ascended, often by walkers who have earlier climbed Helvellyn by way of Striding Edge.

The way down Swirral Edge starts from a prominent cairn 200 yards north-north-west of the summit (past the Ordnance Survey column first), and the descent is immediately steep and stony. It soon becomes rocky as outcrops known as 'the fangs' (for obvious reasons) are reached. You can go either side of these rocks but is probably a little easier to keep right. Further down, a clear path leaves the crest of the ridge to the right, much like the 'below the crest' path on Striding Edge, although Swirral Edge at this point is certainly a lot easier than the crest of Striding Edge.

At the depression between Swirral Edge and Catstycam, a well-blazed path descends right towards Red Tarn (for Glenridding via Red Tarn Beck or Patterdale via Hole-in-the-Wall). A grassier path leads straight on to the shapely peak of Catstycam.

Helvellyn Lower Man

HELVELLYN

The summit of Lower Man

Helvellyn Lower Man is one of only seven tops in the country over 3000'. The full list is:

SCAFELL PIKE	3210'
SCAFELL	3162'
HELVELLYN	3118'
Ill Crag	3068'
SKIDDAW	3054'
Broad Crag	3054'
Lower Man	3033'

Broad Crag and Ill Crag are subsidiary summits of Scafell Pike.

Helvellyn Lower Man (3033'), half a mile to the north-west of the principal top, occupies a key position on the main ridge, which here changes its direction subtly and unobtrusively. Walkers intending to follow the main ridge north may easily go astray hereabouts, the culprit being the wide path from Helvellyn which skirts Lower Man and continues clearly along a broad spur; it appears to be the main ridge but is not (this is the popular route via Browncove Crags to the car park at Swirls). Walkers continuing along the north ridge have to climb Lower Man on the way to White Side and Raise.

For a ridge diagram see Helvellyn 22.

THE SUMMIT

It might be expected that the summit of so popular a mountain would be crowned with a cairn the size of a house, instead of which the only adornment is a small and insignificant heap of stones that commands no respect at all, untidily thrown together on the mound forming the highest point. It is a disappointment to have no cairn to recline against, and as there is no natural seat anywhere on the top visitors inevitably drift into the nearby wall-shelter and there rest ankle-deep in the debris of countless packed lunches. The summit is covered in shale and is lacking in natural features, a deficiency which man has attempted to remedy by erecting thereon, as well as the shelter, a triangulation column and two monuments. And until many walkers learn better manners there is a crying need for an incinerator also, to dispose of the decaying heaps of litter they leave behind to greet those who follow.

The paths across the summit are wide and so well-trodden as to appear almost metalled: they are unnecessarily and amply cairned.

The dull surroundings are relieved by the exciting view down the escarpment to Red Tarn and Striding Edge below.

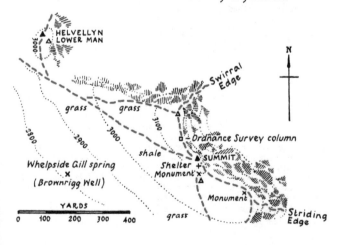

DESCENTS

Descents should not be attempted in the areas shaded. *In general, the eastern slopes are craggy high up and grassy below, but the western slopes are grassy high up and craggy below.*

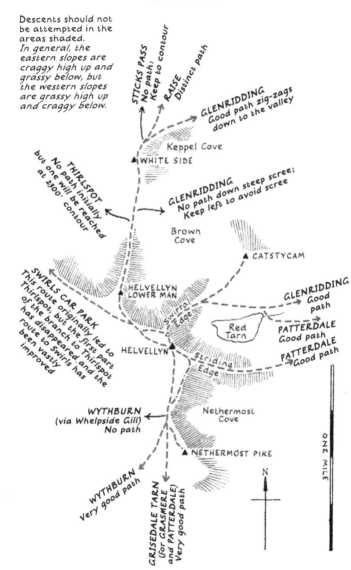

STICKS PASS
No path;
Keep to contour

RAISE
Distinct path

GLENRIDDING
Good path zig-zags
down to the valley

Keppel Cove

▲ WHITE SIDE

THIRLSPOT
No path initially
but one will be reached
at 2300' contour

GLENRIDDING
No path down steep scree;
Keep left to avoid scree

Brown Cove

▲ CATSTYCAM

SWIRLS CAR PARK
This route originally led to
Thirlspot, but the first part
of the branch to Thirlspot
has disappeared, and the
route to Swirls has
been vastly
improved

HELVELLYN
LOWER MAN

Swirral Edge

GLENRIDDING
Good path

Red Tarn

PATTERDALE
Good path

HELVELLYN ▲

Striding Edge

PATTERDALE
Good path

WYTHBURN
(via Whelpside Gill)
No path

Nethermost Cove

▲ NETHERMOST PIKE

N

ONE MILE

WYTHBURN
Very good path

GRISEDALE TARN
(for GRASMERE
and PATTERDALE)
Very good path

RIDGE ROUTES

To HELVELLYN LOWER MAN, 3033': ½ mile : NW
Depression at 2975': 60 feet of ascent

A simple stroll, safe in mist.

Take the Thirlspot path, forking right below the cone of Lower Man. Or, better, follow the edge of the escarpment all the way.

NOTE: *Helvellyn Lower Man stands at the point where the main ridge makes an abrupt and unexpected right-angled turn. Its summit must be traversed for White Side, Sticks Pass or Glenridding.*

To CATSTYCAM, 2917': 1 mile : NW (200 yards), then NE
Depression at 2600': 320 feet of ascent

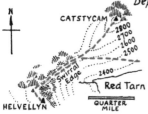

A splendid walk with a fine rock scramble. Safe in mist; dangerous in ice and snow.

200 yards north-west of the top of Helvellyn is a cairn (the Ordnance Survey column is midway), and just beyond, over the rim, is the start of the steep rock stairway going down to Swirral Edge: the descent is less formidable than it looks. Midway along the Edge the main path turns off to the right: here continue ahead up the grass slope to the summit.

The Monuments of Helvellyn —

The Gough Memorial

Erected 1890 on the edge of the summit above the path to Striding Edge to mark the death in 1805 of artist Charles Gough, whose body was found below Striding Edge three months after he went missing. His pet dog Foxie was still alive beside his master, which prompted famous lines from Wordsworth and Tennyson.

Aircraft Memorial

This small stone tablet, 40 yards south of the shelter, commemorates the landing of an aeroplane in 1926. It is inscribed:

The first aeroplane to land on a mountain in Great Britain did so on this spot on December 22nd 1926. John Leeming and Bert Hinkler in an Avro 585 Gosport landed here and after a short stay flew back to Woodford.

The Dixon Memorial

Situated on a platform of rock on Striding Edge near High Spying High overlooking Nethermost Cove and not often noticed. It is inscribed:

In memory of Robert Dixon of Rooking, Patterdale who was killed on this spot on the 27th day of November 1858 following the Patterdale Foxhounds.

RIDGE ROUTES

To BIRKHOUSE MOOR, 2356': 2 miles : ESE then NE
Minor depressions only : 100 feet of ascent

An unpleasant descent on loose scree, followed by an exhilarating scramble along a narrow rock ridge and an easy walk. Dangerous in snow and ice; care necessary in gusty wind; safe in mist.

Turn down the scree for Striding Edge 30 yards beyond the monument. The Edge begins with a 25' chimney, well furnished with holds : this is the only difficulty. From the rock tower of High Spying How at the far end the path slants across the slope but it is pleasanter to follow the crest.

BIRKHOUSE MOOR

2300
2200
2100
2000

PATTERDALE

2200
2300

N

HELVELLYN
2400
2500
2600
2700
Monument —×—
3000
Striding Edge

HALF A MILE

To NETHERMOST PIKE, 2920'
¾ mile : S then SE
Depression at 2840': 80 feet of ascent

A very easy walk. Safe in mist.

HELVELLYN
3100
3000
2900
× Monument
N
2800
2700

HALF A MILE

NETHERMOST PIKE

A broad path leads south to the depression known as Swallow Scarth. Here the path divides, one branch descending to Wythburn, and the other continuing over the flat top of Nethermost Pike. To visit the summit-cairn bear left at the fork, and left again in about fifty yards, along a distinct path. A more interesting route follows the edge of the escarpment from the Gough Memorial, the views being very impressive.

Whelpside Gill Spring (Brownrigg Well)

Few visitors to Helvellyn know of this spring (the source of Whelpside Gill), which offers unfailing supplies of icy water. To find it, walk 500 yards south of west from the top in the direction of Pillar. In the nineteenth century a leat was built to carry water from the spring into the gill to its north to serve the needs of the Helvellyn Mine lower down the gill. The leat has long since fallen into disuse ; only a groove now remains.

THE VIEW
(with distances in miles)

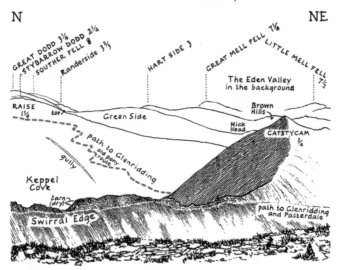

N   NE

GREAT DODD 3½
STYBARROW DODD 2¼
SOUTHER FELL 8
Randerside 3⅓
HART SIDE 3
GREAT MELL FELL 7¼
LITTLE MELL FELL 7½

The Eden Valley
in the background

RAISE 1¾
tor?
Green Side
Brown Hills
Nick Head
CATSTYCAM ¾

Path to Glenridding
old pony route
gully

Keppel Cove
tarn (dry)
Swirral Edge

path to Glenridding
and Patterdale

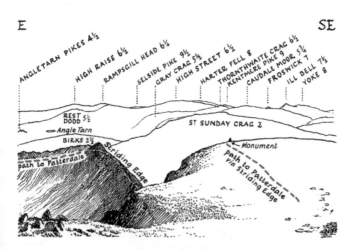

E   SE

ANGLETARN PIKES 4½
HIGH RAISE 6½
RAMPSGILL HEAD 6¼
SELSIDE PIKE 9½
GRAY CRAG 5½
HIGH STREET 6½
HARTER FELL 8
THORNTHWAITE CRAG 6½
KENTMERE PIKE 9
CAUDALE MOOR 5¾
FROSWICK 7
ILL BELL 7½
YOKE 8

REST DODD 5½
Angle Tarn
BIRKS 2½
St SUNDAY CRAG 2
Monument

path to Patterdale
Striding Edge
Path to Patterdale
via Striding Edge

The summit of Hartsop Dodd is just visible, in front of Gray Crag
and immediately to the left of St Sunday Crag.

THE VIEW

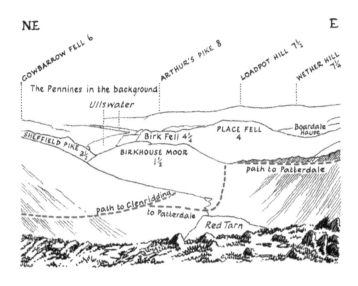

NE   E

GOWBARROW FELL 6

The Pennines in the background

Ullswater

ARTHUR'S PIKE 8

LOADPOT HILL 7½

WETHER HILL 7¼

SHEFFIELD PIKE 2½

Birk Fell 4¼

PLACE FELL 4

Boardale Hause

BIRKHOUSE MOOR 1½

path to Patterdale

path to Glenridding

to Patterdale

Red Tarn

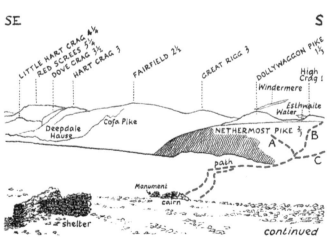

SE   S

LITTLE HART CRAG 4½

RED SCREES 5¼

DOVE CRAG 3½

HART CRAG 3

FAIRFIELD 2½

GREAT RIGG 3

DOLLYWAGGON PIKE 1⅓

High Crag 1

Windermere

Esthwaite Water

Deepdale Hause

Cofa Pike

NETHERMOST PIKE ⅔

A

B

C

path

Monument

cairn

shelter

continued

A : to NETHERMOST PIKE
B : to Grisedale Tarn (for Patterdale and Grasmere)
C : to Wythburn

THE VIEW

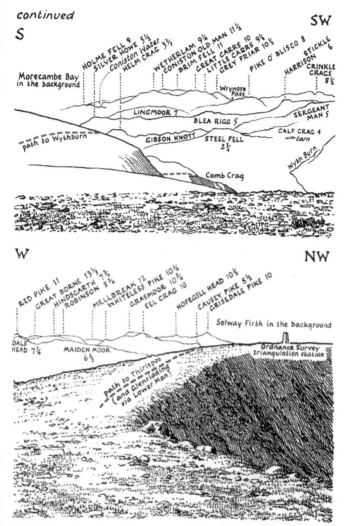

continued

S   SW

HOLME FELL 9
SILVER HOWE 5½
Coniston Water
HELM CRAG 3⅓
WETHERLAM 9½
CONISTON OLD MAN 11½
BRIM FELL 11
GREAT CARRS 10
LITTLE CARRS 9½
GREY FRIAR 10½
PIKE O' BLISCO 8
HARRISON
STICKLE 6
CRINKLE
CRAGS
8½

Morecambe Bay
in the background

Wrynose
Pass

LINGMOOR 7

BLEA RIGG 5

SERGEANT
MAN 5

path to Wythburn

GIBSON KNOTT

STEEL FELL
2¾

CALF CRAG 4
— tarn

Wyth Burn

Comb Crag

W   NW

RED PIKE 11
CREAT BORNE 13½/7⅓
HINDSCARTH 7½
ROBINSON
8½
MELLBREAK 12
WHITELESS PIKE 10½
GRASMOOR 10¾
EEL CRAG 10
HOPEGILL HEAD 10½
CAUSEY PIKE 8½
CRISEDALE PIKE 10

Solway Firth in the background

DALE
HEAD 7¼

MAIDEN MOOR
6⅔

Ordnance Survey
triangulation station

path to Thirlspot
(and Glenridding
via Lower Man)

Knott Rigg, Ard Crags, Sail and Scar Crags are also visible from
the summit, backed by north-western giants Grasmoor and Eel
Crag. Hopegill Head is sometimes known as Hobcarton Pike.

THE VIEW

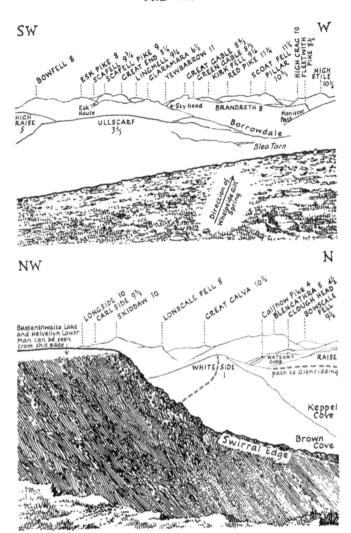

SW   W

BOWFELL 8 · ESK PIKE 8 · SCAFELL 9¼ · SCAFELL PIKE 9 · GREAT END 8½ · LINGMELL 9¼ · GLARAMARA 6½ · YEWBARROW 11 · GREAT GABLE 8⅓ · GREEN GABLE 9¼ · KIRK FELL 9½ · RED PIKE 11½ · SCOAT FELL 11½ · PILLAR 10⅔ · HIGH CRAG 10 · FLEETWITH PIKE 8¼ · HIGH STILE 10½

HIGH RAISE 5 · Esk Hause · ULLSCARF 3⅔ · Sty Head · BRANDRETH 8 · Honister Pass · Borrowdale · Blea Tarn

Direction of Whelpside Gill spring

NW   N

LONGSIDE 10 · CARL SIDE 9⅔ · SKIDDAW 10 · LONSCALE FELL 8 · GREAT CALVA 10½ · Calfhow Pike 4 · BLENCATHRA 8 · CLOUGH HEAD 4½ · BOWSCALE FELL 9¼

Bassenthwaite Lake and Helvellyn Lower Man can be seen from this edge

WHITE SIDE · WATSON'S DODD · RAISE · path to Glenridding

Keppel Cove

Brown Cove

Swirral Edge

The fell immediately to the right of Esk Hause in the SW–W sector is Allen Crags. Base Brown and Grey Knotts are both visible, near Brandreth.

Heron Pike

2008'

OS grid ref: NY356083

from Grasmere

▲ FAIRFIELD

▲ GREAT RIGG

▲ STONE ARTHUR

▲ HERON PIKE

● Grasmere ▲ NAB SCAR

● Rydal

Ambleside ●

MILES

0   1   2   3   4

Heron Pike is a grassy mound on the long southern ridge of Fairfield. From no direction does it look like a pike or peak nor will herons be found there. It is a viewpoint of some merit but otherwise is of little interest. It is climbed not, as a rule, for any attraction of its own, but because it happens to lie on a popular route to Fairfield. The ridge beyond it undulates with little change of altitude before rising sharply to Great Rigg, and this hinterland of Heron Pike is generally referred to as Rydal Fell: for convenience it will be described in this chapter as a part of Heron Pike.

NATURAL FEATURES

Heron Pike is the watershed between Rydale and the short Greenhead valley. Grass predominates on its slopes but there is much bracken on the Rydale flank and rock outcrops on both. Its streams are small and flow into the Rothay. A dreary sheet of water named Alcock Tarn, once a reservoir, occupies a shelf above Grasmere; here are many low crags. A nameless summit on the ridge to the north of Heron Pike has a steep east face, which at one point falls away abruptly in a formidable wall of rock, Erne Crag (or Earing Crag), and, further north, the fellside is cleft from top to bottom by a straight stony gully, beyond which the ground becomes rough as Great Rigg is approached. In contrast, the western slopes adjoining Great Rigg are entirely grassy.

At 2039', the north summit is higher than its parent summit, but does not have the bulk or shape to justify claims that it is the true summit.

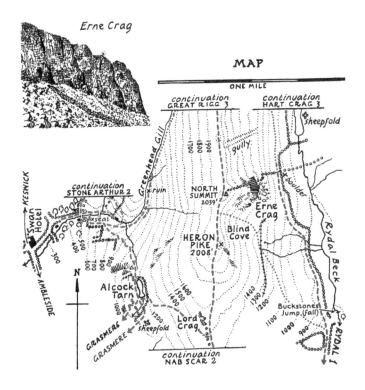

Erne Crag

MAP

ASCENT FROM GRASMERE
1750 feet of ascent : 1½ miles

ASCENT FROM RYDAL
1750 feet of ascent : 2¼ miles

Usually the summit of Heron Pike is visited only incidentally on the way to or from Fairfield, but it may be recommended as the objective of an easy and remunerative half-day's walk from Grasmere (using the path from the south end of Alcock Tarn reached via Dove Cottage or from the Swan Hotel) or from Rydal (climbing Nab Scar en route). Gully-addicts will rejoice to learn that a long straight gully, full of shifting scree but with no difficulty other than steepness, falls from the ridge half a mile north of the summit, directly above the sheepfold in mid-Rydale beyond Erne Crag : this offers a scramble they (and they alone) will enjoy, but not even the most avid of them would find any pleasure in *descending* by this route.

THE SUMMIT

The summit is by a little outcrop of rock, distinguished by quartz. All else is grass. There is no cairn and nothing of interest except the view. The nameless north summit is better : at least it has a wall and a cairn and a few rocks suitable for backrests.

DESCENTS : Any route of ascent (except the gully) may be used for descent. A quick way off to Rydal, in a season when the bracken is short, is by Blind Cove. *In mist, keep strictly to the path going south to Nab Scar and Rydal.*

RIDGE ROUTES

To GREAT RIGG, 2513'
1½ miles : N then NNE
Minor depressions
550 feet of ascent

A pleasant high-level traverse. A good path undulates over grass and finally climbs the cone ahead. *Safe in mist.*

To NAB SCAR, 1450'
⅔ mile : S
Downhill all the way

A very easy descent. The path keeps to the left of the ridge for much of the way, then it follows an old wall. *Safe in mist.*

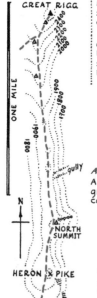

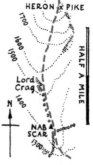

THE VIEW

The smallness of the summit gives depth to the views, which are particularly rich in lakes and tarns, with the vista of Windermere being especially good. Nearby are the fells of the Fairfield Horseshoe, but the best of the mountain scene is formed by the finely grouped Coniston and Langdale fells with Scafell Pike overtopping all.

Principal Fells

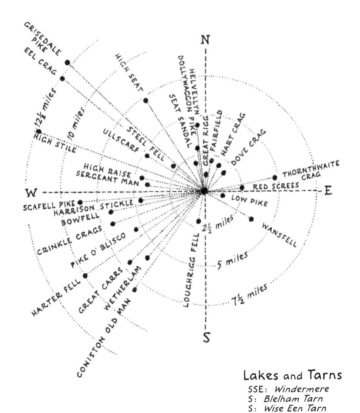

Lakes and Tarns

SSE: *Windermere*
S: *Blelham Tarn*
S: *Wise Een Tarn*
S: *Esthwaite Water*
SSW: *Coniston Water*
SSW: *Elterwater*
W: *Easedale Tarn*

High Hartsop Dodd 1702'

OS grid ref: NY394108

from Dovedale Beck

Patterdale

Hartsop

Hartsop
Hall

HIGH
HARTSOP
DOVE CRAG ▲ ▲ DODD

LITTLE ▲
HART CRAG

RED ▲ SCREES

MILES
0   1   2   3

High Hartsop Dodd, seen from the valley near Brothers Water, has the appearance of an isolated mountain with a peaked summit and steep sides, a very shapely pyramid rising from green fields. But in fact it is merely the termination of a spur of a higher fell, Little Hart Crag, which it partly hides from view and its uninteresting grassy summit has little distinction, though it is always greeted with enthusiasm by walkers who attain it direct from the valley, for the upper slopes above the sparsely wooded lower flanks are excessively steep. A high ascending ridge links the Dodd with the rough top of Little Hart Crag.

MAP

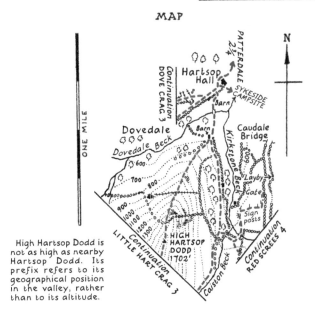

High Hartsop Dodd is not as high as nearby Hartsop Dodd. Its prefix refers to its geographical position in the valley, rather than to its altitude.

ASCENT FROM HARTSOP HALL
1200 feet of ascent : 1 mile

High Hartsop Dodd may be climbed from the barn at its foot — note here the symmetry between the pitch of the roof of the barn as it is approached across the boulder-dotted pastures from Hartsop Hall, and the sides of the pyramid of the Dodd behind — but the steepness of the slope, especially as the top wall is neared, makes the ascent laborious, despite the addition of some welcome zig-zags in the upper stages. It is really much better first to ascend Little Hart Crag (preferably by way of Dovedale) and to return to the valley over the top of the Dodd.

Hartsop Hall can be reached from the Cow Bridge car park to the north and from the Brotherswater Inn via Sykeside Camping Park. The ascent can also be made from the layby to the south of Caudale Bridge.

THE SUMMIT

There is a tiny cairn in a sea of grass indicating the highest point, which is usually assumed to be the top of the *first* rise above the broken wall, although there is clearly higher ground beyond this point and the main depression before Little Hart Crag.

‖ DESCENTS: *In mist*, remember that the wall does not cross the ridge at right-angles, but at a tangent. Do NOT follow the wall down : on both flanks it leads to crags.

Dove Crag and Hogget Gill, from High Hartsop Dodd

THE VIEW

Brothers Water

The most striking feature in a moderate view is the exceptionally fine picture of Dovedale, which is seen intimately in all its strong and impressive contrasts.

Lakes and Tarns
NNE: *Brothers Water*

Principal Fells

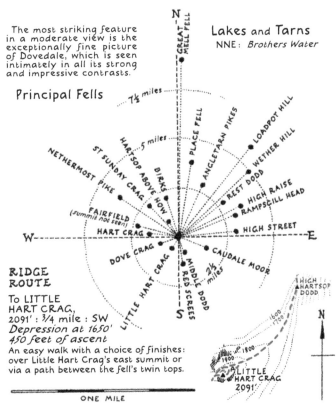

N

GREAT MELL FELL

7½ miles

5 miles

PLACE FELL

ANGLETARN PIKES

LOADPOT HILL

HARTSOP ABOVE HOW

WETHER HILL

ST SUNDAY CRAG

BIRKS

REST DODD

NETHERMOST PIKE

HIGH RAISE
RAMPSGILL HEAD

FAIRFIELD
(summit not seen)

HIGH STREET

HART CRAG

W — — — — — — — — — — — E

DOVE CRAG

CAUDALE MOOR

2½ miles

LITTLE HART CRAG

MIDDLE DODD

RED SCREES

S

RIDGE ROUTE

To LITTLE HART CRAG, 2091' : ¾ mile : SW
*Depression at 1650'
450 feet of ascent*
An easy walk with a choice of finishes: over Little Hart Crag's east summit or via a path between the fell's twin tops.

HIGH HARTSOP DODD

1600
1700
1800
1900

LITTLE HART CRAG 2091'

N

ONE MILE

High Pike

2155'

sometimes referred to as
Scandale Fell

OS grid ref: NY374088

from High Sweden Bridge

▲ DOVE CRAG

▲ HIGH PIKE

▲ LOW PIKE

● Rydal

● Ambleside

MILES
0   1   2   3

Everest enthusiasts will liken the two pronounced rises on the long southern spur of Dove Crag to the 'first and second steps' on the famous north-east ridge (but imagination would indeed have to be vivid to see in the grassy dome of Dove Crag any resemblance to the icy pyramid of that highest of all peaks!). The first rise is Low Pike, the second is High Pike. The latter, with its cairn perched on the brink of a shattered cliff, is the most imposing object seen from Scandale which lies far below.

Some authorities refer to High Pike as Scandale Fell, but the latter name is more properly applied in a general way to the whole of the high ground enclosing Scandale Bottom to north and west.

High Pike is the second fell on the popular Fairfield Horseshoe ridge walk (when walked in an anti-clockwise direction).

NATURAL FEATURES

Viewed from the south, High Pike has the appearance of an isolated peak; viewed from the parallel ridges to the east (Great Rigg–Heron Pike–Nab Scar) and west (Red Screes) it is seen in its true proportions as merely the flat top of a rise in Dove Crag's long southern ridge; viewed from the north, it is entirely insignificant. High Pike, therefore, cannot be regarded as having enough qualifications to make it a mountain in its own right. Its level top, however, marks a definite change in the character of the ridge, which is narrow and rocky below and broad and grassy above. The western flank of High Pike descends to Rydale in uninteresting slopes relieved by occasional outcrops of rock; the eastern face is much rougher and steeper, with an ill-defined stony shoulder going down into Scandale. High Pike's most significant feature is, in fact, man-made; the high wall over its spine is visible from Ambleside.

MAP

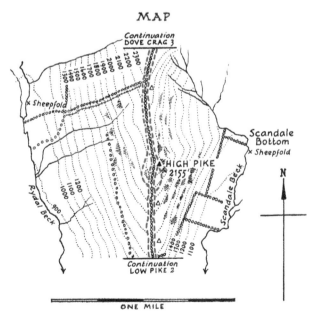

ONE MILE

The Scandale High Pike, at 2155', is just two feet lower than its namesake in the northern fells.

ASCENT FROM AMBLESIDE
2000 feet of ascent : 4 miles

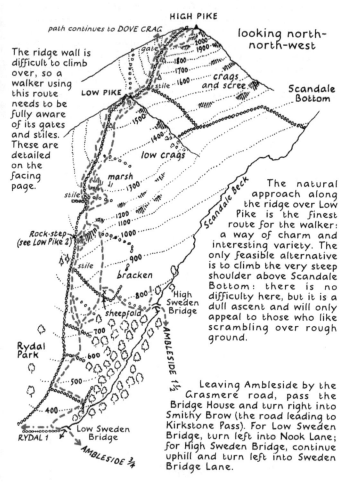

HIGH PIKE

path continues to DOVE CRAG

looking north-north-west

The ridge wall is difficult to climb over, so a walker using this route needs to be fully aware of its gates and stiles. These are detailed on the facing page.

gate

2000
1900
1800
1700
1600
1500
1400
1300
1200
1100
1000
900
800
700
600
500
400

crags and scree

Scandale Bottom

LOW PIKE

stile

low crags

marsh

stile

Rock-step (see Low Pike 2)

stile

bracken

Scandale Beck

High Sweden Bridge

AMBLESIDE 1½

sheepfold

Rydal Park

Low Sweden Bridge

RYDAL 1

AMBLESIDE ¾

The natural approach along the ridge over Low Pike is the finest route for the walker: a way of charm and interesting variety. The only feasible alternative is to climb the very steep shoulder above Scandale Bottom: there is no difficulty here, but it is a dull ascent and will only appeal to those who like scrambling over rough ground.

Leaving Ambleside by the Grasmere road, pass the Bridge House and turn right into Smithy Brow (the road leading to Kirkstone Pass). For Low Sweden Bridge, turn left into Nook Lane; for High Sweden Bridge, continue uphill and turn left into Sweden Bridge Lane.

This route, commonly used as the initial stage of the 'Fairfield Horseshoe', provides a pleasant walk along a good ridge, with a choice of two paths either side of a very prominent wall. The lower approaches (via the bridges) are equally attractive.

THE SUMMIT

The summit is a flat grassy promenade with a cairn standing at the northern end on the edge of a decaying crag, overlooking Scandale. These days the cairn is nowhere near as imposing as the illustration above. The inescapable summit wall is nearby, with a gate directly opposite the highest point.

The wall

Walkers starting (or completing) the Fairfield Horseshoe ridge walk cannot help but notice the ridge wall between Low Sweden Bridge and Dove Crag: it accompanies them all the way and its intimacy becomes a nuisance. However, it is well worthy of notice, particularly on the steepest rises south of High Pike's summit, where the method and style of construction, in persevering horizontal courses despite the difficulties of the ground, compel admiration. It should be remembered, too, that all the stone had to be found on the fell and cut to shape on the site. Witness here a dying art!

Such is the height and sturdy construction of this wall that there are very few places where it can be scaled (the summit of Low Pike being one of them though this is not recommended). Hence, the diagram to the left which indicates the best places to cross and re-cross the wall in ascent and descent.

IN ASCENT: the summit of High Pike can be reached via the western path from either of the first two gates north of Low Pike.

IN DESCENT: below the marsh, the path that hugs the east side of the wall leads to the tricky rock step, but this can be avoided (see Low Pike 2).

The path on the west of the wall is generally drier and offers the best views. The older (eastern) path is sheltered from westerlies.

The wall: well constructed, but this section is starting to show signs of wear and tear.

RIDGE ROUTES

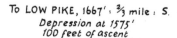

To DOVE CRAG, 2598' : 1 mile : N.
Slight depression : 470 feet of ascent

An easy, gradual climb on a good path. Perfectly safe in mist.

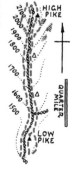

Follow the wall north; there are good paths on both sides, and it is possible to switch sides at a gate and at a gap in the wall. The cairn does not come into sight until a broken fence is reached.

To LOW PIKE, 1667' : ⅔ mile : S.
Depression at 1575'
100 feet of ascent

An easy downhill walk beside the wall, with a choice of switching sides. Safe in mist.

The summit is straddled by the wall; the cairn is to the east, but whichever path is chosen, the wall can be climbed at the summit.

from Scandale

DESCENTS: The ridge path should always be used when leaving the top: nothing but discomfort is to be gained by attempting a direct descent to east or west.

In bad weather, a safe descent may be made to Ambleside by following the ridge over Low Pike, keeping to the path or to the wall, although the tricky rock step south of Low Pike's summit may then be encountered (see *Low Pike 2* for details about this obstacle).   continued

continued

A journey to Patterdale need not be abandoned in the event of bad weather on High Pike: the safe conclusion of the walk is ensured if the wall is followed north to a broken fence, which leads down grassy slopes to Dovedale or, alternatively, Scandale Pass. *See Dove Crag 6 for details.*

THE VIEW

The ridge wall obstructs the view westwards from the cairn but is worth peeking over for the prospect of the Central Fells, which is good. In other directions, neighbouring higher fells hide the distance, but much of the High Street range is seen over Scandale Pass.

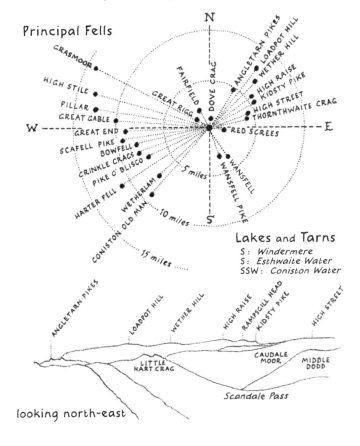

Principal Fells

N

GRASMOOR
HIGH STILE
PILLAR
GREAT GABLE
GREAT END
SCAFELL PIKE
BOWFELL
CRINKLE CRAGS
PIKE O' BLISCO
HARTER FELL
WETHERLAM
CONISTON OLD MAN

FAIRFIELD
GREAT RIGG
DOVE CRAG
ANGLETARN PIKES
LOADPOT HILL
WETHER HILL
HIGH RAISE
KIDSTY PIKE
HIGH STREET
THORNTHWAITE CRAG
RED SCREES

WANSFELL
WANSFELL PIKE

W
E
S

5 miles
10 miles
15 miles

Lakes and Tarns

S: *Windermere*
S: *Esthwaite Water*
SSW: *Coniston Water*

ANGLETARN PIKES
LOADPOT HILL
WETHER HILL
HIGH RAISE
RAMPSGILL HEAD
KIDSTY PIKE
HIGH STREET

LITTLE
HART CRAG
CAUDALE
MOOR
MIDDLE
DODD

Scandale Pass

looking north-east

Little Hart Crag

2091'

OS grid ref: NY387100

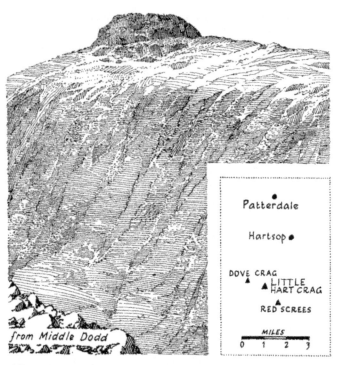

from Middle Dodd

Patterdale

Hartsop

DOVE CRAG ▲   ▲ LITTLE
HART CRAG

▲
RED SCREES

MILES
0   1   2   3

Little Hart Crag is the sentinel of Scandale Pass, four miles north of Ambleside, and takes its duty of guarding the Pass very seriously and proudly. It has the appearance, in fact, of a crouching watchdog, facing Scandale and missing nothing of the happenings there, while its spine curves down to the fields of Hartsop; the path from one place to the other climbs over its shoulder just beneath the hoary head and beetling brows.

It is really a very junior member in a company of grand hills and quite overshadowed by Red Screes and Dove Crag; but it has individuality and an interesting double summit which commands delightful views of Scandale and Dovedale.

NATURAL FEATURES

Little Hart Crag descends in uninteresting slopes of grass and bracken to Scandale in the south; it is connected in the west to Dove Crag by the broad marshy depression of Bakestones Moss; south-east is the lower depression of Scandale Pass and the vast soaring flank of Red Screes. North-east is a narrow spur running at a high elevation before plunging sharply to the valley of Hartsop: this is High Hartsop Dodd, and its steep-sided pyramidal form, seen from Brothers Water,

The summit, from the south

gives it the appearance of being a separate height. Just below the summit, west, is a long wall of impressive crags, Black Brow. The eastern slopes, falling to Caiston Glen, are rough and unattractive.

Hartsop, from the summit

The fell is usually climbed either as part of the Scandale Horseshoe from Ambleside, comprising Low Pike, High Pike, Dove Crag, Little Hart Crag and Red Screes, or as part of the Dovedale Horseshoe, from Brothers Water: Hartsop above How, Hart Crag, Dove Crag, Little Hart Crag and High Hartsop Dodd.

MAP

ONE MILE

Tiny Scandale Tarn is well worth a visit, with a fine location on a shelf overlooking Scandale. Grassy shores make this a fine place for a summer picnic.

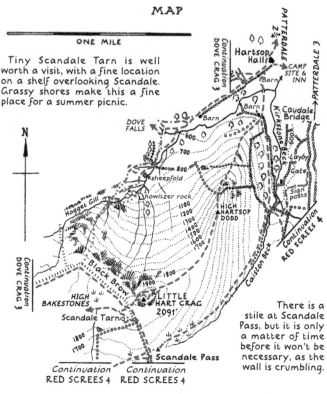

There is a stile at Scandale Pass, but it is only a matter of time before it won't be necessary, as the wall is crumbling.

ASCENT FROM AMBLESIDE
2,000 feet of ascent : 4¼ miles

The climb from Scandale Pass is on a clear path throughout, the final section from a small col to the west of the summit up a steep spine. *It is safe in mist.* For details on getting to Scandale Pass from Ambleside, see Dove Crag 5.

An easy walk that gives a good flavour of the quiet valley of Scandale.

ASCENT FROM PATTERDALE
1700 feet of ascent : 5 miles from Patterdale village

No poet ever sung the praises of Hogget Gill, and few walkers go there, but it is worth a visit for its impressive scenery. However, the direct route via the gill and the steep slope below Black Brow is adventurous *and must not be attempted in mist.*

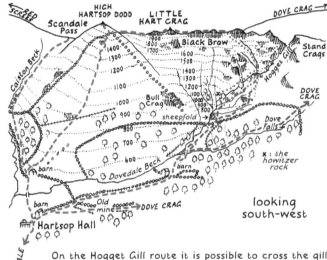

looking
south-west

On the Hogget Gill route it is possible to cross the gill upstream of the sheepfold near a prominent boulder that resembles the summit rocks of Helm Crag (The Howitzer) and proceed on Hogget Gill's left (south) bank. However, this is an awkward, pathless approach. It is better to cut the corner from the valley floor directly to a weakness in Hogget Gill, where it is easy to cross at a flat section after a short descent from a steep bank.

Two routes are in use : the first begins with a thin path just after the gap in the wall and follows a beck in its early stages before angling left up a grassy rake. A simple walk follows across grass with an intermittent path leading to the crossing point of the gill ; the second begins from further up the valley and follows a beck in a shallow gully to the right of a rock outcrop.

Little Hart Crag may be best known and most visited from the Scandale side, but its finest aspect faces north to Dovedale. The easiest route is via Caiston Glen, turning right at Scandale Pass (see facing page); the most direct route is over High Hartsop Dodd, which is airy but steep ; the most interesting way up is via Hogget Gill, *which must not be attempted in mist.*

THE SUMMIT

There are two well defined tops. The higher is that nearer to Dove Crag; it is surmounted by a cairn perched on the extreme edge of a rocky platform. The lower summit, to the north-east, is less conspicuous, but is easily identified in mist by markings of quartz in the stones near the insignificant cairn: this cairn is the key to the ridge going down to High Hartsop Dodd. Both summits are buttressed to the south by sheer walls of black rock.

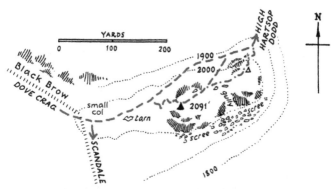

DESCENTS: The descent to Patterdale is best made directly by the grassy ridge over High Hartsop Dodd, the last 1000 feet down to the valley being steep on a clear path throughout. Scandale, for Ambleside, may be reached by cutting off a corner at the top of the pass.

In mist, the summit can be confusing and dangerous, although in recent years the path from the small col to the west of the summit has become much clearer, and a useful new path from the depression between the two summits connects to the 'bypass' path to the north of the summit. The safest way off is west to the broken fence, following this down south to Scandale Pass for either Patterdale or Ambleside. Descents to Caiston Glen or Dovedale direct should not be attempted.

THE VIEW

Principal Fells

The charming picture of the Hartsop valley compensates for the restricted view. This is the best viewpoint for Scandale.

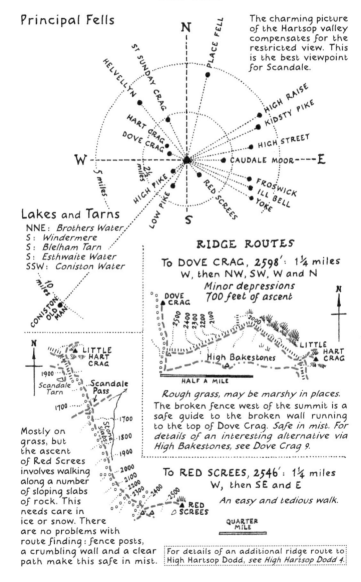

Lakes and Tarns

NNE: *Brothers Water*
S: *Windermere*
S: *Blelham Tarn*
S: *Esthwaite Water*
SSW: *Coniston Water*

RIDGE ROUTES

TO DOVE CRAG, 2598': 1¼ miles
W, then NW, SW, W and N
Minor depressions
700 feet of ascent

HALF A MILE

Rough grass, may be marshy in places.
The broken fence west of the summit is a safe guide to the broken wall running to the top of Dove Crag. *Safe in mist.* For details of an interesting alternative via High Bakestones, see Dove Crag 9.

Mostly on grass, but the ascent of Red Screes involves walking along a number of sloping slabs of rock. This needs care in ice or snow. There are no problems with route finding: fence posts, a crumbling wall and a clear path make this safe in mist.

TO RED SCREES, 2546': 1¼ miles
W, then SE and E

An easy and tedious walk.

QUARTER MILE

For details of an additional ridge route to High Hartsop Dodd, see High Hartsop Dodd 4.

Little Mell Fell

1657'

OS grid ref: NY423240

from Gowbarrow Fell

Little Mell Fell barely merits inclusion in this book. It *is* a fell — its name says so — but it is not the stuff of which the true fells are made. It rises on the verge of Lakeland but its characteristics are alien to Lakeland. It stands in isolation, not in the company of others. Its substance looks more akin to the sandstones of the nearby valley of Eden; its patchwork

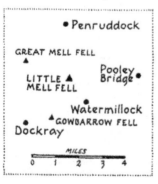

clothing, gorse and ling prominent, is unusual on the other fells; its hedges of stunted, windblown, unhappy trees and tumbledown fences are unsatisfactory substitutes for friendly stone walls. It is ringed by a quiet and pleasant countryside of green pastures and lush hedgerows, and one is as likely to meet a cow as a sheep on its slopes. There is good in all, however, and its heathery top is a fine place for viewing the (greater) merits of other fells.

NATURAL FEATURES

Little Mell Fell is an outlier of the Helvellyn range and the last Lakeland fell in the north-east before the high country falls away to the wide plain stretching to the distant Border. It is an uninspiring, unattractive, bare and rounded hump — the sublime touch that made a wonderland of the district overlooked Little Mell — and few walkers halt their hurried entrance into the sanctuary to climb and explore it. In truth, there is little to explore. As though conscious of its failings it tries to aspire to normal mountain structure by throwing out two ridges, but the effort is weak and not convincing. One feels sorry for Little Mell Fell, as for all who are neglected and forlorn, but at least it is beloved of birds and animals and it is one of the few fells that grouse select for their habitat, and not even the great Helvellyn itself can make such a claim!

MAP

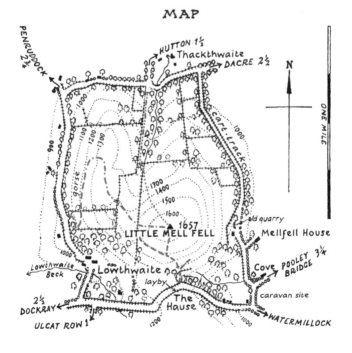

ASCENT FROM THE HAUSE
450 feet of ascent : 1/3 mile

It is difficult to plan a mountaineering expedition within a single square mile of territory, and probably it is best to climb straight up and down from The Hause (the highest point on the minor road between Matterdale End and Watermillock) and get the job done without frills: half an hour is sufficient from here. A gate gives access from the road, and after crossing a field a second gate leads to open fellside where the path bears left. Signposts at a junction indicate the way to Lowthwaite (straight on) and the summit (right). Go straight up a steep, grooved path or preferably a graded path to the right which turns back to join it. Further up, it joins a shepherd's track but soon a steeper path breaks off right to the summit as Blencathra comes into view.

ASCENT FROM THACKTHWAITE
750 feet of ascent : 1 mile

An alternative approach lies along the wooded hollow above the charming bridge near Thackthwaite and makes use of an old droveway with ditches on either side. The route soon deteriorates into a muddy trudge and is not recommended.

ASCENT FROM LOWTHWAITE
550 feet of ascent : 1¼ miles

Take the narrow road leading north-west from Lowthwaite and turn off right onto a farm track after 450 yards. A meandering path leads through gorse bushes and onto the open fell; some agility is needed to scale a wire fence further up.

THE SUMMIT

On the highest point is an Ordnance Survey column in a shallow bowl. The stone wall that formerly stood nearby has gone, and so has all the heather that once covered the top. Penrith can be seen from the summit, with the village of Dacre directly below.

DESCENTS: Descents may safely be made in any direction, in any weather, without the remotest risk of accident by falling over a crag; frisky bullocks are the only obstacles to be feared. The Hause, to which descents will be made usually, is not visible from the summit but comes into sight below by walking south, in the direction of Hallin Fell: beware rabbit holes obscured by bracken on this slope.

Great Mell Fell from Little Mell Fell

THE VIEW

The diagram illustrates effectively the isolated situation of Little Mell Fell on the fringe of mountain country. One half of the view is of Lakeland, the other half of lowlands stretching away to the Pennines and the Border across the lovely Vale of Eden.

This is one of the few good viewpoints for appreciating the shy beauty of Martindale. Gowbarrow Fell hides most of Ullswater, only the unexciting lower reach of the lake being in sight.

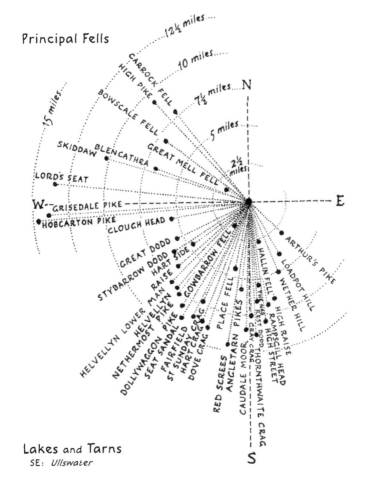

Principal Fells

Lakes and Tarns
SE: *Ullswater*

Low Pike   1667′

OS grid ref: NY373078

from Buckstones Jump

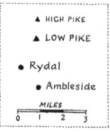

▲ HIGH PIKE

▲ LOW PIKE

● Rydal

● Ambleside

MILES

0   1   2   3

Low Pike is well seen from the streets of Ambleside as the first prominent peak on the high ridge running northwards. The gradient along the crest of the ridge is slight, but Low Pike, halfway along, is sufficiently elevated above the deep valleys of Scandale, east, and Rydale, west, to give an impression of loftiness which exaggerates its modest altitude. There is a good deal of rock on the fell with several tiers of low crag. Below the fell on the Rydale side is the well known local beauty spot of Buckstones Jump.

MAP

Buckstones Jump is a delightful cascade and pool created by a long rib of rock that cuts across the line of Rydal Beck. The pool has a natural shingle beach, making it a fine place for a picnic or a swim.

Continuation HART CRAG 3

Continuation HIGH PIKE 2

N

Buckstones Jump

LOW PIKE 1667'

Rydal Beck

Marsh (with a warning sign!)

800 900 1000

to RYDAL PARK (private)

1400

RYDAL 1

1300

footbridge (closed)

Stile

1200

Continuation RED SCREES 3

1100

Rock step

1000

High Sweden Bridge

ONE MILE

900

sheepfold

AMBLESIDE 1½

The rock-step

It is unusual for a distinct track to have so formidable an obstacle — the explanation is probably that this track was made by walkers *descending* the fell, the turn left to the usual path just above being easily missed.

800

700

600

500

Scandale Beck

400

Low Sweden Bridge

RYDAL 1

AMBLESIDE ¾

Walkers with a degree of agility will not find the step too difficult to climb if the right foot is used first, the right foot in this case being the left. There is no dignity in the proceeding, either up or down. The less agile will be glad to find an easier way up a few yards away to the right of the rock step, starting on a ledge. Some use of hands may be needed on the rocks, but this bypass ascent is without difficulty of any kind; it is certainly far easier than the rock step.

ASCENT FROM AMBLESIDE

1400 feet of ascent : 3⅓ miles

Low Pike is invariably climbed from Ambleside, usually on the way to the high fells beyond; it is, however, an excellent objective for a short walk from that town. The approach, by any of the variations, from pleasant woods and pastures leading to a craggy ridge is very attractive. The routes up via High Sweden Bridge and down via Low Sweden Bridge give the best views; the vista of Ambleside backed by Windermere is very beautiful. Only the wall along the watershed and the marsh above the rock step (very boggy in wet weather) detract from the merits of this enjoyable walk.

ASCENT FROM RYDAL
1400 feet of ascent : 1²/₃ miles

There is little merit in the approach from Rydal apart from a visit to the wonderful water feature of Buckstones Jump. Leave Rydal via the route to Nab Scar but turn off on a track just before the first sharp left. Beside a gate is a kissing gate that used to give access to a footbridge, but this is now closed. Continue on the track to a stile on the right leading to the cascade and pool. Crossing the beck needs care and is difficult when it is in spate. Turn left and leave the thin path for a steep climb to the ridge just north of the summit.

THE SUMMIT

The summit is an abrupt rocky peak, a place of grey boulders and small grassy platforms in the shadow of a substantial stone wall that occupies the highest inches. Some of the rocks near the summit are big enough to afford some simple practice in climbing. A small cairn sits astride the rock.

High Pike

DESCENTS : The way to Ambleside would be obvious even if there were no path; *see High Pike 3 and 4 for details.* If the wall is followed, beware the rock step, which is even more awkward in descent. For Rydal, follow the wall south and go right just before reaching Low Sweden Bridge.

In mist, all descents should be made to Ambleside, keeping to the path, or, if the path is lost, to the wall. There are crags at 1200', alongside the rock step.

stile

1400
1500

Large cairn

AMBLESIDE

YARDS
0 100 200 300

N

HIGH PIKE
gate
gate
1800
1700
1600
1500
stile

LOW PIKE

HALF A MILE

RIDGE ROUTE

To HIGH PIKE, 2155' : ²/₃ mile : N
Depression at 1575' : 600 feet of ascent

A straightforward walk, safe in mist.

A path follows the wall, climbing steadily. It is possible to switch sides at the stile for better views on the west of the wall.

THE VIEW

All the attractiveness of the scene is centred between south and west, where the Coniston and Langdale fells rise grandly from a lowland of lakes. Lingmoor Fell also can be seen, backed by Pike o'Blisco.

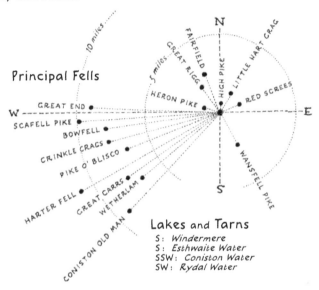

Principal Fells

Lakes and Tarns
S: *Windermere*
S: *Esthwaite Water*
SSW: *Coniston Water*
SW: *Rydal Water*

HIGH SWEDEN BRIDGE is one of Lakeland's most iconic stone bridges, alongside favourites such as Stockley Bridge, Ashness Bridge, Birks Bridge and Slater's Bridge. Its name derives from the Norse word *sviðinn*, which means 'land cleared by burning'.

Middle Dodd

2146'

OS grid ref: NY397096

from Caiston Glen

Patterdale

Hartsop

Hartsop
Hall

DOVE CRAG ▲
▲ MIDDLE DODD

RED ▲ SCREES

MILES
0   1   2   3

To the traveller starting the long climb up to Kirkstone Pass from Brothers Water the most striking object in a fine array of mountain scenery is the steep pyramid ahead: it towers high above the road like a gigantic upturned boat, its keel touching the sky, its sides barnacled and hoary. This pyramid is Middle Dodd, the middle one of three dodds which rise from the pastures of Hartsop, all exhibiting the same characteristics. When seen from higher ground in the vicinity, however, Middle Dodd loses its regal appearance (as do the other two); its summit then is obviously nothing more than a halt in the long northern spur of Red Screes.

MAP

It is possible to ascend Middle Dodd from the Red Pit car park on the Kirkstone Road, following the wall to the depression of Smallthwaite Band (the name of the ridge between Middle Dodd and Red Screes), but such an unremittingly steep and pathless route is not to be recommended.

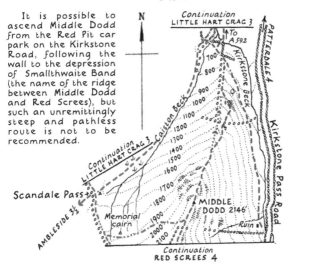

ASCENT FROM HARTSOP HALL

1650 feet of ascent : 2 miles (1½ miles from A592)

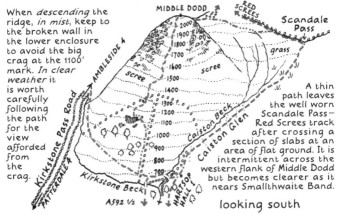

When *descending* the ridge, *in mist*, keep to the broken wall in the lower enclosure to avoid the big crag at the 1100' mark. *In clear weather* it is worth carefully following the path for the view afforded from the crag.

A thin path leaves the well worn Scandale Pass – Red Screes track after crossing a section of slabs at an area of flat ground. It is intermittent across the western flank of Middle Dodd but becomes clearer as it nears Smallthwaite Band.

looking south

The direct climb up the ridge, although free from difficulty, is excessively steep; small outcrops of rock can be avoided on grass. An easier but less attractive route is to proceed to Scandale Pass and slant across the slope to the top; or better still, first ascend Red Screes and descend over the Dodd.

THE SUMMIT

The top of Middle Dodd is a rather narrow grassy promenade. The ground immediately behind the rocky promontory which serves as the triangulation point rises gently to a knoll some forty feet higher — here is the summit cairn, somewhat larger than in the illustration above — before falling imperceptibly to the saddle (known as Smallthwaite Band) linking Middle Dodd to Red Screes.

Near the cairn is a series of curious depressions like a line of sinkholes in limestone country, but as the rock here is volcanic the probability is that they are old earthworks; the detached boulders strewn about in them seem to suggest artificial excavation. Walkers who are neither archaeologists nor geologists will see in the depressions only a refuge from the wind.

Middle Dodd with
Red Screes behind
from
High Hartsop Dodd

THE VIEW

Considering that Middle Dodd is hemmed in on all sides by higher fells, the view is remarkably good, and unexpectedly extensive in the south-west.

Principal Fells

Lakes and Tarns

N: *Ullswater*
N: *Brothers Water*
SW: *Greenburn Tarn (below Great Carrs)*

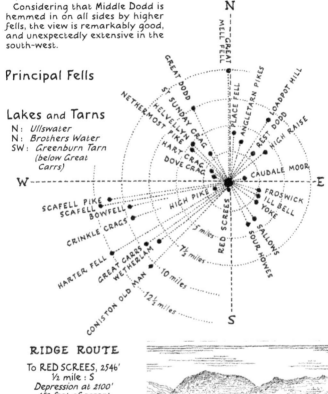

RIDGE ROUTE

To RED SCREES, 2546'
½ mile : S
Depression at 2100'
450 feet of ascent
An easy walk. Safe in mist.
Follow the good path from the summit, which curves around the north-east combe.

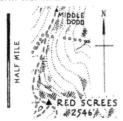

Looking north: Brothers Water backed by Place Fell and Angletarn Pikes.

Nab Scar

1450'

OS grid ref: NY355072

▲ FAIRFIELD

▲ GREAT RIGG

▲ STONE ARTHUR

▲ HERON PIKE

● Grasmere ▲ NAB SCAR
● Rydal

Ambleside ●

MILES
0 1 2 3 4

from Rydal Water

NATURAL FEATURES

Nab Scar is well known. Its associations with the Lake Poets who came to dwell at the foot of its steep wooded slopes have invested it with romance, and its commanding position overlooking Rydal Water brings it to the notice of the many visitors to that charming lake. It is a fine abrupt height, with a rough, craggy south face; on the flanks are easier slopes. Elevated ground continues beyond the summit and rises gently to Heron Pike at the start of the western arm of the popular Fairfield Horseshoe walk. Nab Scar is not a separate fell, but is merely the butt of the long southern ridge of Fairfield.

Dockey Tarn, a shallow rocky pool less than 250 yards west-north-west of the summit, is one of the smallest tarns to be named on Ordnance Survey maps.

MAP

William Wordsworth lived in Dove Cottage from 1799 to 1808 and at Rydal Mount from 1813 to 1850. The two are linked by the Coffin Route. Inhabitants of Nab Cottage, now a language school, have included poet Thomas De Quincey and Hartley Coleridge, eldest son of Samuel Taylor Coleridge.

ASCENT FROM RYDAL
1250 feet of ascent : 1¼ miles

ASCENT FROM GRASMERE
1250 feet of ascent : 2 miles

The popular ascent is from Rydal, a charming climb along a good path, steep in its middle reaches, much of which has been repaired because of its popularity; this is the beginning of the Fairfield Horseshoe when it is walked clockwise.

Nab Scar can also be reached from Grasmere by means of the path that rises from the south end of Alcock Tarn. There are two options to reach this point. From the Swan Hotel, initially take the path to Stone Arthur but turn right and cross Greathead Gill by footbridge and follow the steepening zig-zags to the tarn. From Dove Cottage, take the back road to White Moss and turn left at a small tarn then left again.

THE SUMMIT

Strictly, Nab Scar is the name of the craggy south face, not of the fell rising above it, but its recognised summit is a tall edifice of stones built well back from the edge of the cliffs, near a crumbled wall that runs north towards Heron Pike. Hereabouts the immediate surroundings are uninteresting, the redeeming feature being the fine view.

DESCENTS: The path to Rydal, steep in places but well pitched, is the best way down in any weather.

Nab Scar has a subterranean watercourse: below its surface the Thirlmere aqueduct runs through a tunnel. The scars of this operation are nearly gone, but evidence of the existence of the tunnel remains alongside the Rydal path above the steepest part: here may be found a block of stone a yard square set in the ground; it bears no inscription but marks the position of the tunnel directly beneath.

HERON PIKE

1800
1700
1600
1500

HALF A MILE

Lord
Crag

N

1400

NAB
SCAR

1300

RIDGE ROUTE

To HERON PIKE, 2008': ⅔ mile : N
570 feet of ascent

An easy climb on grass.
A plain path accompanies the old wall, then it keeps to the right of the ridge.

THE VIEW

This is an 'unbalanced' view, most of it being exceptionally dull, particularly the section between north and east where the Fairfield Horseshoe and the 'back' of Red Screes restrict the distant vista. The rest is exceptionally charming. Lakes and tarns are a very special feature of the delightful prospect to south and west and the grouping of the Coniston and Langdale fells is quite attractive.

Principal Fells

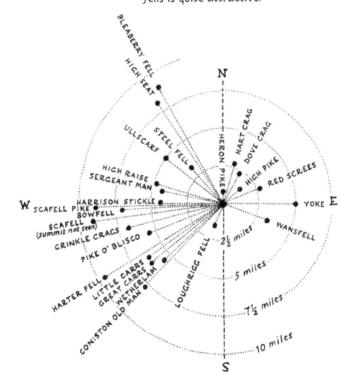

Lakes and Tarns

SSE: *Windermere*
S: *Blelham Tarn*
S: *Esthwaite Water*
SSW: *Coniston Water*

SW: *Elterwater*
WSW: *Grasmere*
WNW: *Easedale Tarn*
NW: *Alcock Tarn*

Nethermost Pike 2920'

OS grid ref: NY344142

from Grisedale

Patterdale

▲ HELVELLYN

▲ NETHERMOST PIKE

Wythburn

▲ FAIRFIELD

Grasmere

MILES

0   1   2   3   4   5

NATURAL FEATURES

Thousands of people cross the flat top of Nethermost Pike every year, and thousands more toil up its western slope. Yet their diaries record 'climbed Helvellyn today'. For Helvellyn is the great magnet that draws the crowds to Nethermost Pike: the latter is climbed incidentally, almost unknowingly, only because it is an obstacle in the route to its bigger neighbour. The grassy west slope trodden by the multitudes is of little interest, but the fell should not be judged accordingly: it is made of sterner stuff. From the east, Nethermost Pike is magnificent, hardly less so than Helvellyn and seeming more so because of its impressive surroundings. On this side a narrow rocky ridge bounded by forbidding crags falls steeply between twin hollows, deeply recessed, in a wild and lonely setting; here is solitude, for here few men walk. Here, too, is a gem of a tarn, Hard Tarn, which is one of the more secluded stretches of water in Lakeland.

looking north

The North Face

1 : The summit
2 : High Crag
3 : Ridge continuing to Helvellyn
(the depression between Nethermost Pike
and Helvellyn is known as Swallow Scarth)
4 : Ridge continuing to Dollywaggon Pike
5 : Comb Crag
6 : Eagle Crag
7 : Thirlmere
8 : Whelpside Gill
9 : Comb Gill
10 : Birkside Gill
11 : Nethermostcove Beck
12 : Ruthwaite Beck
13 : Grisedale Beck
14 : Hard Tarn
15 : Nethermost Cove
16 : Ruthwaite Cove

MAP

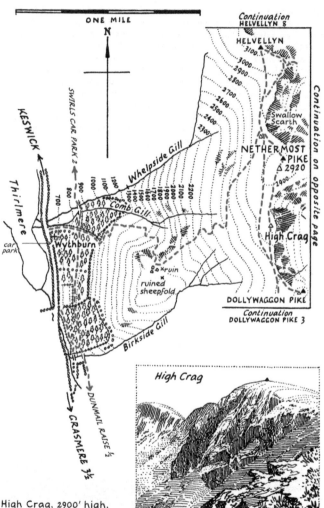

ONE MILE

N

Continuation
HELVELLYN 8

HELVELLYN ▲ 3100

Continuation on opposite page

Swallow Scarth

NETHERMOST ▲ PIKE △ 2920

KESWICK ←

SWIRLS CAR PARK 2

Whelpside Gill

Thirlmere

car park

Comb Gill

Wythburn

High Crag

Continuation
DOLLYWAGGON PIKE 3

ruin
ruined sheepfold

DOLLYWAGGON PIKE

Birkside Gill

DUNMAIL RAISE ½

GRASMERE 3½

High Crag

High Crag, 2900' high, appears from the north to be a mountain in its own right, but is quite clearly a subsidiary summit of Nethermost Pike. In the past few years a well worn path has developed, due to the popularity of this route from Nethermost Pike to Dollywaggon Pike.

MAP

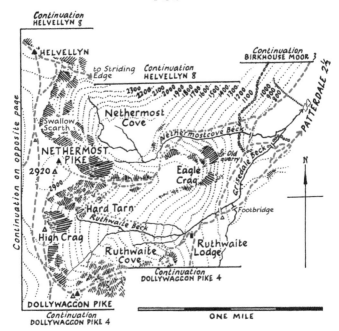

Hard Tarn

Nethermost Pike's eastern slopes are part of a Site of Special Scientific Interest, designated because parts of the area include some of the best examples of arctic alpine and tall herb vegetation found in England.

ASCENT FROM WYTHBURN
2400 feet of ascent : 2 miles

It is possible to cut directly up to the summit
from the spring but preferable to follow the
path to Helvellyn before turning right and taking
the left fork.

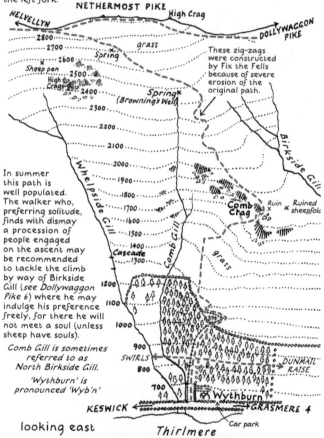

In summer
this path is
well populated.
The walker who,
preferring solitude,
finds with dismay
a procession of
people engaged
on the ascent may
be recommended
to tackle the climb
by way of Birkside
Gill (see Dollywaggon
Pike 6) where he may
indulge his preference
freely, for there he will
not meet a soul (unless
sheep have souls).

Comb Gill is sometimes
referred to as
North Birkside Gill.

'Wythburn' is
pronounced 'Wyb'n'

looking east

These zig-zags
were constructed
by Fix the Fells
because of severe
erosion of the
original path.

HELVELLYN
NETHERMOST PIKE
High Crag
DOLLYWAGGON PIKE
2800
2700
grass
2600
Spring
Sheep pen
2500
High
Crag
2400
Spring
(Browning's Well)
2300
2200
2100
2000
1900
Whelpside Gill
1800
Birkside Gill
1700
1600
Comb
Crag
Ruin
Ruined
sheepfold
1500
Cascade
1400
1300
grass
Comb Gill
1200
1100
1000
900
SWIRLS
DUNMAIL RAISE
800
700
Wythburn
KESWICK
GRASMERE 4
Car park
Thirlmere

The popular path to Helvellyn from Wythburn climbs
steeply up the side of Nethermost Pike, almost reaching its
summit before turning off to the higher fell: the top is
attained by a short detour. The path is very distinct and
has been extensively repaired over the years; in the lower
stages walkers' boots have worn many of the stones smooth.

ASCENT FROM GRISEDALE
2500 feet of ascent : 5 miles from Patterdale village

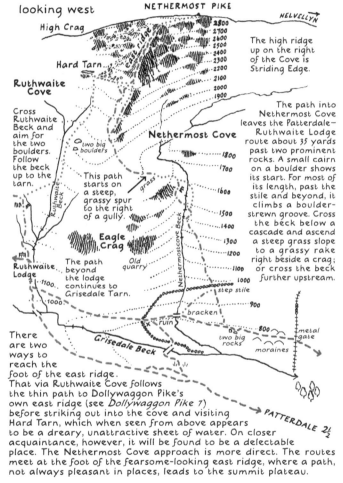

looking west

NETHERMOST PIKE

HELVELLYN

High Crag

2800
2700
2600
2500
2400
2300
2200
2100
2000
1900

east ridge

The high ridge up on the right of the Cove is Striding Edge.

Hard Tarn

Ruthwaite Cove

Cross Ruthwaite Beck and aim for the two boulders. Follow the beck up to the tarn.

two big boulders

This path starts on a steep, grassy spur to the right of a gully.

Nethermost Cove

grass

Ruthwaite Beck

Eagle Crag

Old quarry

The path beyond the lodge continues to Grisedale Tarn.

1800
1700
1600
1500
1400
1300
1200
1100
1000

The path into Nethermost Cove leaves the Patterdale–Ruthwaite Lodge route about 35 yards past two prominent rocks. A small cairn on a boulder shows its start. For most of its length, past the stile and beyond, it climbs a boulder-strewn groove. Cross the beck below a cascade and ascend a steep grass slope to a grassy rake right beside a crag ; or cross the beck further upstream.

Nethermostcove Beck

step stile

Ruthwaite Lodge

1100
1000

bracken

900

ruin

Grisedale Beck

800

two big rocks

moraines

metal gate

There are two ways to reach the foot of the east ridge. That via Ruthwaite Cove follows the thin path to Dollywaggon Pike's own east ridge (see *Dollywaggon Pike 7*) before striking out into the cove and visiting Hard Tarn, which when seen from above appears to be a dreary, unattractive sheet of water. On closer acquaintance, however, it will be found to be a delectable place. The Nethermost Cove approach is more direct. The routes meet at the foot of the fearsome-looking east ridge, where a path, not always pleasant in places, leads to the summit plateau.

PATTERDALE 2½

These are first-class routes for scramblers, but staid walkers should avoid them and proceed via Grisedale Tarn. The east ridge is steep and exciting, finishing with an arête like a miniature Striding Edge. *Avoid the eastern flank in bad weather conditions.*

THE SUMMIT

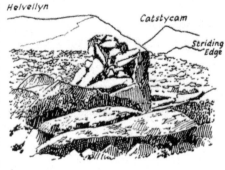

The summit is of considerable extent and so remarkably flat that it is not easy to understand why the name 'Pike' was given to the fell (the top of the east ridge, however, has the appearance of a peak when seen from mid-Grisedale). It is mainly grassy — a field on top of a mountain — with many thin flakes of rock around the cairn.

The broad top is level, and it is difficult to locate the highest point exactly, but the cairn illustrated appears to be slightly higher than the small crescent-shaped wind shelter, facing west, which lies approximately 100 yards to the south-west.

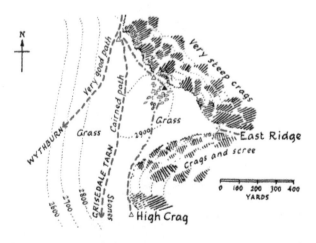

DESCENTS: The popular cairned Helvellyn-Grisedale Tarn path crosses the top but does not visit the actual summit. This path may be followed south to Grisedale Tarn for Grasmere or Patterdale. For Wythburn, cross this path to another running lower along the fellside. The east ridge is a quick way down to Patterdale, but is for experienced walkers only.

‖ In bad weather conditions, leave the summit by one of the two paths mentioned: these are quite safe — the east ridge is not.

RIDGE ROUTES

To HELVELLYN, 3118': ¾ mile : NW then N.

Depression at 2840' : 280 feet of ascent

An easy walk on a broad path, safe in mist.

The path west of the cairn on Nethermost Pike continues north to Helvellyn, developing into a wide uninteresting highway. It is far better, in clear weather, to avoid the path and follow the edge of the cliffs on a thinner path, the views of Nethermost Cove and Striding Edge being very impressive.

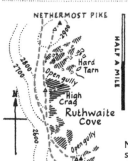

To DOLLYWAGGON PIKE, 2815' 1 mile : S then SE

Depression at 2700': 120 feet of ascent

A very easy walk, safe in mist.

The path west of the cairn on Nethermost Pike continues south, skirting High Crag. At the depression, a direct path leads easily to the summit of Dollywaggon Pike. A much more interesting route, *but only in clear weather*, is to follow the recent path on the edge of the cliffs overlooking Hard Tarn and Ruthwaite Cove, the rock scenery being impressive.

Cascades in Birkside Gill

Northwards, nearby Helvellyn shuts out the distant view, but in all other directions the panorama is very extensive. Nevertheless, the cairn is not a satisfactory viewpoint because the wide expanse of the summit plateau occupies too much of the picture. A much more attractive and better balanced view is obtained from the big cairn on High Crag to the south, which is barely 20' lower: from here the mountain scene is more pleasing, and additional lakes are visible: *Bassenthwaite Lake, Coniston Water* and *Esthwaite Water*.

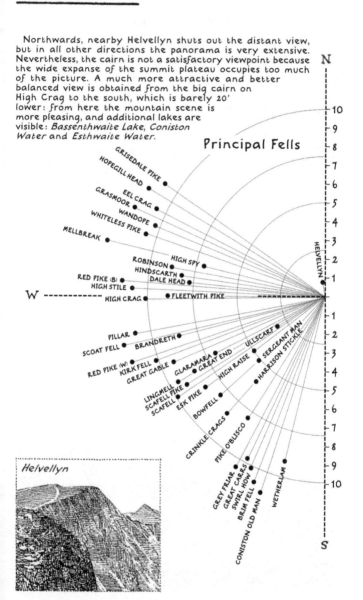

Principal Fells

N

W

S

Helvellyn

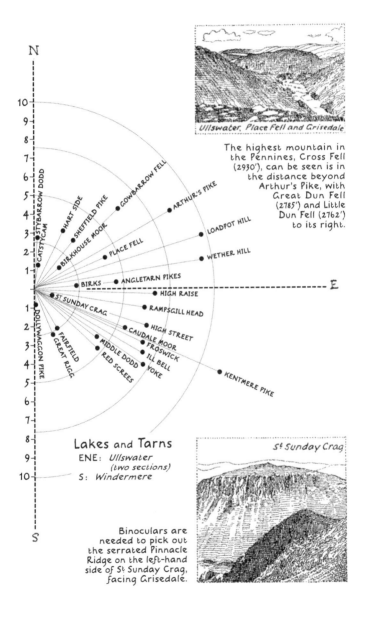

Ullswater, Place Fell and Grisedale

The highest mountain in the Pennines, Cross Fell (2930'), can be seen is in the distance beyond Arthur's Pike, with Great Dun Fell (2785') and Little Dun Fell (2762') to its right.

N

10
9
8
7
6
5
4
3
2
1

CATSTYCAM
STYBARROW DODD
HART SIDE
SHEFFIELD PIKE
BIRKHOUSE MOOR
GOWBARROW FELL
ARTHUR'S PIKE
LOADPOT HILL
PLACE FELL
WETHER HILL
BIRKS
ANGLETARN PIKES

E

HIGH RAISE
1
ST SUNDAY CRAG
RAMPSGILL HEAD
2
HIGH STREET
DOLLYWAGGON PIKE
FAIRFIELD
CAUDALE MOOR
3
GREAT RIGG
MIDDLE DODD
FROSWICK
ILL BELL
4
RED SCREES
YOKE
KENTMERE PIKE
5
6
7
8
9
10

Lakes and Tarns
ENE: *Ullswater*
(two sections)
S: *Windermere*

S

St Sunday Crag

Binoculars are needed to pick out the serrated Pinnacle Ridge on the left-hand side of St Sunday Crag, facing Grisedale.

Raise   2897'

OS grid ref: NY343174

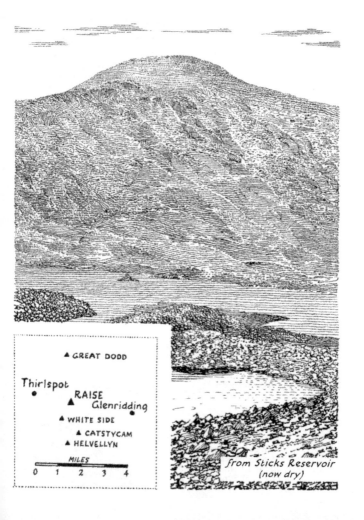

▲ GREAT DODD

Thirlspot
●

RAISE ▲
Glenridding ●

▲ WHITE SIDE

▲ CATSTYCAM

▲ HELVELLYN

MILES
0   1   2   3   4

from Sticks Reservoir
(now dry)

NATURAL FEATURES

Raise deserves a special cheer. It is the only summit in the Helvellyn range adorned with a crown of rough rocks — and they make a welcome change from the dull monotony of the green expanses around Sticks Pass. But in general the fell conforms to the usual Helvellyn pattern, the western slopes being grassy and the eastern slopes more scarred. It further differs from its fellows on the main ridge, however, in that its western slopes do not reach down to the valley; they are sandwiched between the more extensive, sprawling flanks of Stybarrow Dodd and White Side and are crowded out completely at the 1600' contour where Brund Gill meets Sticks Gill (West). Similarly, to the east, Raise does not extend to the Patterdale valley, being squeezed out by lower neighbour, Sheffield Pike.

looking north

1 : The summit
2 : Rock Tor
3 : Sticks Pass
4 : Ridge continuing to White Side
5 : Stang
6 : Stang End
7 : Keppel Cove
8 : Keppelcove Tarn (dry)
9 : Sticks Reservoir (dry)
10 : Sticks Gill (East)
11 : Sticks Gill (West)
12 : Brund Gill
13 : Glenridding Beck
14 : Rowten Beck

The Rock Tor

This small outcrop, about 25' in length, rises from a slope of lichened scree. It is not remarkable in itself, but stands out so prominently that it forms a ready means of identifying Raise in all views where the east slope is seen in profile.

Raise 3

MAP

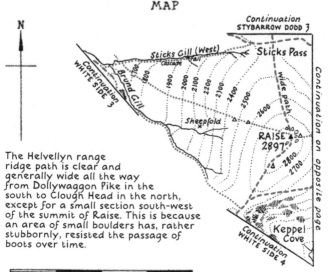

N

Continuation
STYBARROW DODD 3

Sticks Gill (West)
Cascade
Fall

Sticks Pass

Continuation
WHITE SIDE 3

Brund Gill

1700
1800
1900
2000
2100
2200
2300
2400
2500

wide path

Continuation on opposite page

Sheepfold

2600

RAISE
2897

2800

2700

Keppel
Cove

Continuation
WHITE SIDE 4

The Helvellyn range ridge path is clear and generally wide all the way from Dollywaggon Pike in the south to Clough Head in the north, except for a small section south-west of the summit of Raise. This is because an area of small boulders has, rather stubbornly, resisted the passage of boots over time.

ONE MILE

The lower eastern slopes of Raise are pock-marked with the scars of industry. The illustrations above show the now-disused and derelict chimney (marked by the x on the map on the facing page) and the stone aqueduct which formerly served the Glenridding lead mine. Only a small portion of the aqueduct remains intact (see picture on right) but it is sufficient to indicate the skill of the masons who built it and to make one envy their pride in the job, and be glad they are not here to see the ruins.

MAP

Continuation
STYBARROW DODD 4

Sticks Pass

Continuation
SHEFFIELD PIKE 3

Sticks Gill (East)

Former Reservoir

Weir

Ski lift

Ski hut

Disused Aqueduct

Stang End

Disused Lead Mine

Rock tor

X Ruin ▲Stang

RAISE 2897

Water Cut

2800 2700 2600 2500 2400 2300

Rowten Beck

1500 1400 1300 1700

Continuation
on opposite page

wide path

Keppel Cove

2200 2100 2000 1900 1800

wide path 1700 1600

Glenridding Beck

Sheepfold

Keppelcove Tarn (dry)

Dam

Continuation
CATSTYCAM 3

There are many notices in the vicinity of Keppelcove Tarn. On the burst dam, there are three warnings for walkers: a) *Danger. Unstable structure. Do not walk or climb on*; b) *Danger of falling*; and c) *Danger. Falling debris.* Fences at either end of the structure have been put in place to deter crossings. The nearby sheepfold has a notice warning that camping inside it is not allowed. As if to emphasise the point, a wire fence around the structure has been installed to make such overnight stays particularly difficult.

Glenridding and Ullswater, from Stang End

ASCENTS FROM STANAH AND THIRLSPOT
2400 feet of ascent : 2½ miles

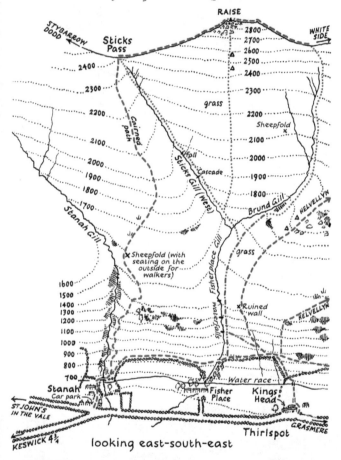

looking east-south-east

As a variation, consider climbing White Side first, via Brown Crag and the upper path to Helvellyn, or reserving this as a route of descent. *See White Side 5 for details.*

Raise overlooks Sticks Pass, from which it is climbed very easily; the path from Stanah to the top of the pass is therefore a convenient route of ascent. Routes from Thirlspot are more direct but lack paths much of the way. All the western approaches are grassy and rather dull.

ASCENT FROM GLENRIDDING
2500 feet of ascent : 4 miles from Glenridding village

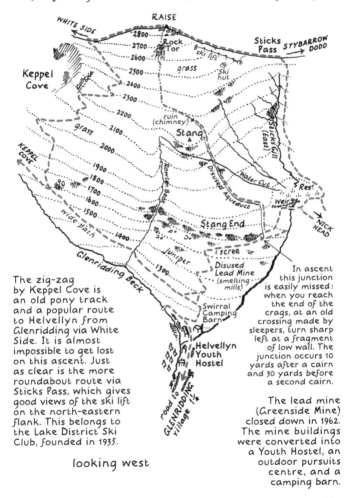

RAISE

WHITE SIDE

2800
2700 Rock Tor
2600 ski lift

Sticks Pass STYBARROW DODD

Keppel Cove

2500
2400 grass
2300 ski hut
2200
2100 ruin (chimney)
2000 Stang

grass

KEPPEL COVE

1900
1800
1700
1600
1500
Wide path
1400

Keppel Cove

Rowten Beck

Disused Aqueduct

Sticks Gill (East)

Water Cut

Res.

Weir

NICK HEAD

Stang End

scree

Disused Lead Mine (smelting mills)

1300 Juniper

Glenridding Beck

Swirral Camping Barn

Helvellyn Youth Hostel

road to GLENRIDDING village 1¼

The zig-zag by Keppel Cove is an old pony track and a popular route to Helvellyn from Glenridding via White Side. It is almost impossible to get lost on this ascent. Just as clear is the more roundabout route via Sticks Pass, which gives good views of the ski lift on the north-eastern flank. This belongs to the Lake District Ski Club, founded in 1935.

looking west

In ascent this junction is easily missed: when you reach the end of the crags, at an old crossing made by sleepers, turn sharp left at a fragment of low wall. The junction occurs 10 yards after a cairn and 30 yards before a second cairn.

The lead mine (Greenside Mine) closed down in 1962. The mine buildings were converted into a Youth Hostel, an outdoor pursuits centre, and a camping barn.

All routes from the east are marred by the inescapable evidences of the lead mine. The Keppel Cove route is easy, and gives impressive views of Catstycam. The approach by Sticks Pass is dull, that by the old aqueduct and the Rock Tor rather better.

THE SUMMIT

SKIDDAW

The summit is a level, grassy plateau with patches of gravelly stones, capped at its higher end by an outcrop of very rough gnarled rocks. The main cairn takes the form of a wind shelter facing north. Smaller cairns on nearby rocks indicate other viewpoints.

DESCENTS : In good weather all routes of ascent are suitable also for descent. The quickest way to Thirlspot is down the western slope, joining a path by Fisher Gill. For Glenridding, the route by the old aqueduct is quickest; if the zig-zag by Keppel Cove is preferred, a big corner may be saved initially by descending to it south-east from the summit.

In bad conditions, head for the top of Sticks Pass, north, whatever the destination.
In mist, remember that the wind shelter faces north.

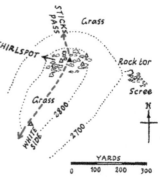

BIRKHOUSE MOOR

The summit of Stang

RIDGE ROUTES

To STYBARROW DODD, 2770' : 1 mile : N, then NE
Depression at 2420' (Sticks Pass)
350 feet of ascent

Grass all the way after initial stones.
Easy. Distinct path. Safe in mist.

Cross Sticks Pass at its highest point, and continue up the steepening slope opposite. The cairn on the south-west top used to be accepted as the summit of Stybarrow Dodd, but there is higher ground beyond, which is now marked by a summit cairn. This is the actual top.

To WHITE SIDE, 2832' : ¾ mile : SW

Depression at 2650'. 200 feet of ascent.

Over rocks at first. Then easy walking on well cairned path.

Cross the summit plateau to the south-west cairn and descend therefrom to meet the good path coming up on the left: it climbs easily to the top of White Side.

This slope is a favourite with skiers and, on snowy winter days, presents an animated scene: a ski lift operates.

Raise from Sticks Pass

The small tarn illustrated is that to the right (west) of the main path just south of Sticks Pass. It tends to dry up in summer and is not always visible.

THE VIEW
(with distances in miles)

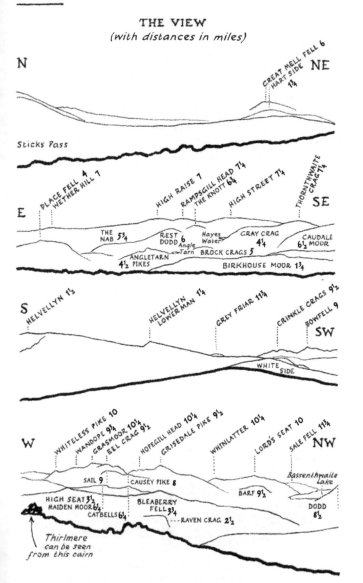

THE VIEW

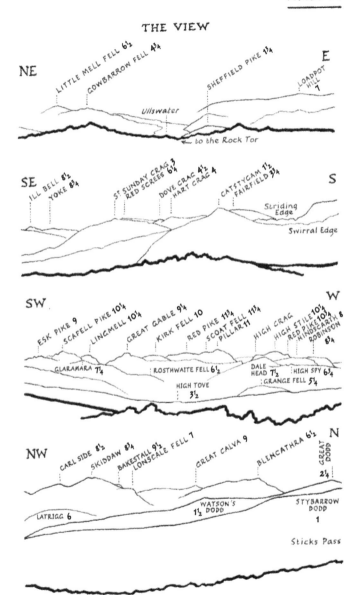

NE

LITTLE MELL FELL 6½ COWBARROW FELL 4¾

Ullswater

SHEFFIELD PIKE 1¾

E

LOADPOT HILL 7

← to the Rock Tor

SE

ILL BELL 8½ YOKE 8¾

ST. SUNDAY CRAG 3 RED SCREES 6¼ DOVE CRAG 4½ HART CRAG 4

CATSTYCAM 1½ FAIRFIELD 3¾

S

Striding Edge

Swirral Edge

SW

ESK PIKE 9 SCAFELL PIKE 10¼ LINGMELL 10¼ GREAT GABLE 9¼ KIRK FELL 10 RED PIKE 11¾ SCOAT FELL 11¾ PILLAR 11 HIGH CRAG HIGH STILE 10¼ RED PIKE 10½ HINDSCARTH 8 ROBINSON 8¾

W

GLARAMARA 7¼ ROSTHWAITE FELL 6½ DALE HEAD 7½ HIGH SPY 6¾

HIGH TOVE 3½ GRANGE FELL 5¼

NW

CARL SIDE 8½ SKIDDAW 8¾ BAKESTALL 9½ LONSCALE FELL 7 GREAT CALVA 9 BLENCATHRA 6½ GREAT DODD 2¼

N

LATRIGG 6 WATSON'S DODD 1½ STYBARROW DODD 1

Sticks Pass

Red Screes

2546'

OS grid ref: NY397088

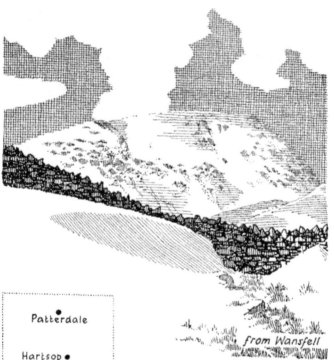

from Wansfell

Patterdale

Hartsop

▲ DOVE CRAG

▲ RED SCREES

● Ambleside

MILES

0   1   2   3

Prominent in all views of the fells from the lesser heights of southern Lakeland is the high whale-backed mass of Red Screes, rising in a graceful curve from the head of Windermere and descending abruptly at its northern end. Some maps append the name 'Kilnshaw Chimney' to the summit, but Red Screes is its name by popular choice — and Red Screes it should be because of the colour and character of its eastern face. It is a friendly accommodating hill, holding no terrors for those who climb to its summit by the usual easy routes and being very conveniently situated for sojourners at Ambleside; moreover, it offers a reward of excellent views.

NATURAL FEATURES

All travellers along the Kirkstone Pass are familiar with Red Screes, for it is the biggest thing to be seen there: for four miles it forms the western wall of the pass. In general structure it is a long broad ridge of considerable bulk. The southern slopes are at an easy gradient, with rock outcrops in abundance and a quarry which produces beautiful green stone; in places the rough ground steepens into crags. The shorter north ridge, after a gradual descent to the lesser height of Middle Dodd, plunges steeply to the fields of High Hartsop. The western slopes are of no particular interest and the pride of Red Screes is undoubtedly its eastern face, where natural forces have eroded two combes which carve deeply into the mountain on both flanks of a wide buttress: runs of fine red scree pour down these hollows. This side of the fell has many crags and tumbled boulders, one of which gave the pass its name; high up is Kilnshaw Chimney, which is hardly as significant as the maps would imply, being only a steep, narrow gully choked with rocks and scree.

Red Screes, although in the midst of high country, contrives to appear more isolated from its fellows than any other of the eastern fells. It is independent and is unsupported, not buttressed by its neighbours: to this extent, it may be said to have the purest mountain form among the eastern fells.

Of the many streams which have their birth on Red Screes, the best known is Stock Ghyll, flowing south and breaking in lovely waterfalls on its way to join the Rothay; on the west innumerable watercourses feed Scandale Beck; northwards, Kirkstone Beck and Caiston Beck carry its waters to Ullswater.

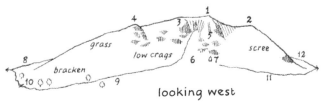

looking west

1 : The summit
2 : Middle Dodd
3 : Raven Crag
4 : Snarker Pike
5 : Kilnshaw Chimney
6 : Kirkstone Pass
7 : The Kirk Stone
8 : Scandale Beck
9 : Stock Ghyll
10 : Stock Ghyll Force
11 : Kirkstone Beck
12 : Caiston Beck

Snarker Pike's unusual name is thought to come from the Old English word *snaca*, a snake.

MAP

Continuation on opposite page

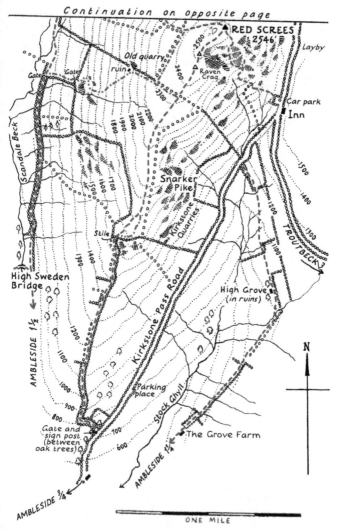

For details about the popular path to High Sweden Bridge from Ambleside, see *Dove Crag 5*.

MAP

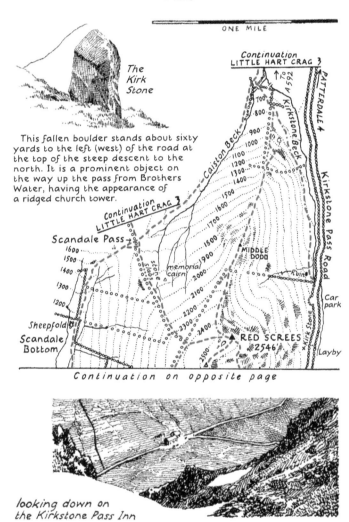

ONE MILE

The Kirk Stone

This fallen boulder stands about sixty yards to the left (west) of the road at the top of the steep descent to the north. It is a prominent object on the way up the pass from Brothers Water, having the appearance of a ridged church tower.

Continuation
LITTLE HART CRAG 3

Caiston Beck

Kirkstone Beck

PATTERDALE 4

Continuation
LITTLE HART CRAG 3

Scandale Pass →

1600
1500
1400
1300
1200

memorial cairn

MIDDLE DODD

Ruin

Kirkstone Pass Road

Car park

Sheepfold

Scandale Bottom

RED SCREES 2546'

The Kirk Stone

Layby

Continuation on opposite page

looking down on the Kirkstone Pass Inn

The Kirkstone Pass Inn stands close to the summit of Lakeland's highest pass open to motor traffic, at 1489'. Formerly an important coaching inn, it now caters primarily for tourists. It is the third highest public house in England.

ASCENT FROM AMBLESIDE
2400 feet of ascent : 4 or 5 miles

looking north

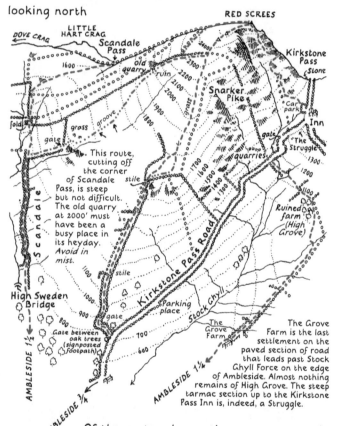

RED SCREES

DOVE CRAG

LITTLE HART CRAG

Scandale Pass

old quarry

ruin

1600

Snarker Pike

Kirkstone Pass

Stone

Car park

Inn

fold

gate

grass

groove

"The Struggle"

1300

This route, cutting off the corner of Scandale Pass, is steep but not difficult. The old quarry at 2000' must have been a busy place in its heyday. Avoid in mist.

stile

quarries

1200

1100

Scandale

stile

Ruined farm (High Grove)

Kirkstone Pass Road

Stock Ghyll

High Sweden Bridge

gate

Parking place

The Grove Farm

AMBLESIDE 1½

Gate between oak trees (signposted footpath)

AMBLESIDE ¾

AMBLESIDE ¼

The Grove Farm is the last settlement on the paved section of road that leads past Stock Ghyll Force on the edge of Ambleside. Almost nothing remains of High Grove. The steep tarmac section up to the Kirkstone Pass Inn is, indeed, a Struggle.

Of the routes shown, three are commonly in use: the direct ridge route (which is better in descending); the longer Scandale Pass route (the safest in bad weather); and the most attractive route via The Grove Farm and Kirkstone. This is a 'natural' approach, following the stream up with the objective ahead. Years ago it was a rough scramble from the pass, but a good clear path (steep in places and much repaired) now leads from the far corner of the car park to the top of Red Screes.

The upper section of the ascent via Kirkstone

The path crosses a beck (A) and continues on a fairly flat course for 200 yards. This is followed by the first paved section (B), rising steeply towards the first ridge (C). A steep rise follows on a paved section. At the second ridge (D), the path skirts the impressive south-east combe. Switching back to the Kirkstone side of the ridge (E), the path bypasses a band of crags to the right and then doubles back on itself by a slab of pinkish rock (F, *look for a small footpath sign*). Finally (G) there are two steep scrambly sections (both easy) followed by a gentle rise to the summit.

Kilnshaw Chimney looks steep, stony and nasty, and it is. It will appeal only to scramblers.

looking north-west
from the corner of the Kirkstone Pass Inn car park

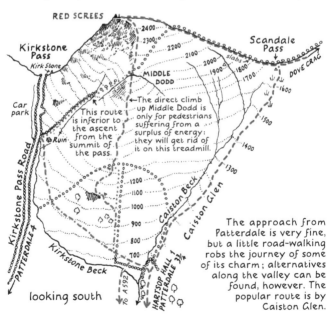

ASCENT FROM PATTERDALE
2200 feet of ascent : 6½ miles from Patterdale village

RED SCREES

Kirkstone Pass
Kirk Stone

Scandale Pass

DOVE CRAG

slabs

MIDDLE DODD

Car park

⊕ Ruin

This route is inferior to the ascent from the summit of the pass.

←The direct climb up Middle Dodd is only for pedestrians suffering from a surplus of energy: they will get rid of it on this treadmill.

Caiston Beck

Caiston Glen

Kirkstone Pass Road

PATTERDALE 4

Kirkstone Beck

HARTSOP HALL 1
PATTERDALE 3½

TO A 592

looking south

The approach from Patterdale is very fine, but a little road-walking robs the journey of some of its charm; alternatives along the valley can be found, however. The popular route is by Caiston Glen.

THE SUMMIT

   The summit is a large grassy plateau, having three
principal cairns widely spaced and differing little in
altitude. There is no mistaking the highest, a substantial
mound of stones situated at the extreme corner of the
plateau: a dramatic site, for here the ground seems to
collapse at one's feet and plunge steeply down to the
winding road far below. An Ordnance Survey column
stands alongside, and twenty yards west is a small tarn
with another to the south-west of it. Below and east of the
highest point is a cluster of rocks known as The Horn,
which appears prominently in views from Patterdale and
the A592; a thin path leads from the summit to this
outcrop. It is a good vantage point and a pleasant place
to eat sandwiches if the top is crowded, but it is well to
tread cautiously here: beware crag! The x on the map
below indicates the location of a natural rocky shelter,
which is a good place to take cover during a westerly gale.

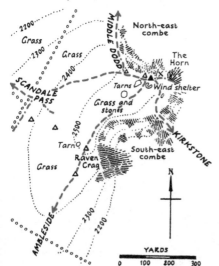

DESCENTS: The best
way down to Ambleside
is by the south ridge —
it is so easy a saunter
that the hands need be
taken from the pockets
only to negotiate gates
and stiles. Also easy, but
longer, is the Scandale
Pass route. For thirsty
walkers, the direct
descent to Kirkstone
is now good underfoot
throughout and easy
to follow, but is steep.
   For Patterdale, the way
over Middle Dodd is
excellent, but steep. The
Caiston Glen path is easy.
*In bad weather, the
safest course of all is
to aim for the top of
Scandale Pass — for
either Ambleside or
Patterdale.*

Patterdale, from the summit

RIDGE ROUTES

TO LITTLE HART CRAG, 2091': 1¼ miles
W, then NW and E

Depression at 1675'
430 feet of ascent

An easy and tedious walk.

Red Screes
has no high
connecting link
with any other
major fell. On the
Fairfield round, the
next adjacent fell
is Little Hart Crag.

On grass, following the wall
across Scandale Pass. Little
Hart Crag needs care in mist.

TO MIDDLE DODD, 2146': ⅔ mile, W, then N
Depression at 2100', 50 feet of ascent

Strictly speaking, Middle Dodd is just the northern spur of Red Screes,
and it certainly looks it on this easy stroll, most of which is downhill.
Details of this walk can be found on *Middle Dodd 3.*

THE VIEW
(with distances in miles)

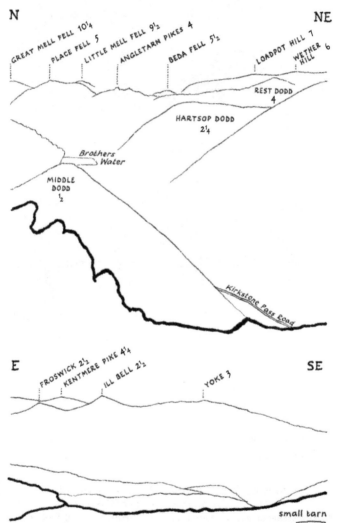

THE VIEW

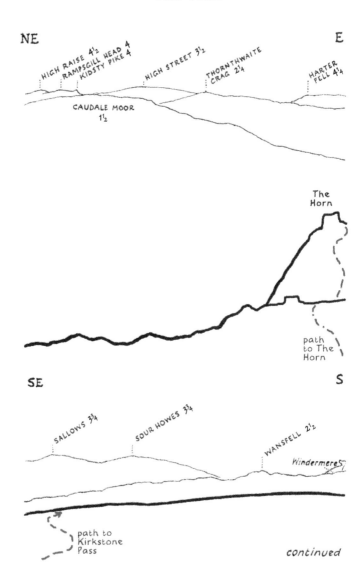

NE

HIGH RAISE 4½
RAMPSGILL HEAD 4
KIDSTY PIKE 4
HIGH STREET 3½
THORNTHWAITE CRAG 2¼
HARTER FELL 4½

E

CAUDALE MOOR 1½

The Horn

path to The Horn

SE

S

SALLOWS 3¾

SOUR HOWES 3¾

WANSFELL 2½

Windermere

path to Kirkstone Pass

continued

THE VIEW

continued

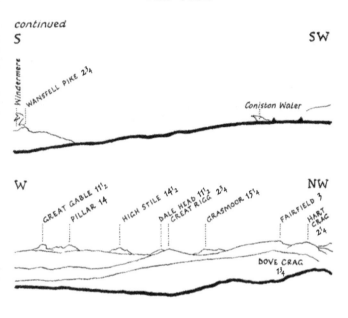

S   SW

Windermere

WANSFELL PIKE 2¾

Coniston Water

W   NW

GREAT GABLE 11½
PILLAR 14
HIGH STILE 14½
DALE HEAD 11½
GREAT RIGG 2¾
GRASMOOR 15¼
FAIRFIELD 3
HART CRAG 2¼

DOVE CRAG 1¾

The south-east combe

The north-east combe

THE VIEW

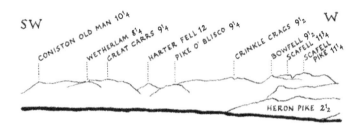

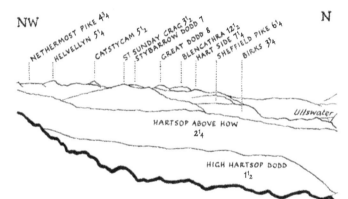

Red Screes has more claims to distinction than any other high fell east of the Keswick/Windermere road ———

(a) *it has the biggest cairn, although perhaps no longer now that many of its stones have been taken to form the summit shelter;*

(b) *it has the greatest mileage of stone walls;*

(c) *it has one of the highest sheets of permanent standing water, and, in springtime, the highest resident population of tadpoles;*

(d) *it has the purest mountain form;*

(e) *it has the reddest screes and the greenest stone;*

(f) *it has one of the finest views (but not the most extensive nor the most beautiful) and the finest of the High Street range;*

(g) *it has the easiest way down;*

(h) *it offers alcoholic beverages at 1480';*

(i) *it gives birth to the stream with the most beautiful waterfalls.*

[Some of these statements are expressions of opinion; others, especially (h), are hard facts.]

Saint Sunday Crag   2756'

OS grid ref: NY369134

Glenridding

Patterdale

▲ HELVELLYN

ST SUNDAY
CRAG ▲

Hartsop

▲ FAIRFIELD

MILES

0   1   2   3   4

from Ullswater

NATURAL FEATURES

The slender soaring lines of St Sunday Crag and its aloof height and steepness endow this fine mountain with special distinction. It stands on a triangular base and its sides rise with such regularity that all its contours assume the same shape, as does the final summit plateau. Ridges ascend from the corners of the triangle to the top of the fell, the one best defined naturally rising from the sharpest angle: this is the south-west ridge connecting with Fairfield at Deepdale Hause. A shorter rougher ridge runs down north-east to Birks. Due east of the top is a subsidiary peak, Gavel Pike, from which a broadening ridge falls to Deepdale. A fringe of crags, nearly a mile in length, overtops the Grisedale face, which drops nearly 2000' in height in a lateral distance of half a mile: in Lakeland, only Great Gable can show greater concentrated steepness over a similar fall in altitude. The south-east face is also steep but less impressive, and the easy slopes to the north-east break into foothills before dropping abruptly to valley level in Patterdale: these slopes are the gathering grounds of Coldcove Gill, the main stream.

Every walker who aspires to high places and looks up at the remote summit of St Sunday Crag will experience an urge to go forth and climb up to it, for its challenge is very strong. Its rewards are equally generous, and altogether this is a noble fell. Saint Sunday must surely look down on his memorial with profound gratification.

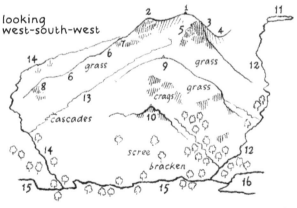

looking
west-south-west

1 : The summit	7 : Lord's Seat	13 : Coldcove Gill
2 : Gavel Pike	8 : Latterhaw Crag	14 : Deepdale Beck
3 : South-west ridge	9 : Birks	15 : Goldrill Beck
4 : Deepdale Hause	10 : Arnison Crag	16 : Ullswater
5 : North-east ridge	11 : Grisedale Tarn	
6 : East ridge	12 : Grisedale Beck	

NATURAL FEATURES

St Sunday Crag has an imposing appearance from whatever direction it is seen, an attribute rare in mountains. From Ullswater and from Grisedale its outline is very familiar. Less well known (because less often seen) is its fine eastern aspect, with the subsidiary summit of Gavel Pike particularly prominent.

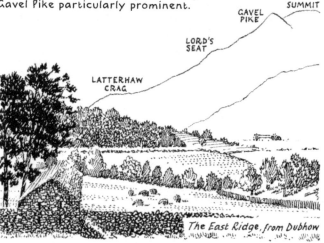

The East Ridge, from Dubhow

There is a glimpse, often unnoticed, of the lofty east ridge soaring high above Deepdale, from the roadway near Bridgend. A much better view is obtained from Dubhow, nearby on the old cart track across the valley.

Cascades, Coldcove Gill

Summit of Gavel Pike

MAP

The ascent of St Sunday Crag via
Pinnacle Ridge is not featured
in this book. It is NOT a way
up for fellwalkers, being
steep and exposed. It is
more of a rock climb
than a scramble.

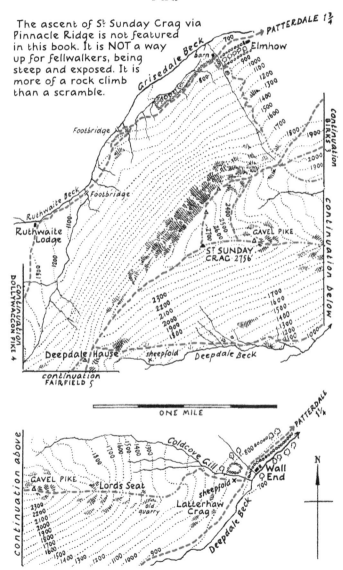

ONE MILE

ASCENT FROM PATTERDALE
2300 feet of ascent : 3 miles (4 by East Ridge)

Climbing on the East Ridge route starts immediately after crossing Coldcove Gill, with a path snaking right that goes *through* a sheepfold. On the way up to Latterhow Crag it becomes intermittent, and on reaching the ridge (which is surprisingly wide at this point) it is easy to be tempted by sheep tracks heading left. Instead, find the old quarry and continue up the ridge, which narrows once past Lord's Seat and is a delightful approach to Gavel Pike.

Further details of Arnison Crag and Birks are given in the separate chapters on those fells.

The Elmhow 'zig-zag', once the popular route has now fallen from favour and is not easy to find.

There is free parking for 3 or 4 cars here, just across the road from the red telephone box.

looking south-west

The *easiest* route (not depicted) follows Deepdale to its head at Deepdale Hause, then ascends the south-west ridge. Apart from a short sharp pull on to the Hause there is no steep climbing. There are intimate views of the crags of Fairfield.

The popular route is via Thornhow End and the western flank of Birks (in clear weather it is better to proceed over the top of Birks). The Trough Head route is easier but dull. The East Ridge is an interesting alternative and technically the best line of ascent.

ASCENT FROM GRISEDALE TARN
1000 feet of ascent · 1¾ miles

looking north-east   St SUNDAY CRAG

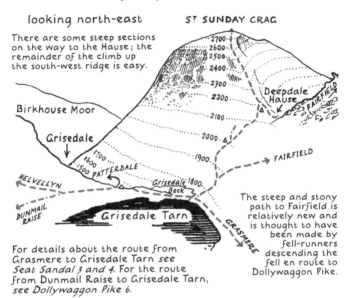

There are some steep sections on the way to the Hause; the remainder of the climb up the south-west ridge is easy.

Birkhouse Moor

Grisedale

2700
2600
2500
2400
2300
2200
2100
2000

Deepdale Hause

FAIRFIELD

1900

FAIRFIELD

HELVELLYN

1700
1600
1500 PATTERDALE

Grisedale Beck

1800

DUNMAIL RAISE

Grisedale Tarn

GRASMERE

The steep and stony path to Fairfield is relatively new and is thought to have been made by fell-runners descending the fell en route to Dollywaggon Pike.

For details about the route from Grasmere to Grisedale Tarn *see Seat Sandal 3 and 4.* For the route from Dunmail Raise to Grisedale Tarn, *see Dollywaggon Pike 6.*

St Sunday Crag is commonly and correctly regarded as the preserve of Patterdale, yet it is interesting to note that the summit is less than three miles from the Keswick-Ambleside road at Dunmail Raise: it may be ascended easily and quickly from here. And from Grasmere via Tongue Gill. In either case, the first objective is Grisedale Tarn.

St Sunday Crag
from Grisedale Tarn

THE SUMMIT

The summit hardly lives up to the promise of the ridges: it is merely a slight stony mound set on the edge of a plateau — a pleasant place of mosses and lichens and grey rocks, but quite unexciting. A sprawling cairn adorns the top, and there is also a well built column of stones a quarter of a mile away across the plateau to the north.

Gavel Pike has a much more attractive summit than the main fell: here are bilberries and heather and natural armchairs among the rocks of the tiny peaked top, and splendid views to enjoy. A delectable place for (packed) lunch!

NORTH-EAST RIDGE

× Best viewpoint for Ullswater

grass

Path joins north-east ridge path

big gully

△ North cairn

crags

cairns

2400
2500
2600
2700

stones

△

GAVEL PIKE
△

EAST RIDGE

saddle

grass

N

HALF A MILE

SOUTH WEST RIDGE

DESCENTS: The royal way down to Patterdale is by the north-east ridge, traversing the flank of Birks and descending the steep woodland of Glenamara Park — a delightful walk with charming views. Other routes are very inferior. For Grisedale Tarn, use the south-west ridge to Deepdale Hause, thence taking the clear path, right, to the tarn, which is in view.

In bad conditions, the danger lies in the long line of crags on the Grisedale face, this fortunately being preceded by steep ground which serves as a warning. For Patterdale, the path from the saddle is safest.

Ullswater
from the
north-east ridge

RIDGE ROUTES

To FAIRFIELD, 2863' : 1½ miles : SW then S
Depression at 2150' : 750 feet of ascent

ST SUNDAY CRAG

A simple descent followed by rough scrambling.

A very pleasant stroll down the south-west ridge, on a clear path, much of which is grassy, leads to the depression of Deepdale Hause. From here, Cofa Pike looks quite formidable, but a plain path climbs steeply up the stony slope to the interesting crest of the Pike; it is also possible to bypass the crest on the right. A loose scree slope (which can be avoided via a sweeping zig-zag to the right) is then climbed to the grassy shoulder above and the summit cairn is just beyond. *In mist, Fairfield is a dangerous place for strangers.*

HALF A MILE
N

Deepdale Hause
DEEPDALE
GRISEDALE TARN
Cofa Pike
FAIRFIELD

To BIRKS, 2040' : 1¼ miles : NE
Minor depressions : 50 feet of ascent

ELMHOW
THORNHOW END
BIRKS
Col
TROUGH HEAD

An easy walk with delightful views.

Cross the tilted summit plateau to the north cairn; beyond, the north-east ridge goes down to a col, whence a level grassy path leads on to the small summit cairn on the top of Birks.

ST SUNDAY CRAG
Gavel Pike

GREAT MELL FELL
LITTLE MELL FELL
GOWBARROW FELL
BIRK FELL
PLACE FELL
GLENRIDDING DODD
BIRKHOUSE MOOR
BIRKS

Ullswater from the north cairn
(The cairn is no longer as well constructed as it is in the illustration.)

THE VIEW

Principal Fells

Lakes and Tarns
NE: *Ullswater*
E: *Angle Tarn*

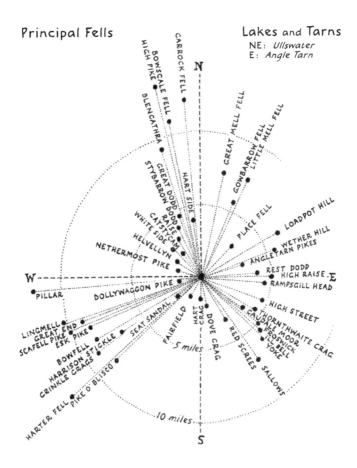

Walkers who reach the summit eagerly expecting to see the classic view of Ullswater from St Sunday Crag will be disappointed — they must go to the bristly rocks at the top of the north-east ridge for that. The lake makes a beautiful picture also from the saddle leading to Gavel Pike. Helvellyn is a fine study in mountain structure, and the best aspect of Fairfield is seen, but these two fells restrict the view. The High Street range, however, is well seen.

Seat Sandal 2415'

OS grid ref: NY344115

from Grasmere

HELVELLYN ▲

FAIRFIELD ▲

SEAT SANDAL ▲

Grasmere ●

MILES
0   1   2

Cascade, Raise Beck

NATURAL FEATURES

Prominent in the Grasmere landscape is the lofty outline of Seat Sandal, soaring gracefully from Dunmail Raise to the flat-topped summit and then suddenly falling away in a steep plunge eastwards. This view reveals its character well: the western flanks are smooth curves of grass and bracken, but the eastern face is a rough slope of shattered cliff and tumbled rock and loose scree from which rises abruptly an overhanging crag. Seat Sandal is a simple straightforward fell, uninteresting except as a viewpoint, with no dramatic effects, no hidden surprises. Geographically it belongs to Fairfield, to which it is connected by a low ridge crossed by the Grisedale Pass.

looking north

Seat Sandal has one distinction: its waters reach the sea at more widely divergent points than those of any other Lakeland fell. This has been so since the diversion of Raise Beck to feed Thirlmere.

(Dollywaggon Pike shares this distinction only when Raise Beck is flowing south at Dunmail Raise.)

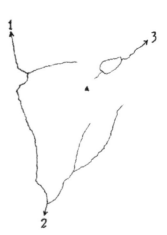

1 : Raise Beck —
    to Thirlmere and (that which escapes being sent south over Dunmail to Manchester) via Derwent Water to the sea at Workington.

2 : Raise Beck and Tongue Gill —
    to Grasmere, Windermere and Morecambe Bay.

3 : Grisedale Beck —
    to Ullswater and the Solway Firth.

MAP

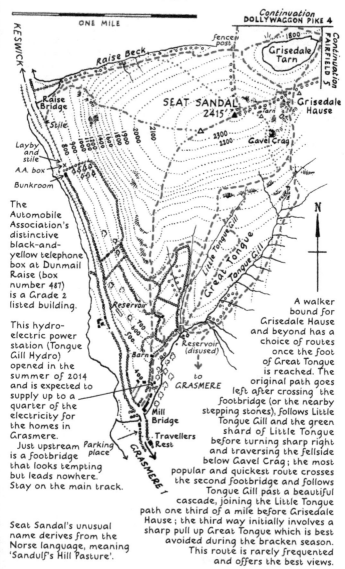

ONE MILE

Continuation
DOLLYWAGGON PIKE 4

Continuation FAIRFIELD 5

KESWICK

Raise Beck

fence post

Grisedale Tarn

1800

SEAT SANDAL 2415'

Grisedale Hause

Raise Bridge

Stile

Layby and stile

A.A. box

Bunkroom

2300
2200

Gavel Crag

Tarn

N

Reservoir

Little Tongue Gill

Great Tongue

Great Tongue Gill

Reservoir (disused)

Barn

to
GRASMERE

Mill Bridge

Travellers Rest

Parking place

GRASMERE 1

The Automobile Association's distinctive black-and-yellow telephone box at Dunmail Raise (box number 487) is a Grade 2 listed building.

This hydro-electric power station (Tongue Gill Hydro) opened in the summer of 2014 and is expected to supply up to a quarter of the electricity for the homes in Grasmere.

Just upstream is a footbridge that looks tempting but leads nowhere. Stay on the main track.

Seat Sandal's unusual name derives from the Norse language, meaning 'Sandulf's Hill Pasture'.

A walker bound for Grisedale Hause and beyond has a choice of routes once the foot of Great Tongue is reached. The original path goes left after crossing the footbridge (or the nearby stepping stones), follows Little Tongue Gill and the green shard of Little Tongue before turning sharp right and traversing the fellside below Gavel Crag; the most popular and quickest route crosses the second footbridge and follows Tongue Gill past a beautiful cascade, joining the Little Tongue path one third of a mile before Grisedale Hause; the third way initially involves a sharp pull up Great Tongue which is best avoided during the bracken season. This route is rarely frequented and offers the best views.

ASCENT FROM GRASMERE
2200 feet of ascent: 3½ miles from Grasmere Church

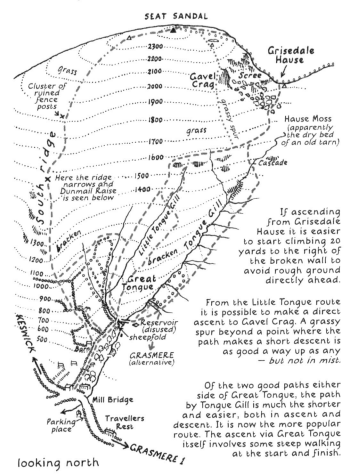

SEAT SANDAL

Grisedale Hause

Gavel Crag

Scree

grass

Cluster of
ruined
fence
posts

south ridge

2300
2200
2100
2000
1900
1800
1700
1600
1500
1400
1300
1200
1100
1000
900
800
700
600
500

grassy spur

Hause Moss
(apparently
the dry bed
of an old tarn)

Cascade

Here the ridge
narrows and
Dunmail Raise
is seen below

bracken

bracken

Little Tongue Gill

Tongue Gill

Great
Tongue

KESWICK

Barn

Reservoir
(disused)
sheepfold

GRASMERE
(alternative)

Mill Bridge

Parking
place

Travellers
Rest

GRASMERE 1

looking north

If ascending
from Grisedale
Hause it is easier
to start climbing 20
yards to the right of
the broken wall to
avoid rough ground
directly ahead.

From the Little Tongue route
it is possible to make a direct
ascent to Gavel Crag. A grassy
spur beyond a point where the
path makes a short descent is
as good a way up as any
— but not in mist.

Of the two good paths either
side of Great Tongue, the path
by Tongue Gill is much the shorter
and easier, both in ascent and
descent. It is now the more popular
route. The ascent via Great Tongue
itself involves some steep walking
at the start and finish.

Seat Sandal is clearly in view from Grasmere, and the
obvious way up is via the south ridge. However, the
ascent via Grisedale Hause offers better scenery, and the
south ridge has better views in descent. For
alternative ways to Grisedale Hause, *see facing page*.

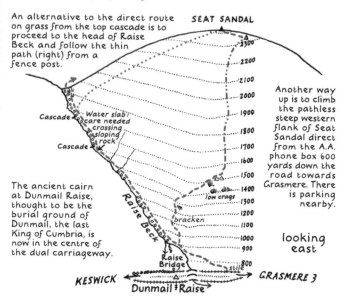

ASCENT FROM DUNMAIL RAISE
1700 feet of ascent : 1½ miles

An alternative to the direct route on grass from the top cascade is to proceed to the head of Raise Beck and follow the thin path (right) from a fence post.

SEAT SANDAL

2300
2200
2100
2000
1900
1800
1700
1600
1500
1400
1300
1200
1100
1000
900
800

Cascade

Water slab: care needed crossing sloping rock

Cascade

Another way up is to climb the pathless steep western flank of Seat Sandal direct from the A.A. phone box 600 yards down the road towards Grasmere. There is parking nearby.

low crags

bracken

The ancient cairn at Dunmail Raise, thought to be the burial ground of Dunmail, the last King of Cumbria, is now in the centre of the dual carriageway.

Raise Beck

Raise Bridge

stile

looking east

KESWICK ← → GRASMERE 3
Dunmail Raise

Seat Sandal is very easily climbed from Raise Bridge. The usual route is to follow sheltered Raise Beck, which has a number of attractive cascades. The direct route now has a clear path up the initial steep section, which is a little less distinct when the slope eases. In descent, this way offers the best views.

from the north

arête

Gavel Crag

looking down on the arête

The name 'Gavel Crag' was invented by the author, but it is now recognised by the Ordnance Survey.

The main object of note on the fell is Gavel Crag on the east face. From the path below it resembles a miniature Pillar Rock. It rises from rough ground but can be reached from below mainly on grass; a fine rock arête connects it to the easier fellside above.

THE SUMMIT

The summit is a flat grassy plateau with small stony outcrops. A broken wall crosses the top. The main cairn stands 30 yards west of the wall, but is not appreciably higher than two other cairns, which indicate alternative viewpoints.

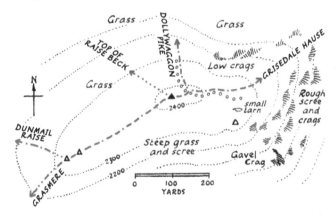

DESCENTS : The best way off the summit, *in clear weather*, is by the south ridge to Grasmere, the views being excellent and the gradient exactly right — this is one of the quickest descents in the area. All routes are safe in good conditions. The east face is steep, and should be avoided.

In mist, the safest descent is to Grisedale Hause (by the wall) where good paths lead to Grasmere and Patterdale; the path to the south ridge from the south-west cairn is just a little too indistinct in its early stages to be recommended. *In snow and ice*, the Grisedale Hause path is the least comfortable way down.

THE VIEW

Principal Fells

Most of the interest in the view is in the western arc, where the panorama is excellent. In other directions, nearby Helvellyn and Fairfield limit the distant view.

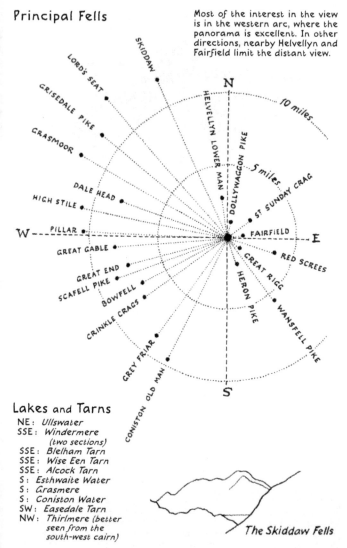

Lakes and Tarns

NE: *Ullswater*
SSE: *Windermere (two sections)*
SSE: *Bleiham Tarn*
SSE: *Wise Een Tarn*
SSE: *Alcock Tarn*
S: *Esthwaite Water*
S: *Grasmere*
S: *Coniston Water*
SW: *Easedale Tarn*
NW: *Thirlmere (better seen from the south-west cairn)*

The Skiddaw Fells

Grisedale Tarn is seen by walking NE 150 yards from the summit cairn.

RIDGE ROUTES

To FAIRFIELD, 2863' : 1⅓ miles : E then NE and E
Depression at 1929' : 950 feet of ascent

A rough descent followed by a steep continuous climb. The top of Fairfield is confusing and dangerous in mist to anyone who is not familiar with it, but there is no difficulty in clear weather.

The wall is a guide down to Grisedale Hause: the last part of the descent is rough but there is easier ground just to the left. The wall continues up the shoulder of Fairfield to 2400' and gives up the struggle but the determined walker toils on along a fair path. The final part of the climb, easier on a thinner path, follows a line of cairns across grass to the stony top.

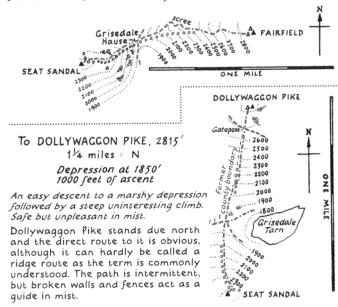

To DOLLYWAGGON PIKE, 2815'
1¼ miles : N

Depression at 1850' 1000 feet of ascent

An easy descent to a marshy depression followed by a steep uninteresting climb. Safe but unpleasant in mist.

Dollywaggon Pike stands due north and the direct route to it is obvious, although it can hardly be called a ridge route as the term is commonly understood. The path is intermittent, but broken walls and fences act as a guide in mist.

Ullswater and St Sunday Crag from Seat Sandal

Sheffield Pike

2215′

OS grid ref: NY369182

from Glenridding

GREAT DODD ▲

Glencoyne ●

SHEFFIELD PIKE ▲

Glenridding ●

Patterdale ●

HELVELLYN ▲

MILES

0   1   2   3   4   5

NATURAL FEATURES

Stybarrow Dodd, on the main Helvellyn watershed, has a long eastern shoulder falling in stages to the shore of Ullswater. Midway, the shoulder rises to a distinct and isolated summit: this is Sheffield Pike, which assumes the characteristics of a separate fell. It soars abruptly between the valleys of Glenridding and Glencoyne and it presents to each a continuous fringe of steep crags. The eastern aspect is pleasing, with rock and heather and an occasional rowan mingling above the well wooded slopes, but westwards the fell is drab and, in the environs of an old lead mine, downright ugly. Since the closing of the mine in 1962, the whole area has been immaculately restored. Tips are partially grass-covered and all the buildings have been demolished or put to new uses, including an outdoor pursuits centre, a bothy and a youth hostel (Helvellyn YHA). Students of old mine workings will find little of interest here.

looking north-west

Heron Pike, from the east

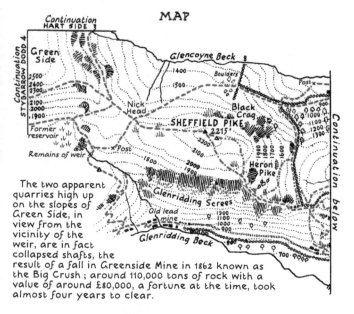

MAP

The two apparent quarries high up on the slopes of Green Side, in view from the vicinity of the weir, are in fact collapsed shafts, the result of a fall in Greenside Mine in 1862 known as the Big Crush ; around 110,000 tons of rock with a value of around £80,000, a fortune at the time, took almost four years to clear.

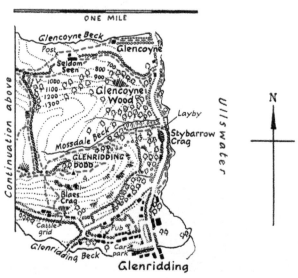

ASCENT FROM GLENRIDDING
1800 feet of ascent : 2 (or 3¼) miles

The two small iron posts on the top of the fell are inscribed 'H 1912' on one side and 'M 1912' on the other. They were erected to mark the boundary between the Howard estate of Greystoke and the Marshall estate of Patterdale.

Sheffield Pike should not be climbed in mist.

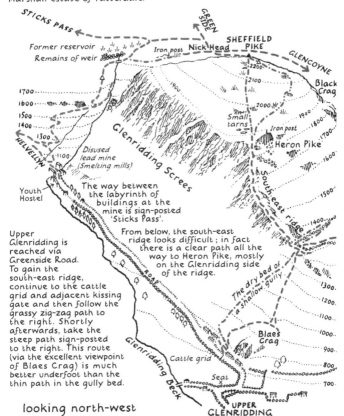

STICKS PASS

Former reservoir
Remains of weir

GREEN SIDE

Iron post   Nick Head

SHEFFIELD PIKE

GLENCOYNE

2200

2100

Black Crag

2000

1900

1800

1700

Small tarns

Iron post

Heron Pike

1600

1700

1600

1500

1400

1300

1100

HELVELLYN

Disused lead mine (Smelting mills)

Glenridding Screes

The way between the labyrinth of buildings at the mine is sign-posted 'Sticks Pass'.

From below, the south-east ridge looks difficult; in fact there is a clear path all the way to Heron Pike, mostly on the Glenridding side of the ridge.

South-east ridge

1500

1400

1300

1200

1100

1000

900

800

700

The dry bed of a shallow gully

Youth Hostel

Upper Glenridding is reached via Greenside Road. To gain the south-east ridge, continue to the cattle grid and adjacent kissing gate and then follow the grassy zig-zag path to the right. Shortly afterwards, take the steep path sign-posted to the right. This route (via the excellent viewpoint of Blaes Crag) is much better underfoot than the thin path in the gully bed.

ROAD

Glenridding Beck

Cattle grid

Seat

Blaes Crag

UPPER GLENRIDDING

looking north-west

Of the two routes illustrated, the climb up the south-east ridge is much to be preferred but it is steep. The path zig-zagging above the former smelting mills and approaching Sheffield Pike from behind via Nick Head is longer and easier — but much less inspiring and not at all exhilarating.

ASCENT FROM GLENCOYNE
1800 feet of ascent : 2½ miles

The mystery of the two iron posts on the top of the fell is solved on the previous page.

Sheffield Pike should not be climbed in mist.

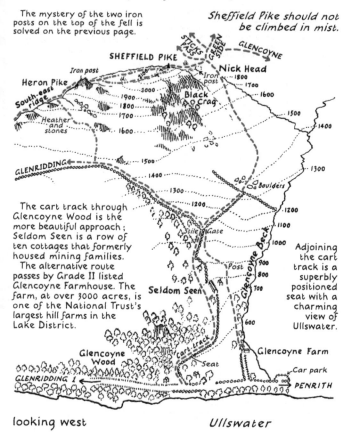

looking west

Ullswater

The cart track through Glencoyne Wood is the more beautiful approach; Seldom Seen is a row of ten cottages that formerly housed mining families.
The alternative route passes by Grade II listed Glencoyne Farmhouse. The farm, at over 3000 acres, is one of the National Trust's largest hill farms in the Lake District.

Adjoining the cart track is a superbly positioned seat with a charming view of Ullswater.

The section of the route via Heron Pike between the wall and the south-east ridge requires some route-finding when the thin path peters out in places, and thus needs clear weather. The way from Heron Pike to the summit is boggy unless walked after a particularly dry spell.

It is usual to follow the path to Nick Head and there turn east to the summit: this is the easiest of all ways on to the fell. Far more attractive, however, is a route traversing below Heron Pike to the top of the south-east ridge, the walking being easy and the views excellent: this is one of the pleasantest short climbs in Lakeland.

THE SUMMIT

Even on a sunny summer day the top of the fell seems a dismal, cheerless place; the area above Black Crag, and the top of Heron Pike, where there is heather, are both nicer.

There are many slight undulations and craggy outcrops. Marshy ground occurs in several places and there are many small tarns.

Beside the summit cairn, which is now a fairly squat edifice, is an inscribed stone bearing the date 1830.

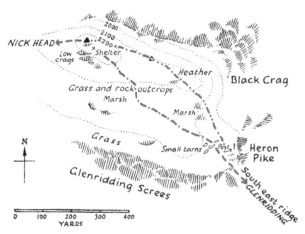

DESCENTS: Any of the routes of ascent may be reversed in clear weather, the south-east ridge being incomparably the best. Some care is necessary in getting off Heron Pike on to the ridge. The summit plateau has crags on three sides, and the main path between the summit cairn and Heron Pike, while very easy to keep to in clear weather, is surprisingly difficult to follow *in mist*. *In bad weather conditions*, the *only* safe way is due west to Nick Head (very gradual descent, boggy in places), from there preferably following the good path down to Glencoyne.

THE VIEW

Ullswater is the main feature of a restricted view. Westwards the prospects is dull; it is really good only between north-east and south. Heron Pike is a much finer viewpoint.

Principal Fells

N

5 miles

2½ miles

GREAT MELL FELL

LITTLE MELL FELL

COWBARROW FELL

GREAT DODD

HART SIDE

STYBARROW DODD

W —————————————————————— E

LOADPOT HILL

RAISE

WHITE SIDE

HELVELLYN LOWER MAN

CATSTYCAM

HELVELLYN

BIRKHOUSE MOOR

FAIRFIELD

ST SUNDAY CRAG

RED SCREES

CAUDALE MOOR

THORNTHWAITE CRAG

HIGH STREET

RAMPSGILL HEAD

HIGH RAISE

WETHER HILL

PLACE FELL

S

Lakes and Tarns

NE: *Ullswater (better seen from the cairn above Black Crag and from Heron Pike)*
SE: *Lanty's Tarn*
W: *Reservoir below Sticks Pass (now dry)*

Black Crag

Heron Pike

RIDGE ROUTES

To STYBARROW DODD, 2770' : 2 miles : W then NW and W.
Depression at 1925' : 1000 feet of ascent

A simple walk with a long climb on grass midway.

An easy descent westwards, boggy in places, leads to Nick Head. Cross the clear paths here and climb the good path on a long grassy slope ahead to the cairn on Green Side. Stybarrow Dodd is then in view in front, across a shallow depression. The paths on this route are now clear enough for it to be safe *in bad weather conditions.*

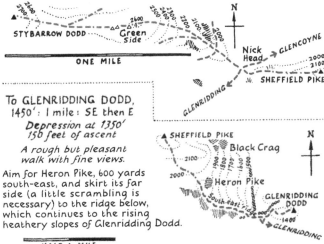

To GLENRIDDING DODD, 1450' : 1 mile : SE then E
Depression at 1350' 150 feet of ascent

A rough but pleasant walk with fine views.

Aim for Heron Pike, 600 yards south-east, and skirt its far side (a little scrambling is necessary) to the ridge below, which continues to the rising heathery slopes of Glenridding Dodd.

Ullswater from Heron Pike

Stone Arthur 1652'

sometimes referred to as Arthur's Chair

OS grid ref: NY348092

from Grasmere

▲ FAIRFIELD

▲ GREAT RIGG

▲ STONE ARTHUR

▲ HERON PIKE

Grasmere ▲ NAB SCAR
● Rydal

Ambleside ●

MILES
0   1   2   3   4

Without its prominent tor of steep rock, Stone Arthur would probably never have been given a name, for it is merely the abrupt end of a spur of Great Rigg, although it has the appearance of a separate fell when seen from Grasmere. The outcrop occurs where the gradual decline of the spur becomes pronounced and here are the short walls of rock, like a ruined castle, that give Stone Arthur its one touch of distinction.

MAP

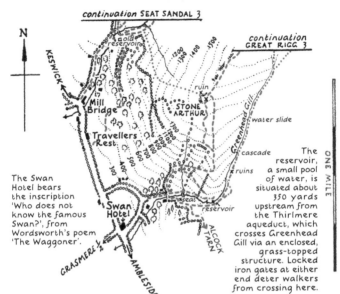

continuation SEAT SANDAL 3

continuation GREAT RIGG 3

N

KESWICK

Mill Bridge

Travellers Rest

gold reservoir

1700 1300 1400 1500

ruin

STONE ARTHUR

Greenhead Gill

water slide

cascade

ruins

1200

900 700 800 600 500

300

400

The Swan Hotel bears the inscription 'Who does not know the famous Swan?', from Wordsworth's poem 'The Waggoner'.

Swan Hotel

seat

reservoir

ALCOCK TARN

GRASMERE ½

AMBLESIDE

ONE MILE

The reservoir, a small pool of water, is situated about 350 yards upstream from the Thirlmere aqueduct, which crosses Greenhead Gill via an enclosed, grass-topped structure. Locked iron gates at either end deter walkers from crossing here.

Alongside Greenhead Gill are the remains of a mine that flourished for nearly ten years in the 16th century. The ruins of two buildings stand on the west side of the gill, just across the beck from a number of exposed veins, which can still be seen today on the eastern bank.

Grasmere, from the summit

ASCENT FROM GRASMERE
1450 feet of ascent : 1½ miles

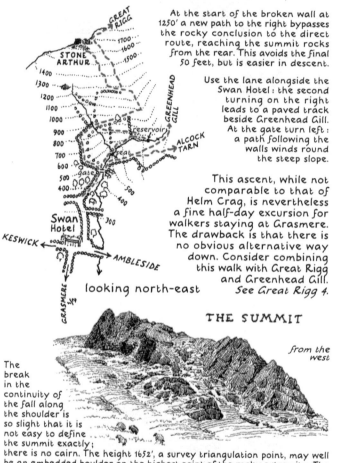

At the start of the broken wall at 1250' a new path to the right bypasses the rocky conclusion to the direct route, reaching the summit rocks from the rear. This avoids the final 50 feet, but is easier in descent.

Use the lane alongside the Swan Hotel: the second turning on the right leads to a paved track beside Greenhead Gill. At the gate turn left: a path following the walls winds round the steep slope.

This ascent, while not comparable to that of Helm Crag, is nevertheless a fine half-day excursion for walkers staying at Grasmere. The drawback is that there is no obvious alternative way down. Consider combining this walk with Great Rigg and Greenhead Gill.
See Great Rigg 4.

looking north-east

THE SUMMIT

from the west

The break in the continuity of the fall along the shoulder is so slight that it is not easy to define the summit exactly; there is no cairn. The height 1652', a survey triangulation point, may well be an embedded boulder on the highest point of the rocky extremity. The small crags around the summit offer practice for embryo climbers whose main concern is not to drop too far if they fall.

DESCENTS : To find the Grasmere path, aim directly for Alcock Tarn. *In mist*, a 40-yard walk north-eastwards on the path to Great Rigg brings you to the start of the 'bypass' path, which is a clear and easy descent. Once the initial crags have been left behind any way down is safe, but unless the path can be found the thick bracken will prove an abomination.

THE VIEW

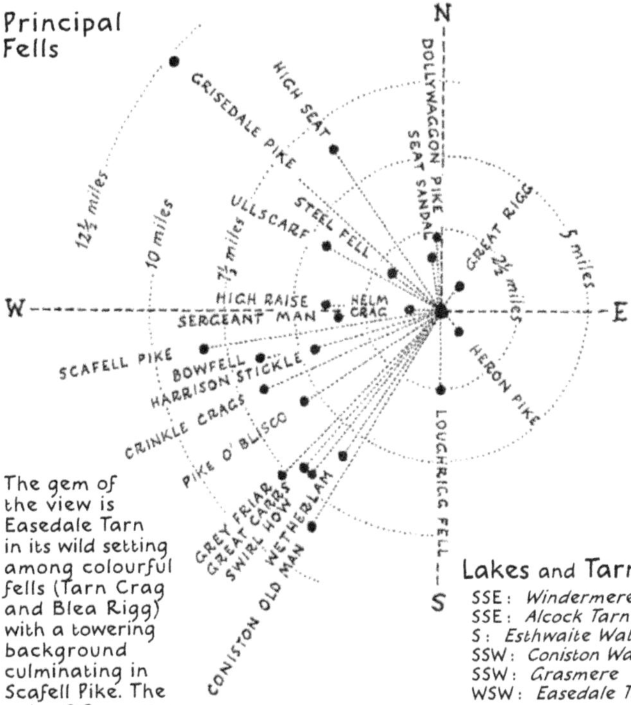
Principal Fells
N
E
S
W
DOLLYWAGGON PIKE
SEAT SANDAL
HIGH SEAT
GRISEDALE PIKE
STEEL FELL
ULLSCARF
GREAT RIGG
HIGH RAISE
HELM CRAG
SERGEANT MAN
SCAFELL PIKE
BOWFELL
HARRISON STICKLE
CRINKLE CRAGS
PIKE O' BLISCO
GREY FRIAR
GREAT CARRS
SWIRL HOW
WETHERLAM
CONISTON OLD MAN
HERON PIKE
LOUGHRIGG FELL
2½ miles
5 miles
7½ miles
10 miles
12½ miles

The gem of the view is Easedale Tarn in its wild setting among colourful fells (Tarn Crag and Blea Rigg) with a towering background culminating in Scafell Pike. The vale of Grasmere, below, is also attractive. The southern ridge of Fairfield occupies the whole horizon to the east, uninterestingly.

Lakes and Tarns

SSE: *Windermere*
SSE: *Alcock Tarn*
S: *Esthwaite Water*
SSW: *Coniston Water*
SSW: *Grasmere*
WSW: *Easedale Tarn*

RIDGE ROUTE

To GREAT RIGG, 2513′
1¼ miles: NE then N

Easy climbing all the way.
Safe in mist.

Follow the shoulder upwards on a clear path (wide in its later stages) which meets the ridge at a cairn.

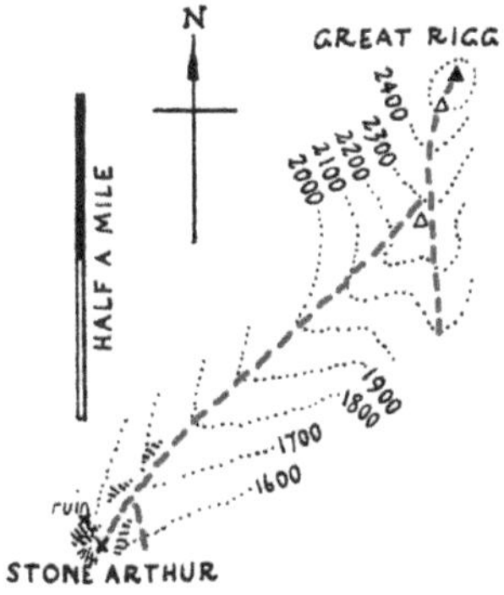
N
HALF A MILE
GREAT RIGG
2400
2300
2200
2100
2000
1900
1800
1700
1600
ruin
STONE ARTHUR

Stybarrow Dodd   2770'

OS grid ref: NY343189

Dockray

▲ GREAT DODD

Stanah
STYBARROW
Thirlspot   ▲ DODD
Glencoyne

▲ RAISE
Glenridding

▲ HELVELLYN
MILES
0   1   2   3   4

from Brown Crag

NATURAL FEATURES

Stybarrow Dodd is the first of the group of fells north of the Sticks Pass and it sets the pattern for them all: sweeping grassy slopes, easy walking for travellers who likes to count their miles but rather wearisome for those who prefer to see rock in the landscape. Rock is so rare that the slightest roughnesses get undeserved identification on most maps, either by distinctive name or extravagant hachures: thus Deepdale Crag is hardly more than a short stony slope. Stybarrow Dodd sends out a long eastern spur that rises to a minor height, Green Side (which, incidentally, gave its name to the lead mine in nearby Glenridding) before falling steeply to Glencoyne; on Green Side there are both crags and dangerous quarries, now disused.

Stybarrow Dodd's one proud distinction is that on its slopes it carries the well known path over Sticks Pass throughout most of its length. Far more people ascend the slopes of Stybarrow Dodd than reach its summit!

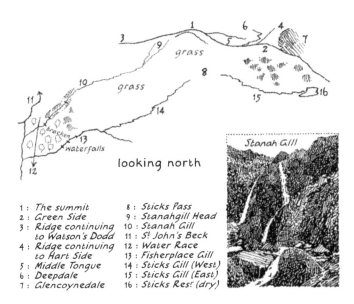

looking north

Stanah Gill

1 : The summit
2 : Green Side
3 : Ridge continuing to Watson's Dodd
4 : Ridge continuing to Hart Side
5 : Middle Tongue
6 : Deepdale
7 : Glencoynedale
8 : Sticks Pass
9 : Stanahgill Head
10 : Stanah Gill
11 : St John's Beck
12 : Water Race
13 : Fisherplace Gill
14 : Sticks Gill (West)
15 : Sticks Gill (East)
16 : Sticks Resr (dry)

According to historical records, 'Dodd' is a relatively recent addition to the fell's name. It was recorded as Stibarro in 1589, Stybrow in 1794 and Stybarrow in 1800.

MAP

ONE MILE

A path follows the intake wall from Stanah to Thirlspot. Where it crosses Fisherplace Gill there is a delightful wooden footbridge with a perfect view of the beck and its waterfalls.

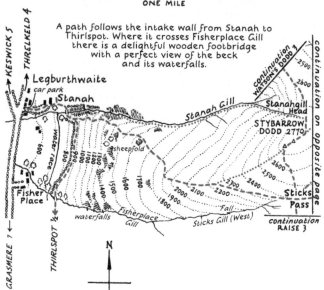

The renovated sheepfold beside the Sticks Pass path from Stanah is a work of great craftsmanship. On its outer wall on the eastern side (away from the prevailing winds) is stone seating ideal for walkers seeking a break.

STICKS PASS —

Sticks Pass, 2420', is the highest pass in Lakeland crossed by a path in common use. The wide summit of the pass was formerly marked by wooden posts, hence the name, but these have now vanished.

Sticks Pass
looking east to Sheffield Pike. The reservoir is now dry.

MAP

continuation GREAT DODD 4
continuation HART SIDE 3
continuation on opposite page
continuation SHEFFIELD PIKE 3
continuation RAISE 4

Green Side is 2608' high. If it were a separate fell only 37 Lakeland fells would be higher.

Browndale Beck · Middle Tongue · Deepdale · Deepdale Crag · STYBARROW DODD · Green Side · White Stones · Glencoyne · Collapsed mine · Nick Head · Sticks Pass · Sticks Gill (East) · Former reservoir · Remains of weir · GLENRIDDING 3

White Stones, straddling the summit area of Green Side, is a cluster of rocks, not particularly white, but in a sea of unremitting green, they stand out sufficiently to deserve a name.

Far more impressive are the rather ugly remains of the weir that once held back the waters of the Sticks Reservoir.

Ullswater
from the east slope of Green Side

ASCENT FROM STANAH
2300 feet of ascent : 2½ miles

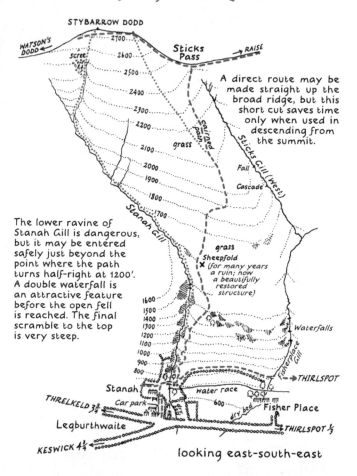

STYBARROW DODD

WATSON'S DODD ←

scree

2700
2600
2500
2400
2300
2200
2100
2000
1900
1800
1700

Sticks Pass

RAISE →

A direct route may be made straight up the broad ridge, but this short cut saves time only when used in descending from the summit.

cairned path

grass

Sticks Gill (West)

Fall

Cascade

Stanah Gill

The lower ravine of Stanah Gill is dangerous, but it may be entered safely just beyond the point where the path turns half-right at 1200'. A double waterfall is an attractive feature before the open fell is reached. The final scramble to the top is very steep.

grass
Sheepfold
✗ (for many years a ruin; now a beautifully restored structure)

1600
1500
1400
1300
1200
1100
1000
900
800

Waterfalls

Fireplace Gill

→ THIRLSPOT

Stanah

THRELKELD 3¾ ←

Car park

water race

600

Fisher Place

dry bed

THIRLSPOT ½ →

Legburthwaite

KESWICK 4¼ ←

looking east-south-east

Conveniently, the good path to Sticks Pass climbs the slopes of Stybarrow Dodd, the summit being easily gained from the top of the pass. This is one of the easiest ways up any fell of such altitude, the only steep section occurring in the first half mile. Stanah Gill is a rough alternative, affording some relief from the dull grassiness of the path.

ASCENT FROM DOCKRAY
1900 feet of ascent : 5½ miles

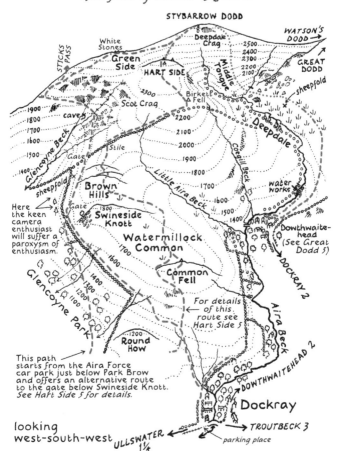

STYBARROW DODD

WATSON'S DODD

Deepdale Crag

GREAT DODD

White Stones

Green Side

HART SIDE

Middle Tongue

STICKS PASS

2500
2400
2300
2200
2100

Birkett Fell

Scot Crag

2300

2200

Deepdale

sheepfold

cave

2100

2000

1900

1800

1700

1600

1500

1400

Glencoyne Beck

Stile

Gate

Little Aira Beck

Coegill Beck

1900

1800

1700

1600

1500

1400

water works

sheepfold

Brown Hills

Gate

Dowthwaite-head (See Great Dodd 5)

Here the keen camera enthusiast will suffer a paroxysm of enthusiasm.

1800

Swineside Knott

Watermillock Common

1700

1600

1500

1400

1300

1200

1100

Glencoyne Park

Common Fell

For details of this route see Hart Side 5

DOCKRAY 2

Aira Beck

1200

Round How

This path starts from the Aira Force car park just below Park Brow and offers an alternative route to the gate below Swineside Knott. See Hart Side 5 for details.

DOWTHWAITEHEAD 2

Dockray

looking west-south-west

ULLSWATER 1¼

TROUTBECK 3

parking place

There is all the difference in the world between the three routes depicted. The direct way up, by Deepdale, is dreary and depressing ; that by the intake wall below Swineside Knott is (after a dull start) a splendid route, with excellent views of Ullswater below ; the high-level approach via Common Fell, Birkett Fell and Hart Side is better as an alternative way down. Swineside Knott is the best viewpoint for Ullswater.

THE SUMMIT

When this book was first published there was no spot height on Stybarrow Dodd and the author suggested that walkers should pass their time on the summit estimating its altitude by this method:

The usually accepted top is the upright slate slab at the south-western end, (2756'), but there is higher ground 300 yards north-east, indicated by a very loose (at the time of writing!) estate-boundary iron post. That it *is* higher is easily proved: from here, the slate slab at 2756' is seen to cover a part of Esk Pike, 9½ miles away, at about 2400'; therefore the view is *downward*. Q.E.D.

The altitude of the highest point can be roughly decided mathematically. It will be noted that the summit of Raise (2889', 7 furlongs) is directly below the summit of Helvellyn (3080' say, 18 furlongs). The walker didn't climb up here to do sums, and is not likely to challenge the statement that the altitude may, from the data, be calculated at 2770' approximately.

Today no such complex calculations are necessary. The 2½" Ordnance Survey map gives the altitude of the highest point as 843 metres (2766'), which is remarkably close to the author's estimate.

On the highest point there is now a large cairn, which incorporates the slate slab. The iron post has gone.

DESCENTS: All ways off are obvious in clear weather. Think twice before dropping down into Deepdale. *In bad conditions* aim south for Sticks Pass.

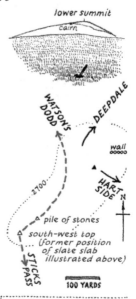

RIDGE ROUTE

To RAISE, 2897': 1 mile : SW then S
Depression at 2420' (Sticks Pass)
470 feet of ascent

An easy walk, mostly on grass. Safe in mist.

From the south-west top, descend south to cross Sticks Pass at its highest point. There are no posts here any more, just a cluster of small rocks. Avoid the small tarn which encroaches close to the path on the right and can easily be overlooked in mist or under snow. The long facing slope of Raise becomes stony towards the summit.

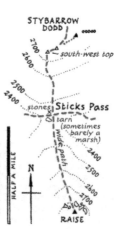

RIDGE ROUTES

To WATSON'S DODD, 2589': ⅔ mile : NW
Depression slight : Ascent negligible

A very easy stroll. Safe in mist.

A short distance beyond the tarn the path divides into three, the left fork slightly ascending across the flat plateau to the summit cairn. Beware of marshy ground in places.

To HART SIDE, 2481' : 1½ miles : E then NE
Depressions at 2525' and 2250': 300 feet of ascent.

An easy walk on grass. Care needed in mist.

Descend east, leaving the wall well to the left, on a thin path to the obvious ridge rising gently to Green Side. Skirt the cairns there and aim directly for Hart Side ahead. Alternatively, bear left at the depression onto the path that skirts Green Side to the north.

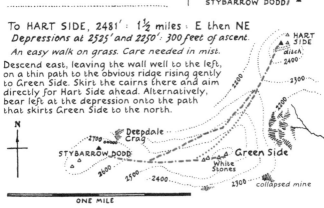

To SHEFFIELD PIKE, 2215' : 2 miles : E then SE and E
Depressions at 2525' and 1925' : 400 feet of ascent

An easy walk. Care needed in mist.

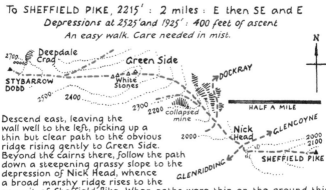

Descend east, leaving the wall well to the left, picking up a thin but clear path to the obvious ridge rising gently to Green Side. Beyond the cairns there, follow the path down a steepening grassy slope to the depression of Nick Head, whence a broad marshy ridge rises to the summit of Sheffield Pike. When paths were thin on the ground this walk was dangerous in mist. The paths are much clearer now, so route-finding dangers are much less: *it still needs care in mist.*

THE VIEW

An extensive and excellent panorama is seen above a dull and dreary foreground.

NOTE: The diagram illustrates the view from the highest point, not from the formerly accepted 'top' (the south-west cairn).

Principal Fells

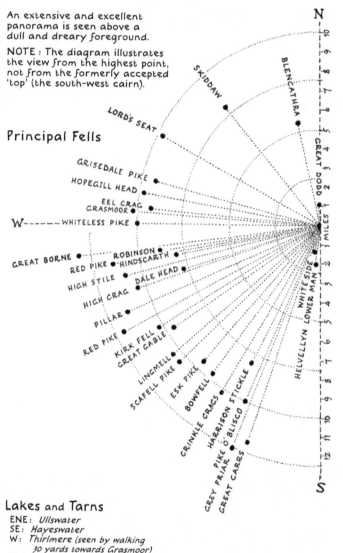

Lakes and Tarns

ENE: *Ullswater*
SE: *Hayeswater*
W: *Thirlmere (seen by walking 30 yards towards Grasmoor)*
NW: *Bassenthwaite Lake*

THE VIEW

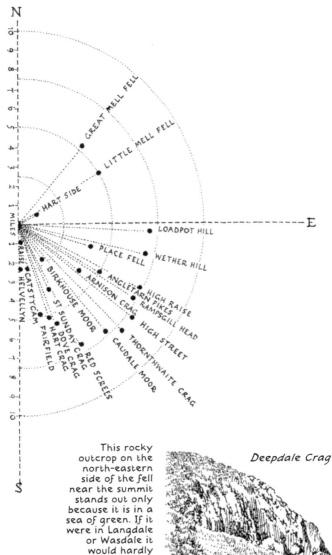

This rocky outcrop on the north-eastern side of the fell near the summit stands out only because it is in a sea of green. If it were in Langdale or Wasdale it would hardly warrant a name.

Deepdale Crag

Watson's Dodd 2589'

OS grid ref: NY336196

▲ GREAT DODD
▲ WATSONS DODD
● Legburthwaite
● Thirlspot

▲ HELVELLYN

MILES
0 1 2 3 4

from Smaithwaite

NATURAL FEATURES

Whoever Mr. Watson may have been, it is a very odd Dodd that has been selected to perpetuate his name. A separate fell it is undoubtedly, with boundaries unusually sharply defined on north and south by deep ravines, but although it conforms to normal mountain structure on three sides — west, north and south — it has no eastern flanks at all : the slope going down east to Deepdale from the summit plateau is bisected by a stream that clearly divides Great Dodd and Stybarrow Dodd, and Watson's Dodd cannot stake a claim to any land on this side. In other respects the fell is normal, taking the form of a steepsided ridge, mainly grass with a fringe of crag. With Great Dodd it shares ownership of a very fine ravine, the little-known Mill Gill, but its especial pride and joy is the Castle Rock of Triermain, an imposing and familiar object that overlooks the Vale of St John, holding a similar position relative to Watson's Dodd as Castle Crag in Borrowdale does to High Spy.

The Castle Rock of Triermain

Castle Rock has a privileged place in literature. Sir Walter Scott selected it as the principal scene for his narrative poem 'The Bridal of Triermain'. Castle Rock is the setting for the magic castle from which the hero of the story, Sir Roland de Vaux of Triermain, must rescue the maiden Gyneth, the illegitimate daughter of King Arthur.

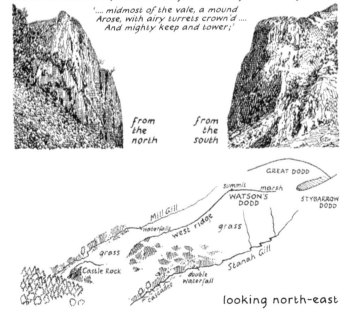

'.... midmost of the vale, a mound
Arose, with airy turrets crown'd ....
And mighty keep and tower;'

from the north

from the south

looking north-east

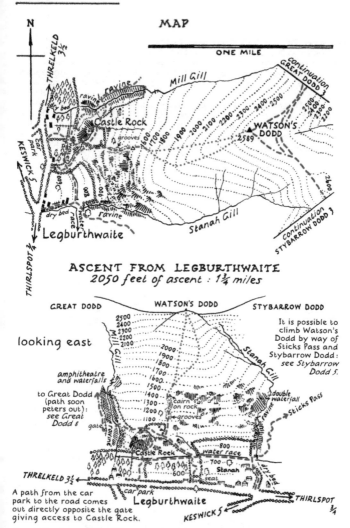

MAP

ONE MILE

N

THRELKELD 3½

ravine ravine

Mill Gill

continuation GREAT DODD 3

Castle Rock

grooves

1600 1700 1800 1900 2000 2100 2200 2300 2400 2500

WATSON'S DODD 2589

2700 2600 2500 2400 2300 2200

KESWICK 5

car park

dry bed

ravine

water race

Legburthwaite

Stanah Gill

continuation STYBARROW DODD 3

2600

THIRLSPOT ¾

ASCENT FROM LEGBURTHWAITE
2050 feet of ascent : 1¼ miles

GREAT DODD   WATSON'S DODD   STYBARROW DODD

looking east

2500 2400 2300 2200 2100

2000 1900 1800 1700 1600 1500 1400 1300 1200 1100

It is possible to climb Watson's Dodd by way of Sticks Pass and Stybarrow Dodd: see Stybarrow Dodd 5.

amphitheatre and waterfalls

to Great Dodd (path soon peters out): see Great Dodd 8

gate

cairn on rock

grooves

double waterfall

ravine

Sticks Pass

800

water race

700

Castle Rock

600

Stanah seat

THRELKELD 3½

car park

Legburthwaite

KESWICK 5

THIRLSPOT ¾

A path from the car park to the road comes out directly opposite the gate giving access to Castle Rock.

Castle Rock and Mill Gill are the highlights, but fencing around Mill Gill, where trees have been planted, means an approach along its southern (right-hand) bank is no longer feasible. On the direct route, once past the shepherd's cairn (perched on a rock) it is as easy to make a beeline for the summit as go right to the ridgeline.

This ascent promises well, but deteriorates into a trudge.

THE SUMMIT

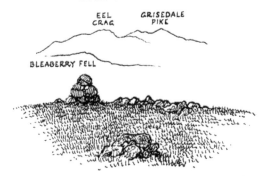

A decent-size cairn (the base much wider than that illustrated above) adorns the highest point, at the western end of the flat triangular top. The stones look strangely alien in the universal grassiness of the surroundings, as though they had been carried there. (Maybe Mr. Watson undertook this task: if so, it is fitting that the fell should bear his name!). There is a suggestion of history in these hoary stones.

DESCENTS: The quickest way down to civilisation is by the west ridge, which commences immediately below the cairn. After half a mile, when the ground becomes rough, incline right to avoid crags ahead and aim for the south corner of the wall behind Castle Rock; the easiest way down is from the shepherd's cairn (perched on a rock) which is indicated in the diagram on the facing page.

In mist, use the same route: the ridge is fairly well defined, but if in doubt incline right rather than left. Avoid getting into Mill Gill or Stanah Gill, both of which are dangerous.

RIDGE ROUTES

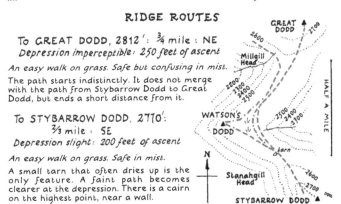

To GREAT DODD, 2812': ¾ mile : NE
Depression imperceptible: 250 feet of ascent

An easy walk on grass. Safe but confusing in mist.

The path starts indistinctly. It does not merge with the path from Stybarrow Dodd to Great Dodd, but ends a short distance from it.

To STYBARROW DODD, 2770':
⅔ mile : SE
Depression slight: 200 feet of ascent

An easy walk on grass. Safe in mist.

A small tarn that often dries up is the only feature. A faint path becomes clearer at the depression. There is a cairn on the highest point, near a wall.

Castle Rock

Castle Rock and Mill Gill

Castle Rock has been an attraction for rock climbers for many years. The higher (250') North Crag has more of the most difficult routes, but it also has a fissure that has been considered dangerous since 2011. A large crack has opened near the top of the crag which could cause a massive rockfall and this is growing wider year by year. A sign at the foot of the path from the road warns of the dangers:

> *It is suggested that climbers visiting the crag avoid the North Buttress of Castle Rock and avoid walking underneath it.*

The ascent of Castle Rock can be made in an easy half-day, but it must be treated with respect: the rewards are spectacular rock scenery and beautiful views.

ASCENT FROM LEGBURTHWAITE
350 feet of ascent : ¾ mile

There are two ways up Castle Rock; the easier is via the rear walled enclosure, accessing the top of Castle Rock by a thin path on a grassy rake from the rear. The direct route starts from the steps and gate just past the car park. Cross the water cut using the left of two stiles. At the foot of the crag, cross a wall (step stile) to the right and follow a well made path that hugs the crag. The grassy top of Castle Rock is on three levels, and a hawthorn bush on the lower level is the key to the upper stages of the ascent. The south viewpoint offers the best views.

NV : north viewpoint
SV : south viewpoint

looking east

In descent, the safest way down is via the rear enclosure; avoid the direct route unless familiar with it. *In mist,* the direct route is dangerous.

THE VIEW

The western half of the view is excellent, the eastern half very disappointing indeed. Watson's Dodd's position to the west of the Helvellyn range ridge line makes it an excellent viewpoint for the central Lakeland fells.

Principal Fells

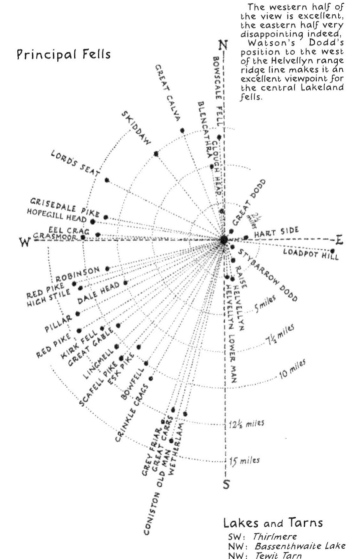

N
BOWSCALE FELL
CLOUGH HEAD
BLENCATHRA
GREAT CALVA
SKIDDAW
LORD'S SEAT
GRISEDALE PIKE
HOPEGILL HEAD
EEL CRAG
CRASMOOR
GREAT DODD
HART SIDE
W — E
LOADPOT HILL
STYBARROW DODD
ROBINSON
RED PIKE
HIGH STILE
DALE HEAD
RAISE
HELVELLYN
HELVELLYN LOWER MAN
PILLAR
RED PIKE
KIRK FELL
GREAT GABLE
5 miles
LINGMELL
SCAFELL PIKE
ESK PIKE
BOWFELL
7½ miles
CRINKLE CRAGS
10 miles
GREY FRIAR
GREAT CARRS
WETHERLAM
12½ miles
CONISTON OLD MAN
15 miles
S

Lakes and Tarns

SW: *Thirlmere*
NW: *Bassenthwaite Lake*
NW: *Tewit Tarn*

White Side 2832'

OS grid ref: NY338167

GREAT DODD ▲

Thirlspot
●
RAISE ▲   Glenridding ●
▲ WHITE SIDE
▲ CATSTYCAM
▲ HELVELLYN

● Wythburn

MILES
0   1   2   3   4

from Catstycam

NATURAL FEATURES

Although White Side presents an intimidating wall of low crags to travellers on the road at Thirlspot its upper slopes on this western side are docile enough, being wholly of grass at easy gradients : two paths to Helvellyn cross this flank, the old pony route and the 'White Stones' route. Very different is the eastern face, which falls sharply and steeply in crag and scree to the silent recesses of the wild upper Glenridding valley.

The summit is no more than a big grassy mound on the high ridge running northwards from Helvellyn and it rises only slightly above the general level of the ridge.

Skiers and sheep share a high regard for White Side.

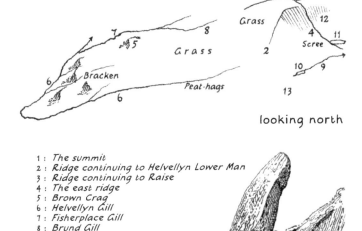

looking north

1 : The summit
2 : Ridge continuing to Helvellyn Lower Man
3 : Ridge continuing to Raise
4 : The east ridge
5 : Brown Crag
6 : Helvellyn Gill
7 : Fisherplace Gill
8 : Brund Gill
9 : Glenridding Beck
10 : Tarn in Brown Cove
11 : Keppelcove Tarn (dry)
12 : Keppel Cove
13 : Brown Cove

Rock pinnacle,
Brown Crag

The habit of the west-flowing streams of White Side is interesting. It seems natural that they should feed Thirlmere, but a strip of higher ground alongside the lake turns them north into the outflow, St John's Beck. This perversity of nature has been corrected by the Manchester engineers, who have constructed a water race along the base of the fell to collect the water and divert it south into Thirlmere.

MAP

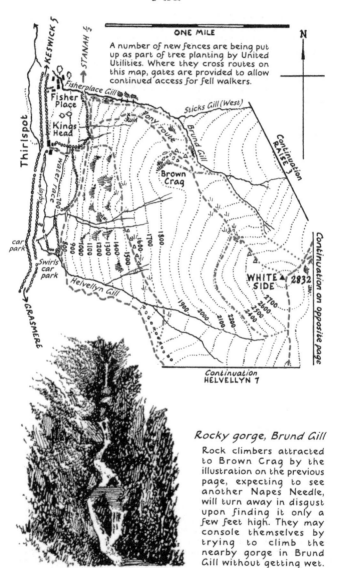

ONE MILE

A number of new fences are being put up as part of tree planting by United Utilities. Where they cross routes on this map, gates are provided to allow continued access for fell walkers.

N

KESWICK 5

STANAH ½

Fisherplace Gill

Fisher Place

Kings Head

Thirlspot

water race

Ruin

Pony route

Sticks Gill (West)

Brund Gill

Continuation RAISE 3

Brown Crag

lay-by

car park

700

800

900

1000

1100

1200

1300

1400

1500

1600

1700

1800

Swirls car park

Helvellyn Gill

1900

2000

2100

2200

2300

2400

2500

2600

2700

WHITE SIDE 2832

Continuation on opposite page

GRASMERE

Continuation HELVELLYN 7

Rocky gorge, Brund Gill

Rock climbers attracted to Brown Crag by the illustration on the previous page, expecting to see another Napes Needle, will turn away in disgust upon finding it only a few feet high. They may console themselves by trying to climb the nearby gorge in Brund Gill without getting wet.

Waterfalls in Fisherplace Gill

MAP

Continuation
RAISE 4

WHITE
SIDE
▲
2832

Continuation on opposite page

2700

2600
2500
2400
2300
2200
2100
2000

Keppel
Cove

Tarn
(dry)

Fold

Dam
1900
2000

Brown
Cove

Ruin
Tarn

GLENRIDDING

Continuation
HELVELLYN 7

Keppel Cove may, on an initial visit, appear to be a very lonely place, but the zig-zags above the cove have seen many thousands of pairs of feet walk this way over the years. Once a favourite way up to Helvellyn for Victorian tourists, the route is now more often used as a fast way down to the Patterdale valley by Helvellyn walkers who would prefer not to descend via the rocky ridges of Striding Edge or Swirral Edge. The scenery on this route is excellent, with Catstycam in particular catching the eye on the far side of Glenridding Beck. From this angle the full length of the impressive north-west ridge can be seen. Also in view is the ruined dam that once held back the waters of Keppelcove Tarn before part of it gave way in 1931.

Tarn in Brown Cove

ASCENT FROM THIRLSPOT
2300 feet of ascent : 2½ miles

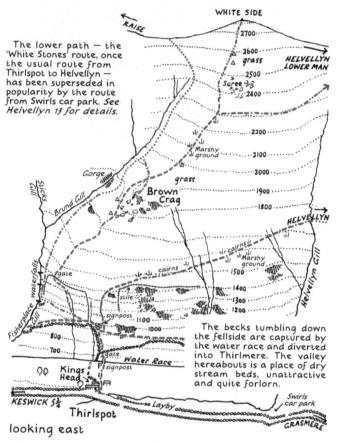

The lower path — the 'White Stones' route, once the usual route from Thirlspot to Helvellyn — has been superseded in popularity by the route from Swirls car park. *See Helvellyn 13 for details.*

WHITE SIDE

RAISE

2700

2600
△ grass

2500
Scree

2400

HELVELLYN
LOWER MAN

2200

Marshy
ground

2100

2000

grass

1900

Gorge

Slicks Gill

Brund Gill

Brown
Crag

1800

HELVELLYN

Helvellyn Gill

cairns

Marshy
ground

1500

gate

cairns

stile

1400

1300

1200

signpost

1100

1000

Fisherplace waterfalls

Fisherplace Gill

800

700

gate

signpost

Water Race

Kings
Head

The becks tumbling down the fellside are captured by the water race and diverted into Thirlmere. The valley hereabouts is a place of dry stream beds, unattractive and quite forlorn.

KESWICK 5¼

Thirlspot

Layby

Swirls
car park

GRASMERE

looking east

The route via Brown Crag is an easy climb, largely on grass after initial steepness. There is some scree to tackle shortly after the old pony route turns off right. The route via Brund Gill has little to recommend it other than a visit to the gorge illustrated on page 3.

Two paths cross the western flank of White Side above Thirlspot, both of which lead to Helvellyn. The lower one, the once-popular 'White Stones' route, does not lead to the summit above, but the upper one (the old pony route) is conveniently placed for the ascent of White Side.

ASCENT FROM GLENRIDDING
2400 feet of ascent : 4 miles from Glenridding village

The course of the east ridge is not obvious, being much broader than, for instance, the dramatic north-west ridge of Catstycam on the other side of the valley. A very thin grass path leaves the track to Brown Cove shortly before the track bends left, but soon peters out. Three fans of scree form a landmark higher up, and a route between the two on the right is feasible, if steep. Higher up, a low rock band is best bypassed on the left. The views to the dry tarn far below become increasingly impressive as height is gained.

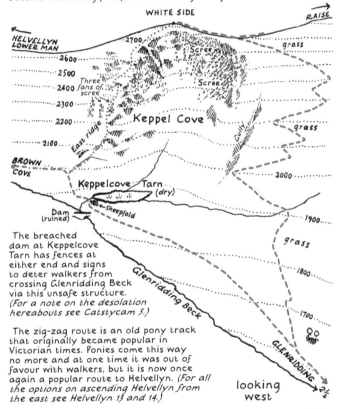

WHITE SIDE

RAISE

HELVELLYN
LOWER MAN

2700

grass

Scree

— 2600

— 2500

Three
fans of
scree

2400

Scree

— 2300

— 2200

Keppel Cove

grass

— 2100

East ridge

Gully

BROWN
COVE

Keppelcove Tarn
(dry)

2000

Dam
(ruined)

Sheepfold

— 1900

The breached
dam at Keppelcove
Tarn has fences at
either end and signs
to deter walkers from
crossing Glenridding Beck
via this unsafe structure.
*(For a note on the desolation
hereabouts see Catstycam 5.)*

Glenridding Beck

grass

— 1800

The zig-zag route is an old pony track
that originally became popular in
Victorian times. Ponies come this way
no more and at one time it was out of
favour with walkers, but it is now once
again a popular route to Helvellyn. *(For all
the options on ascending Helvellyn from
the east see Helvellyn 13 and 14.)*

— 1700

GLENRIDDING

looking
west

2½

There are few high fells more easily climbed than White Side if the zig-zag path from Glenridding is used. The other route shown, by the east ridge, is very different; it is pathless, steep and stony, but not difficult. It does, however, entail some route finding, so should be avoided *in mist*.

THE SUMMIT

The top of White Side is marked by a cairn somewhat different to that illustrated above. The sprawling structure doubles as a wind shelter with three areas for use depending on the prevailing weather. Grassy slopes descend gently away on all sides, although north-eastwards the ground falls away sharply around the rim of Keppel Cove.

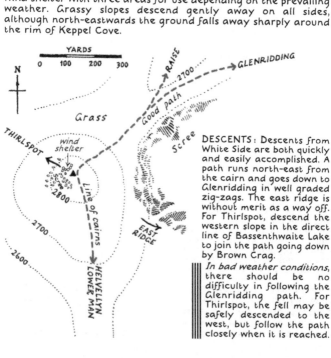

DESCENTS: Descents from White Side are both quickly and easily accomplished. A path runs north-east from the cairn and goes down to Glenridding in well graded zig-zags. The east ridge is without merit as a way off. For Thirlspot, descend the western slope in the direct line of Bassenthwaite Lake to join the path going down by Brown Crag.

In bad weather conditions, there should be no difficulty in following the Glenridding path. For Thirlspot, the fell may be safely descended to the west, but follow the path closely when it is reached.

THE VIEW

Helvellyn shuts out the distant scene southwards, but in all other directions the panorama is very good, especially to the west. The best picture is provided by Skiddaw, with Bassenthwaite Lake at its foot.

Principal Fells

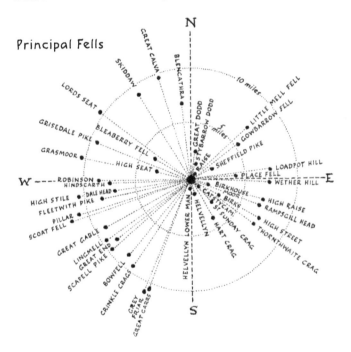

Lakes and Tarns

ENE: *Ullswater (lower reach only seen from the cairn; the upper reach can be seen also by walking 20 yards towards it)*
W: *Thirlmere (a small part — more can be seen by walking 10 yards towards it)*
NW: *Bassenthwaite Lake*

The Skiddaw Group

RIDGE ROUTES

To HELVELLYN LOWER MAN, 3033': 1 mile : S

Depression at 2600'
450 feet of ascent

A grassy descent and a long stony climb. Easy. Safe in mist.

Follow the line of cairns: a fair path leads down to the depression and it continues distinctly up the long ridge ahead, becoming very loose and stony in its latter stages. Helvellyn Lower Man is just a stepping stone to its big brother (Helvellyn, 3118') a further half-mile along the ridge.

WHITE SIDE

N

HALF A MILE

HELVELLYN LOWER MAN

For details of the route from Lower Man to Helvellyn, see Helvellyn 23.

To RAISE, 2897'

¾ mile : NE
Depression at 2650'
250 feet of ascent

RAISE

N

WHITE SIDE

HALF A MILE

Easy walking on a clear path. Safe in mist.

A stony path leads down to the depression (where a branch descends to Glenridding). Strike up the broad shoulder ahead, following a wide ribbon of gravel, and after reaching a cairn cross the level plateau to the stony summit.

Top of Striding Edge · Helvellyn · Top of Swirral Edge · Helvellyn Lower Man

The ridge south

The East Ridge
(In the foreground, the burst
banks of Keppelcove Tarn)

THE EASTERN FELLS
Some Personal Notes
in conclusion

I suppose it might be said, to add impressiveness to the whole thing, that this book has been twenty years in the making, for it is so long, and more, since I first came from a smoky mill-town (forgive me, Blackburn!) and beheld, from Orrest Head, a scene of great loveliness, a fascinating paradise, Lakeland's mountains and trees and water. That was the first time I had looked upon beauty, or imagined it, even. Afterwards I went often, whenever I could, and always my eyes were lifted to the hills. I was to find then, and it has been so ever since, a spiritual and physical satisfaction in climbing mountains —and a tranquil mind upon reaching their summits, as though I had escaped from the disappointments and unkindnesses of life and emerged above them into a new world, a better world.

But that is by the way. In those early Lakeland days I served my apprenticeship faithfully, learning all the time. At first, the hills were frightening, moody giants, and I a timid Gulliver, but very gradually through the years we became acquaintances and much later firm friends.

In due course I came to live within sight of the hills, and I was well content. If I could not be climbing, I was happy to sit idly and dream of them, serenely. Then came a restlessness and the feeling that it was not enough to take their gifts and do nothing in return. I must dedicate something of myself, the best part of me, to them. I started to write about them, and to draw pictures of them. Doing these things, I found they were still giving and I still receiving, for a great pleasure filled me when I was so engaged — I had found a new way of escape to them and from all else less worth while.

Thus it comes about that I have written this book. Not for material gain, welcome though that would be (you see I have not escaped entirely!); not for the benefit of my contemporaries, though if it brings them also to the hills I shall be well pleased; certainly not for posterity, about which I can work up no enthusiasm at all. No, this book has been written, carefully and with infinite patience, for my own pleasure and because it has seemed to bring the hills to my own fireside. If it has merit, it is because the hills have merit.

I started the book determined that everything in it should be perfect, with the consequence that I spent the first six months filling wastepaper baskets. Only then did I accept what I should have known and acknowledged from the start — that nothing created by man is perfect, or can hope to be; and having thus consoled and cheered my hurt conceit I got along like a house on fire. So let me be the first to say it: this book is full of imperfections. But let me dare also to say that (apart from many minor blemishes of which I am already deeply conscious and have no wish to be reminded) it is free from inaccuracies.

The group of fells I have named the
Eastern Fells are old favourites, not quite
as exciting as the Scafell heights, perhaps,
but enjoyable territory for the walker. They
are most conveniently climbed from the west,
which is a pity, for the finest approaches
are from the Patterdale valley to the east.
The walking is easy for the most part; very
easy along the main watershed. The coves
below the summits eastwards are a feature
of these hills: rarely visited, they are very
impressive in their craggy surroundings.
Exploration also reveals many interesting
evidences of old and abandoned industries
— quarries, mines, aqueducts, disused paths.
Somebody should write a geographical history
of these enterprises before all records are lost.

Some of my experiences during
many solitary wanderings while collecting
information for this book would be worth
the telling, but I preserve the memories for
the time when I can no longer climb. One,
however, returns insistently to mind.......I
remember a sunny day in the wilderness
of Ruthwaite Cove: I lay idly on the warm
rocks alongside Hard Tarn, with desolation
everywhere but in my heart, where was peace.
The air was still; there was no sound, and
nothing in view but the shattered confusion
of rocks all around. I might have been the
last man in a dead world. A tiny splash
drew my gaze to the crystal-clear depths
of the tarn .... a newt was swimming there,
just beneath the surface. I watched it for
a long time. And I fell to wondering.......

wondering about it, and its mission as it circled the smooth waters, and the purpose of its life — and mine. A trivial thing to remember, maybe, yet I do. I often think of that small creature, a speck of life in the immensity of desolation in which it had its being.

It is a remarkable thing, now that I come to think of it, that I still set forth for a day on the hills with the eagerness I felt when they were new to me. So it is that I have thoroughly enjoyed my walks whilst this book has been in preparation, much more so because I have walked with a purpose. Yet recently my gaze has been wandering more and more from the path, and away to the fells east of Kirkstone — my next area of exploration.

So, although I take my leave of the Eastern Fells with very real regret, as one parts from good friends, I look forward to equally happy days on the Far Eastern Fells. When this last sentence is written Book One will be finished, and in the same moment Book Two will take its place in my thoughts.

Christmas, 1954   A.W.

STARTING POINTS

AIRA FORCE
Gowbarrow Fell 5

AMBLESIDE
Dove Crag 5
High Pike 3
Little Hart Crag 3
Low Pike 2
Red Screes 5

BROWNRIGG
Great Mell Fell 3

DOCKRAY
Gowbarrow Fell 5
Great Dodd 6
Hart Side 5
Stybarrow Dodd 6

DUNMAIL RAISE
Dollywaggon Pike 6
Seat Sandal 5

FORNSIDE
Great Dodd 7

GLENCOYNE
Sheffield Pike 5

GLENRIDDING
Birkhouse Moor 6
Catstycam 4
Glenridding Dodd 2
Helvellyn 16
Raise 6
Sheffield Pike 4
White Side 6

GRASMERE
(incl. Grisedale Tarn)
Dollywaggon Pike 5
Fairfield 6
Great Rigg 4
Helvellyn 15
Heron Pike 3
Nab Scar 3
St. Sunday Crag 6*
Seat Sandale 4
Stone Arthur 3
* from Grisedale Tarn

HARTSOP HALL
High Hartsop Dodd 2
Middle Dodd 2

HAUSE, THE
Little Mell Fell 3

LEGBURTHWAITE
Great Dodd 8
Watson's Dodd 3

LOWTHWAITE
Little Mell Fell 3

PATTERDALE
(incl. Grisedale)
Arnison Crag 2
Birkhouse Moor 5
Birks 4
Dollywaggon Pike 7
Dove Crag 4
Fairfield 7
Hart Crag 6
Hartsop above How 3
Helvellyn 17
Little Hart Crag 4
Nethermost Pike 6
Red Screes 6
St. Sunday Crag 5

RYDAL
Hart Crag 5
Heron Pike 3
Low Pike 3
Nab Scar 3

STANAH
Raise 5
Stybarrow Dodd 5

THACKTHWAITE
Little Mell Fell 3

THIRLSPOT
Helvellyn 11
Raise 5
White Side 5

TROUTBECK
Great Mell Fell 3

WANTHWAITE
Clough Head 5

WATERMILLOCK CHURCH
(Ullswater)
Gowbarrow Fell 4

WYTHBURN
Helvellyn 12
Nethermost Pike 5

YEW CRAG
(Ullswater)
Gowbarrow Fell 5